The
Simulation
and
Gaming
Yearbook
Volume 2

The
Simulation
and
Gaming
Yearbook
Volume 2

Interactive
Learning

Edited by Roger Armstrong, Fred Percival and Danny Saunders

SAGSET – The Society for Interactive Learning

KOGAN PAGE

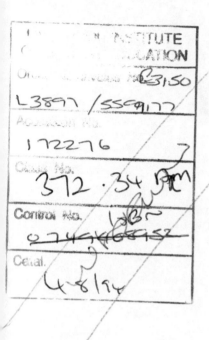
First published in 1994

Kogan Page Limited
120 Pentonville Road
London N1 9JN

British Library Cataloguing in Publication Data

A CIP record for this book is available from the British Library.

ISBN 0 7494 1213 5
ISSN 1351 4644

Typeset by EXCEPT*detail* Ltd, Southport
Printed and bound in Great Britain by
Biddles Ltd, Guildford and King's Lynn.

Contents

Section 4: Applications to business and management

Section 5: Applications to science and engineering

Section 6: Computerized applications

Section 7: Sources of information

Foreword

THE DOLLAR AUCTION by Sivasailam Thiagarajan is a simple game whereby the audience is asked to bid for a dollar. When the auction is concluded the second highest bidder pays. The bidding can go on and on to try and avoid paying and yet winning nothing. It has sometimes seemed that simulation and gaming, and more specifically SAGSET, has been somewhat like THE DOLLAR AUCTION in recent years – going on and on but losing out.

Things have changed in the last year. Two big events have brought this about. First, in 1992 the Edinburgh conference brought together representatives from 28 countries. This indicated the great interest there is worldwide in simulation and gaming. Second, the 1993 publication of the Yearbook by Kogan Page has created an international interest in SAGSET.

It seems very appropriate that the theme of this the second publication is 'interactive learning'. This builds on the Edinburgh conference which was followed by Bucharest in 1993. There would appear to be an upsurge of interest in Eastern Europe in different educational techniques since 1989 so perhaps simulation and gaming will prosper there. Perhaps also the UK has turned in the right direction. There is a retreat on the 'straitjacket' of recent educational legislation. There is a relaxation as regards the publication of statistics and the scope of assessment. This movement will encourage the development of simulation and gaming so it can regain its former prominence.

We are very fortunate indeed to have Kogan Page's support for this publication at a time when the economic situation has not yet fully experienced the 'green shoots of recovery' and budgets are still extremely tight. We trust that sales of the Yearbook will build on the start made in 1993. Our editors – Danny Saunders, Roger Armstrong and Fred Percival – have spent many hours of unseen, unpaid work to produce this edition for which they get precious little credit. Our thanks to them. Mainly, however, thanks to you for reading and using this book as a reference to simulation and gaming and making the effort of the publisher and editors worthwhile.

Peter Walsh
Chair, SAGSET 1989–93

Preface

By way of an introduction we feel it is helpful to our readers if we place the compilation of this Yearbook in the context of economic, political and technological changes that are apparent in Britain, Eastern Europe and the world in general. These are the themes that you will find both mirrored and echoed in the chapters that follow; they are but a microcosm of the changing world in which we live.

Those of you who are engaged in management development and training in further and higher education will have had to explore new paradigms associated with both the theory and practice of learning. Also, many of our readers, particularly those in higher education in Britain, will have the task of developing new teaching and learning strategies. Increasing student numbers within existing cramped teaching accommodation has meant major academic challenges. At a very practical level, for example, teaching accommodation – a scarce resource – has had to be used in what some would consider to be the most efficient way: converting as many rooms as possible into lecture theatres (preferably in tiers and with fixed seating).

On the face of it, this static furnishing and environment is the very thing which militates against the opportunities to develop new and creative learning strategies – most noticeably those which draw upon experiential learning methods and have an interactive focus. The foregoing is but one practical example of the difficulties that simulation games have in promulgating supplementary and alternative learning and teaching strategies to that of the traditional lecture.

It is therefore our belief that the role and contribution our Interactive Learning Society members make in relation to the continuing debate on the applicability and effectiveness of games and simulations in education and training is of crucial importance in fostering a truly dynamic learning environment. Given the ongoing debate concerning the quality of education and the learning experience, it is true to say that we are adherents of the effectiveness school – that which 'does the right thing' – rather than the efficiency school, which would seek to 'do the thing right'. In our view, the latter approach is no more than the end justifying the means! It fails to address the issue of the quality of the learning experience.

Some readers may consider that we are unjustifiably seeking to promote ideas about learning which have no place in the hard economic realities of education and training today. Our retort would be that our position is not grounded in a grand aim or vision of the future, nor is it an idle boast about the effectiveness of interactive methods of learning. Rather it is a stance which draws upon many years' experience of designing, developing, facilitating, debriefing, evaluating and reviewing interactive learning events. Of course we recognize that we do not always achieve our desired learning outcomes (invariably because we have set ourselves over-ambitious targets). Also, we are sometimes left somewhat confused when, even after extensive and deep reflection, we cannot understand or identify why a particular activity had unexpected outcomes. This is not to suggest our inductive reasoning is somehow at fault; rather it is an indication of the complex individual and group processes we are drawing upon, when trying to enhance learning by using various kinds of games and simulations.

We are often astounded at both the breadth and depth to which interactive methods have been applied. In this respect, the contributors to the 1994 Yearbook are no exception. We cannot mention them all, but instead select some key papers which illustrate new as well as recurring issues in the world of simulation and gaming. Our apologies to authors not mentioned, but those of you who have edited manuscripts will appreciate our difficulties!

The effective use of a role-play in an endeavour to address issues as diverse as terrorism, racism, totalitarianism, drug abuse, unemployment and ethnic cleansing was most evident in the work of Claude Bourlés in his introduction to TRAFFIC IN BARABAKH. Given the serious nature of the learning objectives it is pleasing to report that the role play activity was nevertheless both creative and stimulating. Alan Cudworth's HONEYCOMB PROBLEM moved the focus away from social and international issues to that of conflict within the work organization. In particular the classic problem of the tension between personal success and group gains was successfully addressed. This activity amply illustrated that co-operation and communication, a willingness to work for the 'good of all', can achieve more objectives and provide greater satisfaction compared with stereotypical cut-throat competition.

The adaptability and flexibility of interactive learning methods is demonstrated in Laurence Legg's contribution PLANES OR BUST, an optimized production technology (OPT) scheduling game. Originally designed as a core activity for a two day materials management course for British Aerospace, it was subsequently adapted and used to good effect with a wide variety of ages and ability levels (from school children aged 12/13 years through degree students to professionals in related areas). The emphasis on effective teamworking is pursued in Witold Bielecki's computerized simulation business game, MANAGER-93, in which the facilitator is 'able to create different kinds of economic systems, from a pure central planning economic system to a full market-driven system'. Clearly, as the emerging East European economies have to come to terms with free market environments, any tool such as

MANAGER-93 will assist them in learning to work as a free-standing organization in conditions of ambiguity. It is evident that the game has been well received by undergraduates, graduates and postgraduate (MBA) students studying at the University of Warsaw.

The organizational context in relation to the marketing function is further explored by David Tonks and George Long in their chapter considering the use of computer-based simulations to represent and demonstrate the reality of inter-firm relationships. The focus is upon the true effectiveness of learning through simulation, and challenges many of the assumptions about the suitability of models of competition which are built into the software. However, given the apparent success of the simulation as a vehicle for learning, the authors note that this in itself can act as a strong barrier to change.

The difficulties that the tutors of any computerized game or simulation are likely to encounter are illustrated in Jeremy Hall's chapter 'Computerized Tutor Support Systems: The Tutor's Role, Needs and Tasks'. He enters into a discussion about the most appropriate roles for tutors to adopt during the process – administration, facilitation or management. He considers how computerized tutor support systems can release the tutor to focus more on strategic learning issues. This can provide 'the experienced tutor with opportunities to enrich the learning experience'.

Hall's second chapter considers an often neglected aspect of simulations, namely participant support systems. He brings the issue to the fore in his analysis of the case 'EXEC – Management Game System' by his discussion of the functionality and facilities provided by computerized simulation games. He has a real sting to the tale, after taking us through his extensive experience of running this game on executive short courses in the UK and Europe.

Aspects of personal development are explored by a variety of authors, and in the preface we select three papers. In 'Personal Development via the Outdoors', Simon Read seeks to illustrate how outdoor problem-solving tasks can be used to develop a wide range of transferable skills. Read has been successful in designing activities which can be managed by tutors who have no specialist background in outdoor sports or training activities. He very successfully demonstrated not only that it can be fun, but more importantly it can provide participants with opportunities to draw fresh insights into their own abilities, how they are perceived by others and, as a consequence, enhance the probability of more effective and durable personal and working relationships.

The personal development of managers and much of the thrust for continuing professional development in many other specialized fields of work has been stimulated by the ongoing debate on the competence-based approach to the assessment of development. Recent emphasis has been placed upon the demonstration of competences in the workplace. The contribution of Jon Curwin and John Furnival is therefore most welcome as it addresses the assessment of competence through simulation. The authors note the differing perspectives on what is competence, be it holistic or based on checklist and performance criteria. Using the same marketing simulation cited by Tonks and Long as their case study, they present findings and draw conclusions which suggest that the danger in participants focusing on microcompetences is that, as a consequence, they may neglect the macrocompetences of the process of management. Therefore they have been able to highlight both the benefits and limitations of using simulations in competence assessment.

One of the key contemporary debates engaging practitioners in management education and development is that which seeks to answer the question 'Can management be effectively taught at undergraduate level?' The numerous schools of thought embroiled in the debate recognize that the outcome of these discussions is likely to lead to a significant change or re-emphasis in the provision of undergraduate studies within the rapidly expanding business schools.

It is in the context of these changes that the work of Choueke and McCarthy is particularly welcome. In their chapter 'Virtuality and Gaming: The Realization of Paradox' they focus on the development of an undergraduate management programme dedicated to a strong process orientation to learning. Students' personal and professional development is facilitated in an environment which encourages self-management in a group context and a focus on problem-solving and decision-making skills. Their case study examines the contribution that a computer management game – EXECUTIVE 100 – can play in creating an environment of study 'which is analogous to the concept of the virtual organization'. Their metaphor of the virtual organization draws upon the principles of virtual reality: 'this technological development refers to the experience of the world by participating in its simulation and becoming part of the illusion'. We feel this is an advancement in computerized gaming and simulation to which we will be returning in years to come. It could well herald a change in how our work is perceived by both practitioners and the general public. In our view it may well raise ethical issues and confront the facilitators of such interactive learning events with a number of moral dilemmas.

Yes, we live in a rapidly changing world, one in which, as we get older, it can become increasingly difficult to maintain our grasp of technological change in particular. A world in which we are constantly being confronted with fresh challenges, most of which should be grasped as learning opportunities. Therefore it is our pleasure to be able to share with you in the following chapters the experiences of colleagues who have tried to come to terms with the changing world in their own distinct way. We thank them for sharing their experiences and thoughts with us – we also thank our reviewers for all of their comments and suggestions. Further, we hope that you, our readers, will glean as many helpful insights as we the editors have in gathering together the materials we now present to you.

Read on and make your personal contribution to our changing world.

Danny Saunders
Roger Armstrong
Fred Percival
Editors

SECTION 1: Theoretical overviews

Chapter 1

Unnecessary ambivalents - a cause for concern

Ken Jones

ABSTRACT

This chapter develops the concept of an ambivalent event. The term was used by the author (Jones, 1988; 1989; 1991) to cover events in which incompatible methodologies were operating simultaneously and the symptoms were that the facilitator was surprised by the emotions during the event, was unable to produce a plausible explanation for the behaviour, and tended to blame the personalities of the participants. The participants tended to blame each other and a clash of methodologies was considered to be a clash of personalities. The conclusion was that all ambivalents were undesirable and should be avoided by a suitable briefing or by altering faulty design. The present chapter takes a step further, to identify events which are necessary ambivalents, that is to say that if briefed as if they were a single methodology the event would become bland and pointless. Although the class of necessary ambivalents is small, it includes some of the most powerful events used in the field, including STARPOWER, THE COMMONS GAME and (in some cases) PRISONER'S DILEMMA.

The concept of ambivalent events and their potentially hazardous consequences are explained and illustrated elsewhere (Jones, 1988; 1989; 1991). They are a special class of events because they are not games or simulations or exercises, but a muddled and incompatible mixture in which, by definition, some participants behave in accordance with one methodology while others are in a different methodology. Almost by definition ambivalents are undiagnosed as such, and thus the psychological damage to participants and facilitator becomes more hazardous since the cause is not only undetected but attributed to personal failings. Since events are usually reported by the facilitators rather than the participants it is not surprising that the assumption is that the participants are to blame.

It is important to note that the issue is not about the meaning of words, it is about consistent behaviour. This can be demonstrated by considering an event (actual behaviour, not materials) in which everyone concerned used gaming terminology (game, player, etc.) but in which the behaviour was entirely in the simulation mode. This event would be a simulation, not an ambivalent or a game. Similarly, if the terminology of those concerned was in the simulation mode but all the behaviour was in the gaming mode the event would be a game, not a simulation or an ambivalent. To be an ambivalent the behaviour must involve a methodological conflict. For example, if some participants treat the event as an intellectual exercise while others treat it as a play-acting session then the event is an ambivalent.

My previous thinking was that all ambivalents were unnecessary and undesirable, and should be made consistent by either altering the design or by giving an appropriate briefing. This chapter breaks new ground in seeking to identify ambivalents which are necessary and where any change in design or briefing will diminish the effectiveness of the event. Although necessary ambivalents are a very small class, they include some of the most powerful learning events yet devised, including STARPOWER, THE COMMONS GAME and (sometimes) PRISONER'S DILEMMA.

This chapter will outline these three events and give an extract from a report on each. It will note the psychological damage that has been inflicted and suggest that the facilitators probably suffered as much as the participants, and possibly there was undetected damage to the reputations of the facilitators. It will point to evidence that the participants were more aware of incompatible methodology than the facilitators. It will look at the ethical considerations, particularly those issues mentioned by Stewart (1992) and Gredler (1992).

An important part of the argument is the speculation about what would be likely to occur if the facilitator tried to remove the ambivalence from the three events by giving a briefing which asked all the participants to operate in a single methodology, since this is important to establish that the events are necessary ambivalents, not unnecessary ambivalents. The conclusion is that psychological damage which can be caused by all ambivalents can be considerable and that unnecessary ambivalents should not be used and necessary ambivalents should be adequately debriefed, possibly with some follow-up event as well.

THE THREE EVENTS

STARPOWER is a trading situation involving three groups – Squares, Circles and Triangles. During the course of the trading, the facilitator suddenly gives power to the wealthiest group (the Squares) to change the rules about trading in any way they wish.

THE COMMONS GAME has a scoring mechanism and a matrix of points which results in the average group score being reduced to the extent to which individuals increase their own scores at the expense of the group. The artefacts are coloured cards which individuals display. Shields are provided so that the participants may, if they wish, conceal the card they have displayed from everyone but the facilitator. The highest common good can be achieved if participants take it in turn to play the low scoring orange (enhancement) card while everyone else plays the red card.

PRISONER'S DILEMMA involves two people accused of an unspecified crime who separately have to plead guilty or not guilty without consulting their co-defendant. There are several versions but the dilemma is basically a trade-off. If both plead guilty they each receive a relatively high sentence. If both plead not guilty they each receive a relatively low sentence. However, to plead not guilty while the other prisoner pleads guilty is to receive the highest sentence while the co-defendant receives a very low sentence (or is acquitted) as a reward for confessing and cooperating with the prosecution. The event is often run repetitiously with participants informed of how the other prisoner pleaded in the previous round. Unlike the first two events this is sometimes not an ambivalent, particularly if it is run as an intellectual exercise. In fact, it has been run between computers where there is no possibility of methodological ambivalence since the programmes all assume the gaming mode and no real-world ethics become involved.

The following extracts from reports of the three events include accusations of disreputable conduct such as robbery, violence, treachery, greed and betrayal; allegations that the participants were motivated by boorishness, seriousness and forgetfulness, and a stated or implied confession of bewilderment expressed in terms of muddled or inappropriate terminology.

STARPOWER

On one occasion a group of leftish liberal studies lecturers announced 'The name of the game is GRAB', and very shortly afterwards I was knocked to the floor and a pack of bonus cards torn from by hand. This was a pity – a meeting intended to show the hidden violence of our established society showed instead only the boorishness of some of its opponents (Coleman, 1977).

THE COMMONS GAME

Players were directed to accumulate the maximum number of points. The player with the highest number of points received $5. The words 'win' or 'winner' were never used by the game directors. Greed and curiosity to get the commons up or down played significant roles in determining the teams' results. No goals were set at the beginning of the game; however, they tended to evolve during the game. Occasionally, players forgot about the commons and only 'played the game'. Titles of essays by the students reflect the confusion, frustration and complexity of dealing with commons property as shown in the following examples: 1. Can Humanity Survive? 2. Can We Save the Commons? 3. Commons' Cents (Or Don't Be Petty With Your Cash). 4. Managing Commons Property Resources: The Simulation and The Real World (Kirts et al., 1991).

PRISONER'S DILEMMA

One of the most significant aspects of this study, however, did not show up in the data analysis. It is the extreme seriousness with which the subjects take the problems. Comments such as 'If you defect on the rest of us, you're going to live with it for the rest of your life' were not uncommon. Nor was it unusual for people to wish to leave the experimental building by the back door, to claim that they did not wish to see the 'sons of bitches' who double-crossed them, to become extremely angry at other subjects, or to become tearful (Liebrand 1983).

Comment

In common with other ambivalents, whether necessary or unnecessary, these reports contain the symptoms of muddled thinking, hurtful behaviour and failure to find a plausible cause. The gap between the terminology and the behaviour is reflected in the words used to describe the events – meeting, games study – all cosy respectable words suggesting that nothing undesirable had occurred.

Coleman's leftish lecturers said: 'The name of the game is GRAB'. It is unlikely that the lecturers used 'game' in its gaming sense. They may have used the word because that was the label bestowed on the event by the facilitator in the briefing. Another possibility is that they used the phrase in the colloquial sense of meaning 'the essence of a situation' as when an American diplomat (McGeorge Bundy) remarked of European foreign affairs, 'Settlement is the name of the game'. If, as Coleman implies, the words were connected with what followed they could signify (a) resentment about perceived manipulation by the facilitator, (b) a declaration to abandon the gaming mode where players obey rules (otherwise there is no game) and behave in the mode in which participants have the power and authority to do what they think is in their own best interests, and (c) to use this power to create a free-for-all.

Coleman criticizes the robbery with violence as being due to 'boorishness' – a strangely mild word in the circumstances but that is, nevertheless, an accusation of a fairly serious personality fault. It is also surprising that he says the aim of the event is to show violence, albeit hidden violence. What is missing from Coleman's account is any awareness of methodological clash, and if anyone was aware of this it was probably the lecturers.

Kirts *et al.* seem vaguely aware that methodology might have some bearing on the way the event is briefed and run. In the briefing they were careful to set no goals and to avoid mentioning the concept of winning. However, presumably they called the event a game in the briefing. Not only is the methodology enshrined in the title of the event but their article is highly unusual because it employs no interchangeable labels. They themselves make no reference to other methodologies such as simulation, exercise, simulation-game and so forth. They do not explain how a game can have no goals and no winners. Their complaint is that some players 'only played the game'. That is precisely what players of games are supposed to do, otherwise they would be in a different methodology. The players are being blamed for doing what they have been asked to do and the authors do not explain how players who play a game are 'forgetful' because they behave like players. It seems likely that the participants were fortunately more aware of the methodology than the authors of the article, since one participant wrote an essay entitled 'Managing Commons Property Resources: The Simulation and The Real World'. It makes one wonder whether the essay was more cogent, plausible and interesting than the article.

The psychological damage caused in the Liebrand event was horrendous – friendships broken, tears, extreme anger, threats of 'having to live with it for the rest of your life', treachery and escape by the back door. What is not reported is the damage to the facilitator, yet some participants must have thought worse of the person who organized the shattering experience and who failed to debrief it. To attribute the anger, threats and tears to 'extreme seriousness' is unconvincing to say the least. Seriousness, particularly extreme seriousness, suggests calmness, thought and deliberation, not emotional outbursts. Liebrand calls the event a 'study' and the contrast between this label and the behaviour is startling. Elsewhere in his article Liebrand refers to 'social dilemma games'. He defines social dilemmas as 'Situations in which, by the very act of choosing a strategy with negative externalities, the ultimate outcome can be called deficient.' Again there is conflict of terminology, between 'game' (presumably regarded by Liebrand as a non-serious competitive event), 'social' which suggests a simulation, and 'negative externalities with deficient outcomes' which suggests that the event may have dangers of which the facilitator should be aware. The labelling is cerebral and detached, whereas the event was personal and devastating.

In none of the three extracts is there any suggestion that the facilitators (or the authors of the events) were in any way responsible for what occurred. It is as if they all thought, 'How surprising, but it was not my fault so it must be caused by the unfortunate personalities of those particular participants'. (For further examples see the chapter on ambivalents in Jones, 1989, pp. 127–41.)

The argument here is not that ambivalents always cause extreme distress, but that they are far more likely to do so if the facilitator is surprised, caught off balance, and does not have an effective debriefing ready and waiting. Failure to debrief effectively is failure to diagnose the event. Even small amounts of unnecessary distress should be regretted. The other missing element from the three accounts is the identity of the accused. In Coleman's case it appeared to be the group who were in a simulation mode, not a gaming mode. In Kirts et al. the accused are the gamesters and self-seekers, not the simulation participants who are presumably trying to enhance the common good. With Liebrand it seems plausible to suppose that the 'sons of bitches' were the gamesters and their accusers were the 'extremely serious' participants in the simulation mode. In all three examples there are indications that the participants understood far more about what was involved than those who reported the events.

A practical test of whether an event is a necessary ambivalent, as distinct from an unnecessary ambivalent, is whether the briefing can improve the situation by turning it into a one-methodology event. Suppose, for example, that in briefing the three events the facilitators had said something on the following lines:

This event is a game. That is to say, it has its own internal rules and there is only one role, that of player, and the duty of each player is to try to win. Provided players stick to the rules and accept the spirit of fair play, there is no question of anyone later being blamed for real-world unethical behaviour such as greed or deceit. In a game it is morally acceptable to win by acquiring more power within the rules. Nothing personal is involved, someone has to lose. This is not a simulation about real-world ethics and society, it is a game about winning and losing.

With STARPOWER such a briefing would be incompatible with the point in the event when the Squares are given the power to alter the rules since this is designing a game not playing a game. In the time-out for rule discussion no game is in progress; the participants are no longer players, they are game designers. However, if the rule change element was removed from STAR-POWER, the event would become a simple, harmless and largely pointless trading game. No one would learn anything new about themselves and the debriefing would presumably discuss gaming strategies and not real-world ethics. Facilitators would be deprived of drawing an analogy between gaming behaviour and real-world ethics.

The same situation would probably occur if THE COMMONS GAME was so briefed. In this case participants would not dither about whether to support the community or themselves, they would have a duty to put themselves first, irrespective of the fact this this would diminish the total wealth of the group. Thus, they would try to bluff, conceal, deceive and lie, although presumably no one would believe them since everyone would be in the same mode. If they were genuine about increasing the resources of the commons they would not be players in the game, they would be interlopers from an unauthorized simulation.

If PRISONER'S DILEMMA were briefed as a game there would be no threats and no one would be accused of being sons of bitches, since such behaviour would be approved and applauded by the players themselves as being the right way to try to beat one's opponent. (If the two cooperated the event would be non-competitive and therefore not a game but a simulation.) As a game, the outcome is likely to be that everyone would always plead guilty since this is the only way to beat the opponent. To plead not guilty would lead to a draw at the best and at worst would lose. After a dozen or so rounds in which everybody always pleaded guilty the game would presumably be abandoned as being pointless and uninteresting.

What would happen if all three events were briefed as being a simulation, perhaps on the following lines?

This event is a simulation in which you have roles and duties and real-world ethics. This does not mean that you cannot lie and cheat and steal, but that if you do so you should consider real-world consequences and the question of ethics will be discussed in the debriefing. Do not, however, try to imitate the real world by play-acting, simply do whatever you personally believe to be in your own best interests in the situation in which you find yourself.

In the case of STARPOWER the outcome would probably be completely different from what normally occurs. Particpants might set up committees to help the deprived and dispossessed. Charities could be formed. Income tax could be introduced. The Squares would probably either refuse the responsibility of fixing new trading rules and ask for a referendum or else change the rules to equalize the wealth. Not only would such conduct be approved in its own right, it would also be likely to enhance the standing of the participants in the eyes of the facilitator – the good student syndrome.

With THE COMMONS GAME a simulation briefing would reduce the event to about five minutes – the time needed to work out that the participants should take it in turn to play the orange card while everyone else plays the red card. Once this solution was arrived at there would be no point in playing the cards since the result would be inevitable. The reaction would probably be, 'We've solved it. What shall we do now?'

With PRISONER'S DILEMMA everyone would see themselves in prison with ethical duties (honour among thieves) and it would not take much imagination to realize that if they pleaded guilty and sent their companion to gaol they could end up with a knife in their back. In addition, their colleague in real life would not be too happy about being sent to prison while they received a light sentence or went free as a reward for the treachery. For both ethical and real-life reasons it is unlikely anyone would plead guilty. In such circumstances the event might last five or ten minutes before being abandoned as boringly repetitive.

It follows from this analysis that the briefing of all three events must be vague in order to attempt to achieve ambivalence. However, such action will be successful only if the participants are ignorant of the methodology. If the first words of participant interaction are, 'Well, obviously this is intended to be a simulation (or game)' and everyone agreed, then the event would not be an ambivalent.

ETHICAL CONSIDERATIONS AND PSYCHOLOGICAL DAMAGE

As pointed out by Stewart (1992), researchers are concerned about ethics, particularly in experiments involving some type of deception, whereas teachers are concerned about learning. As an example of the nature of the concern of researchers she cites Walster et al. (1967):

There are . . . two frequently mentioned dangers of deception experiments, to which some experiments are more liable than others. First, some critics have voiced their concern that lying to people may lead them to lose faith in their fellow human beings. Because scientists are ordinarily highly respected, the discovery that a scientist will lie might upset subjects even more than lies told by others. Secondly, and perhaps more importantly, it has been pointed out that some deception manipulations are emotionally disturbing to a subject, and the disturbances might not be entirely amenable by debriefing.

Stewart makes the point that there has been little discussion of ethical considerations in experiential learning compared with considerable discussion by research workers in the field of experiments. She urges facilitators who use games and simulations for experiential learning to focus on ethics in their debriefing if the event involves deceit:

> For example, if a simulation-game encourages participants to lie, the debriefer must be prepared to discuss the morality of lying and its negative effect on both the liar and the person being lied to.

She goes on to say, 'It is unethical to conduct an experience-based activity without providing an adequate debriefing'. However, even if we accept Stewart's recommendations about the need for ethical adequacy in the debriefing, four major practical difficulties remain.

First, ambivalents do not normally come with a health warning on the package. Not only is there little discussion of ethics in the literature, there is even less in the facilitator's notes, where the general assumption is that this is a normal event which works well. What may be an adequate debriefing for a normal event could be utterly inadequate for an ambivalent.

Second, the area of concern is not only about the possible harmful consequences of deception by the designer and/or facilitator, but the harm which could be caused in any other way. Although the three events discussed above involve muddle and methodological conflict, they do not involve a hidden agenda as such since all the participants know all the details about the scoring systems. Moreover, the ethics involving the participants are not those of deceit but of such undesirable behaviour as greed, intolerance, violence, hate – as shown in the three reports.

Third, it is impossible to give an adequate debriefing of an ambivalent if there is a faulty diagnosis of the methodology. If the facilitator acquires a concern about ethics without at the same time sorting out the methodology then the situation could be worse than having no ethical discussion at all. Ethics involves judgement about human behaviour and judgement can involve blame and feelings of guilt. If participants get hurt during an event because they falsely assume their fellow participants are in the same behavioural mode as they are and if the facilitator is unaware of the true cause of the conflict, then a facilitator-led discussion about ethics could fan the flames of personal resentment, anguish and guilt which could engulf not only the ex-participants but the facilitator as well. No one, particularly the facilitator, would have the necessary methodological equipment to tackle the blaze. Thus, the debriefing itself could be a cause of hurt and distress.

Fourth, even if the facilitator is aware of the clash of methodologies, then merely to announce this fact in the debriefing may not in itself be enough to expunge the feelings of distress and hurt caused during the event. As Tesch (1977) pointed out, the hidden assumption is that the debriefing will create a magical undoing, 'an eraser for emotional and behavioural residues'. Probably most people who have experienced interactive learning from the inside will remember situations in which being shown someone's role card in the debriefing, or hearing the explanation of the behaviour, was not enough to erase the memory of the emotional distress, and lingering and possibly unspoken accusations remain. (Thinks: 'You said that hurtful remark and you looked really mean. I had always thought you were my friend but now I am not so sure'.)

These issues of deceit, ethics and psychological damage are dealt with very thoroughly by Gredler (1992). Her long analysis of STARPOWER (pp. 130–39) is not only valuable in its own right but touches on key issues involved in many games and simulations. In addition, her view that the event is seriously flawed and has undesirable consequences (and presumably should not be used) is not only relevant to this chapter but to SAGSET conferences where STARPOWER is often run as an example of a classic interactive event. Moreover, Gredler does know the difference between a game and a simulation and has a no-nonsense approach to those who combine the words into a new type of event – simulation-game. On this point she says, 'Games and simulations represent different psychological realities. Thus merging the two categories results in a contradiction in terms and the exercises send conflicting messages to participants' (p. 12). Here are several extracts which I have married together to give her view of STARPOWER:

STARPOWER is an ingenious exercise in that conflict between the groups is established. However, the exercise contains a design flaw that generates undesirable effects when implemented. The design of empathy/insight simulations should be consistent with two basic requirements. First, participants should not be misled about the nature of the situation nor tricked in any way into executing behaviours that are later criticised. Second, like other simulations, empathy/insight simulations are not games and care should be taken that participants do not view them as games. STARPOWER, however, violates both requirements. First, participants are told they are participating in a game and that the three highest scores will win. When given the opportunity to make the rules, the Squares do so in a way that ensures that three of their group will be the winners. There is no difference between this behaviour and the behaviour of bankrupting one's friends in Monopoly. Both actions are entirely legitimate in a game situation. However, the behaviour of the Squares is extrapolated into the real world as though the Squares were not playing a game. They have, in other words, been tricked. In fact, the Director's Instructions include the statement that the Squares sometimes have difficulty in admitting that they abused their power (Shirts, 1969, p. 18). They are quite correct – their behaviour was appropriate for the game they believed they were playing.

The Director's Instructions also describe the concepts that typically emerge from the post-simulation discussion. Two of the concepts are '1. Each of us may be more vulnerable to the temptation to abuse power than we realise' and '2. To change behaviour, it may be necessary to change the system in which that behaviour occurs'. In other words, participants have been asked to judge the Squares' game behaviour as though it were real-world behaviour. Participants are not sophisticated enough to understand the difference between games and simulations and thus do not question the transfer. A more serious problem, however, is issues of trust may be raised: Susan (a Triangle) may wonder if Diane (a Square) is entirely trustworthy. Hard feelings generated by the exercise may persist into the educational or work setting.

Gredler goes on to consider the point that despite these disadvantages STARPOWER could be beneficial if it achieved certain outcomes. She examines several potential behavioural changes (eg, become more vigilant citizens) and concludes that most of the objectives are not clear and those that are clear would be better achieved by a different type of interactive event.

What is missing from Gredler's analysis is an awareness of the crucial distinction between playing a game and designing a game. The two activities are not only different, they are incompatible. A person cannot be engaged in both activities at the same time – a game is automatically suspended if the players are debating the rules. The situation in STARPOWER is not the same as bankrupting one's friends in Monopoly; it is as if a player who was winning in Monopoly was given the right to change the rules of the game. Nor is sophistication required to know the difference between playing and designing. Very young children design games and change rules and playing conditions. Suppose one child says, 'I want to bat first because it is my bat and ball' and another says, 'That's not fair because we can never get you out'. At this point both children know that they are in a real-life discussion and not playing a game. They also know that fairness is a key issue when discussing game rules. Games are designed to be fair, real life is not.

What is unusual in STARPOWER is not the behaviour of the participants but the behaviour of the facilitator – giving the winning side the right to move the goalposts. This is not deceit or trickery. It is obvious, straightforward, mind-boggling unfairness. It completely contradicts the whole ethic of games. The only trickery is telling a lie about the reason for doing so – that the Squares are the more successful players. But this is not what Gredler objects to. She says that the Squares were tricked into behaving badly because they thought it was a game and were then criticized because they were judged as if it were a simulation. But, as pointed out above, there is no way that a rule-changing session can be thought of as playing a game. Presumably, if the Squares fixed the rules in their own favour, they were already in a simulation mode – that is, behaving professionally in an event which included within itself a dominant role for rule-changers. They know that the event is no longer a game, and probably are aware that it is, or is intended to be, an indication of real-world power struggles (in international affairs, in local affairs, in institutions and in families). Naturally, in order to be in the simulation mode they must be prepared to justify their actions, which is different from the play-acting mode where they could say, 'We know it was wrong but we did it because we were imitating the real world'. In the simulation mode they could say (or think) the following: (a) their actions are legal because absolute rule-changing power has been granted, (b) they are ethically entitled to act in the interests of their own group, which presumably includes their families, and (c) they are doing nothing unusual because there are so many real-world precedents. Only Diane herself knows whether or not she gained pleasure from the thought, 'This will be tough on Susan, but I and my upper set will be all right'.

Suppose, however, that one concedes to Gredler the assumption that the Squares are in the gaming mode when they fix the rules. In this case the ethical situation becomes worse, not better. The world takes a very harsh view of those who try to fix gaming rules in their own favour. In any case, to do so would probably mean that the other side would not play. Not only adults but young children refuse to participate in unfair games.

Regarding the victims, Gredler may be too restrictive in implying that only the Squares can suffer. Diane may be surprised and disappointed that her best friend, Susan, whom she thought to be friendly and polite, suddenly becomes a street-corner agitator before her very eyes. Facilitators should also remember that criticizing the referee is learned young – 'Daddy, it is not fair that you always let Diane bat first just because she is the best player'. A mature Susan is likely to be circumspect and would be unlikely to accuse the facilitator openly, perhaps finding it more satisfying to air the complaint later among friends. After all, within STARPOWER, the obvious protest is, 'Who gave you the right to alter the rules?' and the obvious answer is, 'The facilitator did'. All the participants know this. Perhaps the reason that the question is rarely asked or answered is because the participants do not wish to step outside the methodology by mentioning the facilitator, and also to avoid seemingly to criticize the facilitator. So the knowledge about who caused the distress is likely to lie dormant and surface later.

RECOMMENDATIONS

Unnecessary ambivalents should be avoided or made consistent by altering the design or improving the briefing.

Necessary ambivalents should be avoided except in cases where the facilitator is aware that they are ambivalents and can deal with the methodology in the debriefing.

If the necessary ambivalents are potentially powerful events, as in the three examples in this chapter, then the facilitator should consider not just a normal explanatory debriefing but some sort of interactive follow-up involving cooperation and empathy.

In all cases of necessary ambivalents, facilitators should explain their own actions and describe what they were asked to do in the instructions. This could take the form of an apology; for example, at the end of STARPOWER the facilitator might say:

I am sorry about the distress. You must blame me, or blame the designer of the event. It was unfair and contrary to the ethic of gaming to give one group permission to move the goalposts. The reason I gave for doing so, that the Squares were the better players, was a lie. Even if it were true it would not be justified. However, the Director's Instructions said that I had to give you this explanation about the Squares, and then let the event develop in the hope that people could learn something about themselves.

Although Shirts does not mention such a confession by the facilitator, it is good practice in debriefings for facilitators to lay their own cards on the table, otherwise they may not only not know what hit them but may not even realize they have been hit. Quite apart from the trauma of the events, occurrences associated with ambivalents, particularly necessary ambivalents, are potentially damaging to facilitator-student relations and are a particular cause for concern.

REFERENCES

Coleman, V (1997) 'Videorecording and STARPOWER', *SAGSET Journal*, 3,1. Also published in Megarry, J (ed) (1977) *Aspects of Simulation and Gaming*, Kogan Page, London.

Gredler, M (1992) *Designing and Evaluating Games and Simulations: a process approach*, Kogan Page, London.

Jones, K (1988) *Interactive Learning Events: a guide for facilitators*, Kogan Page, London and Nichols Publishing, New York.

Jones, K (1989) *A Sourcebook of Management Simulations*, Kogan Page, London and Nichols Publishing, New York.

Jones, K (1991) *Icebreakers: a sourcebook of games, exercises and simulations*, Kogan Page, London and University Associates, San Diego.

Kirts, C A, Tumeo, M A and Sinz, J M (1991) 'The COMMONS GAME. Its instructional value when used in a national resources management context', *Simulation and Gaming*, 22,1.

Liebrand, W B G (1983) 'A classification of social dilemma games', *Simulation and Gaming*, 14,2.

Powers, R B and Boyle, W (1983) 'Generalization from a commons-dilemma game', *Simulation and Gaming*, 14,3.

Shirts, R G (1969) STARPOWER, McGuiver Shirts, Del Mar, CA.

Stewart, L P (1992) 'Ethical issues in postexperimental and postexperiential debriefing', *Simulation and Gaming*, 23,2.

Tesch, F E (1977) 'Debriefing research participants: though this be method there is madness in it', *Journal of Personality and Social Psychology*, 35, 217–24.

Walster, E, Berscheid, E, Abrahams, D and Aronson, V (1967) 'Effectiveness of debriefing following deception experiments', *Journal of Personality and Social Psychology*, 6, 371–80.

ABOUT THE AUTHOR

Ken Jones has been designing, demonstrating and writing about simulation, exercises and games for more than 25 years. He started his career in journalism on *The Yorkshire Post*, then went to Oxford University as an adult student, graduating in Philosophy, Politics and Economics. Most of his career has been with the BBC's World Service.

Address for correspondence: Ken Jones, 4, Ashdown Lodge, 1c Chepstow Villas, London W11 3EE.

Chapter 2

Simplicity and realism in business games

Clive Loveluck

ABSTRACT

The more articles I read about business games – and the more conferences I attend – the more I become depressed by the tendency, aided and abetted by the increasing availability of computers, toward the construction and use of ever more complex models to underpin games. In particular, I am puzzled by the relationship between simplicity and realism and in this chapter I would like to explore some of the fundamental problems of relating these two criteria.

Consider these views:

> Simplicity is worth striving for only as long as it does not conflict too sharply with realism (Thorelli and Graves, 1964).

> As the complexity of the game increases, the subjective realism will also increase, *ceteris paribus* (Cohen and Rhenman, 1961).

These are propositions with which, I suppose, most game designers would agree. Certainly, I had accepted them even though the *ceteris paribus* condition protects the latter proposition from refutation.

Both quotations, however, raise some basic points which I would now like to consider:

- What do we mean by realism?
- What do we mean by simplicity?
- Is it possible to devise some measures of these game characteristics?

REALISM

I would first like to consider the concept of reality and to suggest that there is no such thing. I will argue that there is a whole 'set' of realities and that we should specify which 'reality set' we are seeking to simulate.

In this context, we can regard the difference between 'subjective' or 'perceived' reality as something of a red herring. Duke (1974) has defined 'perceived reality' as:

impressions of reality as obtained through barriers [which are] impediments to a clear interpretation of reality: barriers of language, knowledge, prejudice, human limitations, and so on.

Such a view is implicitly accepted by Stanislaw (1986), who has written that a simulation 'is an attempt to mimic the behaviour of a real-world system with a computer program'. It follows, therefore, that reality is the ideal and that the greater the fidelity of the simulation, the greater should be our preference for that simulation. I would suggest that this is not true in gaming-simulations, simply because we do not know what the 'real-world system' is.

Let me illustrate by reference to two well-known games, one British and one American: CAR-100 and THE EXECUTIVE GAME by Henshaw and Jackson.

CAR-100 is a game based upon the European car industry and is described by its author, Peppercorn (1988), as 'A real business model':

. . . we could bring our systems analysis and computer modelling experience into use to create what we still believe to be the only commercially available real business model as opposed to a model . . . developed from theory rather than actuality . . .. In our approach to building the market model . . . we opted for the empirical approach.

Clearly, the author has a very fragile grasp of scientific method. By implication, the model has been constructed on an inductivist view and has ignored the now well-accepted notions of Kuhn, Popper and Lakatos and the hypothetico-deductive method. The idea that a complex model of any activity can be constructed from observation alone is clearly absurd. We might ask: what was observed that could be used to construct this 'empirical' model? The answer is:

. . . market surveys, statistics published by the Society of Motor Manufacturers and Traders, regular reports in the *Financial Times* and, of course, the plethora of journals, magazines and TV programmes.

This is a remarkable form of reality: a 'real model' based on the chitchat of the press and TV and prepared without the benefit of any theoretical structures to explain or predict causal relationships. Such a game is dangerous and it is fortunate that it has such a short shelf-life, for if it ever was 'real' in 1987, it is certainly not real in 1994!

THE EXECUTIVE GAME is clearly a superior game, but what 'reality' underlies it? Carvalho (1991) has recently published an excellent article which seeks to use this game as an illustration of different methods of validating business simulations. The technique used is that of response surface methodology (RSM), a set of statistical procedures used to develop an empirical model of the relationships between input and output variables of a system where the internal dynamics of the system are unknown. This canonical analysis seeks to identify the stationary point on the 'surface' and, hence, can be used to explore the relationships embedded in the model. It is the validity of 'realism' of these relationships which determines the 'reality' of the game.

Carvalho writes: 'The principle of profit maximisation is deeply embedded in economic theory and business practice'. It is this principle for which Carvalho is searching with RSM. While the methodology is valid and interesting, it is a matter of some concern that one apparent criterion for judging the validity or realism of the game is the extent to which the profit maximization principle is coded into the model.

This is very questionable indeed. Armen Alchian (1977), an eminent economist, has pointed out that, 'in the absence of complete information and perfect foresight, the assumption of profit maximisation is meaningless as a guide to specifiable action'. More recently, Simon (1984), a Nobel Laureate in economics, has pointed out that 'no one has observed whether the actual positions of business firms are the profit maximizing ones nor has anyone proposed a method of testing this proposition. I [Simon] cannot imagine what this test would be since the tester would be as incapable as business firms are of discovering what the optimal position actually is'. In other words, it is questionable whether or not profit maximization is 'real' and what Carvalho is really testing is not whether the model is 'real' but whether the model is consistent with another (questionable) theory!

I would argue that it is this consistency which represents our reality. As game designers we have neither the time nor the skills to develop original theories which cover all the economic, marketing, sociological and psychological characteristics of the situations which we are presenting in our models. Our problem is to select and integrate appropriate hypotheses from other sources.

It is the appropriateness and integration of these hypotheses and their consistency with our model which represents the reality for which we are searching. The 'real' reality is a chimera which we can never find.

SIMPLICITY

And what about simplicity? Here is an illustrative example.

In an interesting article, Thavilkulwat (1991) proposes some models for capturing the human component of computer-based business simulations which 'take the . . . perspective' of simplicity. I would like to look at one example of simplicity, taken from this article. Thavilkulwat writes:

> Wage directly affects the size of the labor pool, the number of workers willing to work at that wage. The effect of wage, however, is contingent on the productivity of labor. The more productive the labor, the higher the wage that should be required for a labor pool of a given size. Because people are capable of collective action, the labor pool should be subject to discontinuities occasioned by strikes and settlement of strikes. These characteristics can be captured by a cusp catastrophe function. . . .
> . . . the cusp catastrophe function is an element of a catastrophe theory, a

method of applying topographical mathematics to the modelling of divergent and discontinuous functions. . . .

. . . The formula for obtaining the roots of one of the equations involved in this model ($z^3 - bz - a = 0$) exists but is complicated although experimentation with an interactive algorithm indicates that roots will be found within 20 iterations.

Did you understand that? I cannot understand how this is simple. It is rare for any game to have 20 or more decision periods, and even if participants are familiar with catastrophe theory, I doubt that they will be able to disentangle the multiple variables of a game in order to be able to set up any experimental analysis which involves 20 iterations.

Perhaps part of the problem is that what is simple to Thavilkulwat is not necessarily simple to me . . . I am sure it is not simple to my managerial students!

The notion of simplicity, like beauty, is intuitive and we need a more objective characterization before we can hope to agree about the relative simplicities of different games. Basically, of course, simplicity means economy of description and perhaps we should, in the field of games, pursue the concept introduced into mathematics by Solomonoff in 1952 – the complexity of a theory can be taken to be the size of the shortest Turing machine program that, given the experimental setup as input, would produce the empirical observations as output.

The Copernican revolution is a good example of simplicity and Occam's razor: when in doubt, use the simplest theory! The selling point of the Copernican model was not that it gave better predictions than those of Ptolemy but that it was so much simpler.

CONCLUSION

Keys and Wolfe's (1990) supposition that 'the most important function of management games in the future will be as research laboratories' is, I think, a most important notion. I would like to suggest that priority in such a research programme should be in two areas:

■ can we get game designers to tell us the degree of reality of their game – in the sense of specifying the hypotheses on which their models are constructed? And,
■ can we establish a measure of simplicity of games which can be applied to all games?

REFERENCES

Alchian, A (1977) 'Uncertainty, evolution and economic theory' in *Economic Forces at Work*, Liberty Press, New York.

Carvalho, G F (1991) 'Evaluating computerized business simulators for objective learning validity', *Simulation and Gaming*, 22, 3 Sept.

Duke, R (1974) *Gaming: the future's language*, Halsted Press, New York.

Cohen, K J and Rhenman, E (1961) 'The role of management games in education and research', *Management Science*, VII, Jan.

Keys, B and Wolfe, J (1990) 'The role of management games and simulation in education and research', Yearly Review of Management: special issue of *Journal of Management*.

Peppercorn, D (1988) 'CAR-100: a real business model', in Sanders, D, Coote, D and Crookall, D (1988) *Perspectives on Gaming and Simulations*, 13, SAGSET, Loughborough University.

Simon, H A (1984) 'Testability and approximation', in *Philosophy of Economics*, D M Hausmann (ed), HUP, Cambridge, Mass.

Stanislaw, H (1986) 'Tests of computer simulation validity', *Simulation and Gaming*, 17.

Thavilkulwat, P (1991) 'Modeling the human component in computer based business simulations', *Simulation and Gaming*, 22.

Thorelli, H B and Graves, R L (1964) *International Operations Simulation*, The Free Press, New York.

ABOUT THE AUTHOR

Clive Loveluck is an independent consultant specializing in the construction of games and courses based on games.

Address for correspondence: Bryndu, Sennybridge, Powys LD3 8HN, UK.

Chapter 3

The assessment of competence through simulation

Jon Curwin and John Furnival

ABSTRACT

This chapter briefly traces the development of management thinking and practice through the current competence-based approach, with the emphasis now being on what managers can demonstrate they can do in the workplace. The ongoing debate concerning task-based generic competences and underlying personal characteristics is used to illustrate some of the problems with assessment of competence at management level. Simulations are discussed as a competence assessment method using the authors' experience with business managers and undergraduate students.

Business games provide an opportunity for managers and others to develop and demonstrate competence. These competences can be task-based at a micro-level or holistic at a macro-level. The context of the simulation and the expectations of participants are major determinants of learning outcomes. There remains a truth in the old saying that 'you get out what you put in'. Business simulations also reinforce a particular view of business by the structuring of the scenario, the framework of decision making and feedback.

COMPETENCE

The theory of management is usually traced back to Henri Fayol who analysed management activity into five areas: planning, organizing, directing, coordinating and controlling. Management development was, and often still is, based on these five elements. Management theory then developed from criticisms of this 'universal remedy' to include consideration of a variety of situational factors:

social and technical systems – Tavistock Institute
environment – Lawrence and Lorsch
role analysis – Mintzberg
relationships and networks – Kotter

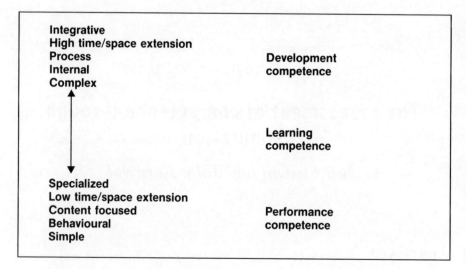

Figure 3.1 *A hierarchical map of managerial competence* (Kolb *et al.*, 1986)

and, of particular relevance to the competency movement, 'the complex interaction of job, organisation environment, competencies of the individual and individual actions' (Boyatzis, 1982).

A major recent development in management has been the development and use of competence-based development with many influential organizations such as Abbey National, British Petroleum and the National Westminster Bank planning their recruitment and development of managers around a competency model.

Some organizations have adopted the generic competences developed by the Council for Management Education as part of the Management Charter Initiative (MCI), whereas others have researched and developed their own competences, hence mirroring the earlier development from a set of generic principles to a situational approach. There is at present some disagreement amongst management thinkers about the most useful competency model to adopt.

Kolb *et al.* (1986) have developed a model, shown in Figure 3.1, which indicates the possible links between generic and situational competences. This model illustrates the hierarchy of competences from simple task-based up to the more complex internal personal characteristics, from performance competences through learning competences up to developmental competences.

Elkin (1990) discusses two approaches to competence which he labels as micro and macro. Micro competences are exemplified by the tasks lists and performance criteria reflected in National Vocational Qualifications (NVQs) and can be derived from the 1988 Manpower Services Commission definition of competence: 'Abilities to perform the activities within an occupation'.

Macro competences indicate a personal qualities approach as shown in the

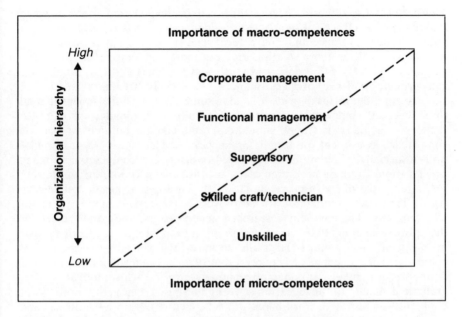

Figure 3.2 *The relative importance of micro and macro competences at different levels in the organizational hierarchy* (Elkin, 1990)

Hay McBer competences which are reflected in Boyatzis' work. The definition adopted by him in *The Competent Manager* illustrates this macro approach: 'An underlying characteristic of a person which results in effective and/or superior performance in a job'.

Elkin shows how the emphasis on macro competences increases as one climbs the organizational hierarchy; see Figure 3.2.

THE ASSESSMENT OF COMPETENCE

Reasearchers and practitioners supporting the macro approach to management argue that competence is holistic and personal and greater than the sum of the elements. This presents a difficulty in assessment as it is not sufficient to assess the individual components of competence and then award the competence. Our research indicates that the approach of participants to a simulation does depend on whether they are seeking to develop micro or macro competence.

Assessment methodology has been categorized as follows:

- performance at work
- performance on specially set tasks
- questioning
- historical evidence (Gealy *et al.*, 1991)

The 'performance at work' category appears to be the preferred approach when looking for evidence of competence against work-based standards but although such evidence may have face validity, it can suffer from many weaknesses such as recency, transferability, cost and range (for a full discussion see SCOTVEC report – Mitchell and Cuthbert (1989)). Simulations can provide evidence of performance on specially set tasks which can supplement other forms of evidence and in some cases can aid assessment at all three levels of competence referred to by Kolb *et al.* Simulations can also reduce or avoid risk (flight simulators) and can be tailored to specific competence assessment for specific organizations. This is not new, as simulations (especially role play) have been used to determine 'competence' in many organizations' training programmes for recruitment, selection and appraisal.

One example of the use of simulation to develop and assess competence comes from a postgraduate Certificate in Management run in house by a major UK company. The company researched and developed the competences for this programme in 1988 via a training needs analysis to identify 'basic management and commercial skills to meet the changing needs of the company'. The competences were revised in 1991 and competence research and development remains an ongoing company project. This innovative programme is mainly distance learning, workplace-based and includes the use of CBT, interactive video, work-based projects, mentors, learning contracts and simulations. Assessment evidence is mainly via project work, case studies, preset exercises and simulations. These are used along with workplace evidence to build a portfolio for final assessment. Many of the managers are engineers and have limited exposure to marketing or other business disciplines. Marketing is one of the key competence areas and has been addressed using a simulation, THE MARKETING GAME (Mason and Perreault, 1987). The results of using such a simulation are reported below.

THE USE OF SIMULATION – SOME FINDINGS

The opportunities to develop and demonstrate competence are clearly limited by the realities of the workplace and the effectiveness of the assessment method. Managers tend to specialize and cannot easily shift from one functional area to another to meet the requirements of a management qualification. The challenge to companies has been how to accommodate vocational qualifications at the same time as their managers are reporting increasing job pressures. It is evident from our initial research that time and opportunity are both limited in the workplace for the achievement of the full range of management competences and that even if the workplace did allow the development of each particular competence, the question would remain as to which, if any, of the competences were transferable.

Simulations, such as business games, can provide insight into many aspects of business and, in particular, those aspects where the managers concerned have limited access. This section considers the results of work undertaken with the participants of several business simulations over the last three years. This summarizes our experience of observing business game participants, the results of questionnaires completed by participants and the assessment completed by participants. The participants were either students at the University of Central England on business-related courses or managers with the major national company already referred to. The managers from the national company were seeking marketing competences on the basis of a three-day workshop on THE MARKETING GAME but were engineers by training and job, and had little direct contact with the marketing function within their organization. The students were mostly between 25 and 35 years old with a range of business experience, taking Stage 2 or Stage 3 of a part-time business studies degree.

Participants from various simulations were generally enthusiastic about business games, giving mean scores between 4 to 5 on a number of satisfaction scales where 0 indicated 'no satisfaction' and 6 indicated 'substantial satisfaction'. It is clear from observing a number of games that things do go wrong but that the games themselves survive and can be considered robust in terms of design. On occasions, computer systems have failed to deliver the correct results, groups have been unable to work together or accommodation has been inadequate but the game overall has been seen as successful. It does seem important that participants percieve the game as an ongoing managed exercise that can cope with any unexpected contingencies and, as such, reflects their own experience of work. How often can a job be repeated in the workplace just because the first printout had missing figures, or employees cannot work together, or factory space was inadequate?

The factors that are reported as particularly important are the formation of groups, the timing of decisions and the purchase of additional (market research) information. Clearly, groups can be formed in many different ways, from the completely random to the completely controlled, but what is critical is that the method is understood and accepted by the participants. If groups are not given sufficient time between decisions, an often reported criticism, they tend to agree decisions quickly without adequate discussion, with the dismissal of dissent and without the use of analytical techniques. Participants also expect wide-ranging information as a simulation progresses in addition to rather technical looking printouts of results. The initial case-study or scenario is accepted but participants often expect this to be elaborated and enriched in the same way that a business becomes better understood in both quantitative and qualitative terms with increased business experience.

The response to a business simulation will depend on expectations. An interesting point of difference emerged between managers on company-sponsored simulations and similar mature students on university courses. When asked about improvement, the managers were concerned with matters such as 'tutors being assigned to groups', 'better identification of learning points' and 'talk by experts', whereas the mature students were concerned with the more operational issues of 'more time', 'networks by computer' and 'fewer groups'. There are a number of indications that the sample of managers seeking competences on a company-sponsored simulation were wanting to be shown how to do things and as such gain the individual competences at this micro level, but were not demonstrating the same independence of action seen with other groups. In response to questions about reasons for the business game, the managers gave 'learning marketing competences' and 'gain competence', whereas other groups were more concerned with the more holistic issues of 'teamwork', 'learning from others' and 'observing group behaviour'. The interesting contrast therefore is that the manager in the company-sponsored simulation may have been developing the micro-level competence whereas other groups were developing competence at a macro level. Clearly what participants get from a simulation depends on what they expect and how the context of the simulation is developed.

Participants were asked a range of questions about how they made decisions. Generally, participants from all simulations gave high positive scores to 'work as a team', 'discuss the decision made' and 'agree most of the time', and much lower scores to 'manage time effectively' and 'have own function or task'. It was observed that most groups quickly became involved with the task and gave little attention to the process. So although decisions were typically made on time, there was little reflection on how the decisions were made and whether there were better ways for the groups to work. Being able to learn from the past, being able to challenge the status quo, and being able to generate innovative solutions are all seen as important aspects of management development and yet are not particularly evident in the way participants approach a business simulation. A business simulation, however, provides a real opportunity for participants to reflect and learn from the way their team managed their problems. In terms of business issues, it was generally reported that business games did 'involve participants', 'did create a problem situation' and 'did present organizational data', but to a much lesser extent 'give realistic results', and 'allow creative responses' and 'present organization issues'. It was generally thought that although a business simulation could present a challenging business scenario and develop the skills of working with such scenarios (important for long-term planning) they could not mirror the reality of the workplace. There was little evidence of groups using business techniques such as breakeven charts, sales forecasting or cashflow forecasts or groups having the dynamics to use such time-consuming techniques. The use of techniques was only likely to happen when participants were encouraged to use them by the game organizer. It was generally observed that students did what they needed to do to meet the requirements of the simulation exercise as described. Game organization is clearly critical in that it provides the framework and the setting for participant expectation which can lead to the seeking of micro or macro competence.

CONCLUSION

Business simulations do provide a context to develop competences at a macro and micro level. The response of participants depends upon their expectations and they may see the simulation as merely an opportunity to confirm task competences at the micro level. In the context of management development, the business simulation introduction provides the learning framework and the final feedback provides the necessary reflection on the learning experience. Participants tend to focus on the task of management (micro competences) and may, to some extent, neglect the importance of the process of management (macro comptences). It is the element of gaming that can make a business game fun but for groups to reach a quick consensus without challenge, analysis or dissent distracts from the reality of the workplace. A business game may adequately provide further evidence of competence development and achievement but is unlikely, in isolation, to prove a competence. Interestingly, a business simulation could provide an opportunity to show that a competence is transferable from a particular workplace. In summary, therefore, a business simulation on its own is unlikely to be sufficient to prove a competence, but this is also true of other forms of management development, including written reports, presentations, role play and on-the-job performance. However, simulations do provide a useful addition to the range of methods available for competence development and assessment.

REFERENCES

Boyatzis, R E (1982) *The Competent Manager*, Wiley, New York.
Elkin, G (1990) 'Competence based human resource development', *Industrial and Commercial Training*, 22, 4.
Gealy, N, Johnson, C, Miller, C and Mitchell, L (1991) 'Designing assessment systems for national certification', in Fennell, E (ed) *Development of Assessable Standards for National Certification*, Employment Department, Sheffield.
Kolb, D, Lublin Spoth and Baker (1986) in Henry, J (ed) *Creative Management*, Sage, London.
Mason, C and Perreault, W (1987) THE MARKETING GAME, Irwin, London.
Mitchell, M and Cuthbert, T (1989) *Insufficient Evidence?*, SCOTVEC 1989, Glasgow.

ABOUT THE AUTHORS

John Furnival, Principal Lecturer External Relations, has a background in financial services, engineering and consultancy. He now lectures and consults in Business Strategy and Management Development.

Jon Curwin is Principal Lecturer in Business Analysis. He has a particular interest in the application of quantitative methods in business and has written a number of computer-based business games.

Address for correspondence: both authors are from the University of Central England Business School, Perry Barr, Birmingham B42 2SU.

Chapter 4

Virtuality and gaming: the realization of paradox

R Choueke, M McCarthy, N Hayes and S Aslam

ABSTRACT

This case study focuses on the development of an undergraduate programme: BSc (Hons) Organization and Management Studies at Edge Hill College. The programme began just three years ago and the first graduates are now completing.

From its inception, the programme has been dedicated to a strong process focus, concentrating primarily upon the personal and professional development of the students with a particular emphasis upon problem-solving, decision-making and group skills. Self-management is seen as particularly important and students are encouraged from the outset to take responsibility within a framework that is progressively more flexible. Thus by the third year, students are meant to be managing their learning effectively within a group learning milieu, with responsibility for time, resources, themselves and reflection. Tutor leadership is concerned with the development of materials, which are supplemented by students' own findings, and the outline of topic area coverage. Increased flexibility over the latter is encouraged to allow for the development of students' interests.

This case study is principally concerned with the development of the third year, the use of games, in particular a computer management game – EXECUTIVE 100 – and the creation of an environment which is analogous to the concept of the virtual organization. The aim is to engender a learning community wherein student groups represent mini-organizations designed to provide:

- Learning sets
- Interactive organisms
- A competitive-collaborative market place
- A political network.

The authors have drawn upon notions of synergistic work teams, holistic learning and the learning organization to develop earlier ideas of student-centred learning in ways which emphasize the legitimacy and value of student contribution. In other words, the right to question implies the right to answer as well as the right to *an* answer. Adopting the principle of loose-tight structures as a means of testing learning within varying degrees of flexibility, the authors sought to provide an environment of safety for individual and group risk-taking.

The notion of games as a means of creating a virtual reality where student decision making counted and where learning could replicate real world negotiation of knowledge became a paramount tool in the construction of the experience.

The chapter will seek to explore some of the issues associated with this course design, to examine student response and to suggest some principles for further development using the virtual organization analogy.

It is interesting to consider that the current fascination with the virtuality principle is based upon the notion of a paradox: namely, that the replication of a reality is its own form of reality. The principle is based upon three elements: that the constructed reality should be inclusive, interactive and occurring in real time. The ancient Taoist principle of virtuality recognizes the natural virtue, the potential for 'becoming' of living organisms. The interplay of these ideas presented the authors with a philosophical base for developing their activity. Communicating this to the student group was a lengthy and fascinating experience.

THE BACKGROUND

The only materialist – be he poet, teacher, scientist, politician or statesman – is the man who gets lost in his material without a gathering metaphor to throw it into shape and order. He is the lost soul. (Robert Frost)

BSc (Hons) Organization and Management Studies began in October 1990, with, from the outset, an experimental focus, as outlined in an earlier paper (McCarthy, 1992). Briefly, the course attempts to present a synthesis of academic knowledge and skills development to students within the subject of management.

The case study presented in this chapter is concerned with the third-year core studies programme and the teaching and learning methodology adopted there as a logical development of what has gone before in the previous years. At this stage, it may be useful to summarize this through a series of questions:

What are we doing?

The programme is planned through a series of topics concerning organizational effectiveness. Topics cover organizational needs in order to establish and maintain effectiveness, techniques related to effectiveness and also critiques of the concepts associated with effectiveness. The approach is highly interactive, based upon packaged material prepared by the team, a number of key lectures, and a computerized management game concerned with the planning, management and marketing of cars within a model of the European market. The game generates its own results at the end of each round, together with market information based upon environmental factors and the interaction of the various teams playing the game.

How are we doing it?

Students are asked to form self-selected study groups according to criteria articulated within the larger group and discussed in seminars. These groups stay together for the full course (126 hours), though of course not all work is group work. The groups work together in a variety of modes:

- working groups – handling packaged learning material produced by the team, and ensuring effective use of resources to meet the challenges thus presented;
- research teams – a similar operation that, nevertheless, extends the work of the group into research activity of various kinds with consequent increased demands upon time, commitment and personal responsibility;
- car production management – the use of the EXECUTIVE MANAGEMENT GAME (April Training, 1990) based upon car manufacturing and marketing, requires each group to act as a management team, making a range of decisions based upon information provided by the game, in competition with the other teams;
- action learning set – each group operates as an action learning set which is self-facilitated for the purposes of extending knowledge and skills (Revans, 1982);
- individual study – students work on their own for some of the time in the conventional way and decide for themselves how much of this will be interactive and the extent to which the results will be shared.

Why?

The approach is rooted ideologically in the commitment of the tutors to notions of the learning organization, the principles of student-centred learning and a belief that learning is an holistic experience which must be supported by valuing of the student. Thus, one arrives at a distillation of the key principles: experiential learning, valuing the individual and exploring meanings.

Learning involves the whole person, not just the intellect; one can, therefore, talk about dimensions of learning which engage interactively and holistically, as shown in Figure 4.1.

Why this way?

The necessity of finding ways of doing this which allowed students to establish their own meanings that somehow were concomitant with the so-called 'real world', led to the establishment of the present working pattern. At the same time, the drive towards greater student independence seemed paramount, given the final-year status of the work being done. It was recognized that students needed to do more than acquire knowledge and develop skills; there needed to

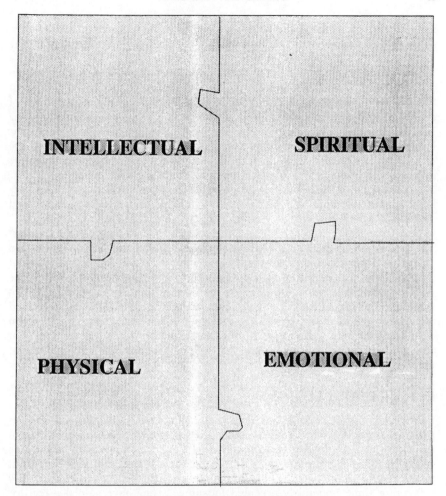

Figure 4.1 *The dimensions of learning*

be a degree of personal development that echoed the progression experienced on management development courses, and established real confidence amongst students as they prepared for the world of work.

Above all, the tutors implicitly acknowledged that human beings develop identity through meaning (Smails, 1984); people therefore have to be free (at both a practical and a psychological level) to develop their own meanings. That, for us, is the real value of learning.

THE FEEDBACK PROCESS: LEARN AND CHANGE

While groups were given the opportunity at the outset to form on the basis of their own criteria, many groups felt driven towards an overriding concern with working with friends and those familiar to them. This was in spite of earlier experiences that showed the need for caution in this respect. Consequently, some groups consisted of two sets of friends joining up together (group size was four to five).

One group, in particular, consisted of two pairs with disparate skills and different ways of working; indeed, the two friendships were two very different types of relationship. As a group they worked through conflict by a process of mediation and negotiation within the group itself. The tutors acted as sounding boards for ideas and for commentaries on the conflict. Gradually, one pair learned to work with the other very effectively. Interestingly, one of the remaining pair learned to work in the style of both pairs, to the extent that he managed the interaction more flexibly than the other three members.

In consequence, three of the four pushed themselves towards a level of very high quality learning, they performed well in the car company mode and developed a more holistic approach to their own management competence.

This particular group exemplified the process that was happening amongst all the groups, albeit at a different pace. Essentially, it was a process of learn and change, through tacit agreement concerning the reality of the environment that had been created with the game at its centre. Students became aware of the vital importance of perception and its relationship both to experience and to learning. The classification of new data according to notions of perceived usefulness and the need for further processing was of particular significance in developing an understanding of personal learning processes (cf. the notion of acquiring and applying knowledge – Argyris, 1957; also, meta-learning models, Bateson, 1972).

INTERIM CONCLUSIONS

Pathway for development – the students have gained knowledge about their personal learning processes; additionally they have learned about ownership of their learning and the struggle to achieve this while participating in the learning of others. This is a greater struggle than many of them realized, because it meant re-examining previous groupwork as well as the current context and rethinking some previously accepted meanings. They have gained a feel for managing diverse resources that is akin to the so-called 'real world' (which may be just as virtual as this one, only not as much fun). Importantly, students recognized that the process which had been encouraged here was not one that ended.

Graduation – they all did! The results were beyond the expectations of the college, to the extent that numerous commentators were somewhat confounded. However, the team had already taken the precaution of ensuring that all work was double-marked and a significant selection was triple-marked.

TO THE LEARNING ORGANIZATION THROUGH THE VIRTUAL ORGANIZATION

Pedler *et al.* (1991) draw attention to the learning organization as an advanced stage of development for organizations. It was a recognition of the importance

Figure 4.2 *Dealing with the familiar and unknown* (Hayes, 1993)

of this concept and the identification of the need for students to be more than simply aware of the concept that underpinned much of the planning for the course discussed here. The learning organization is itself a model for learning (to state the obvious); more difficult was finding a way of using it with students who are caught within the boundaries set by conventional education. The notion of the virtual organization provided the means of escaping or subverting these boundaries in order to create a reality where student decisions mattered and affected their own defined outcomes.

THE FUTURE

The obvious needs to be stated: the experiment can be replicated. However, as the process is organic, it will change and develop. Our reflection is informed by

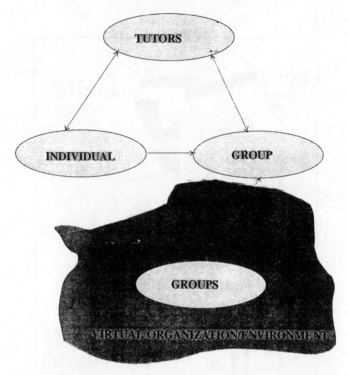

Figure 4.3 *The virtual organization as a learning environment*

student feedback, and the theoretical models that we have used to develop our thinking provide a basis for maintaining the on-going research process. Indeed, a development for us has been in the exploration of the concept of the virtual organization as a holistic learning process. Figure 4.3 models our notion of the virtual organization as a creation of the learning activities of this class of students.

Students needed to be concerned with the multiplicity of roles with which they were being charged. First, they were required to work as learners in their own right; second, they were required to interact with tutors both in an information-exchange mode and in a counselling mode. They had to be part of a small group operating on a number of levels (see below) and, as part of that group, participate in the interactions between the groups. The basis of these interactions changed regularly, as dictated by the requirements of the task, which therefore affected the nature of the relationship within and between the groups.

Figure 4.4 is broadly similar to Kolb's (1984) Learning Circle, but with two important differences. Exploration is seen to precede reflection and it is a stage in which the tutor is actively involved through the use of counselling techniques. Students are encouraged to examine what was happening during the completion of the task both at the level of task operation and at the level of

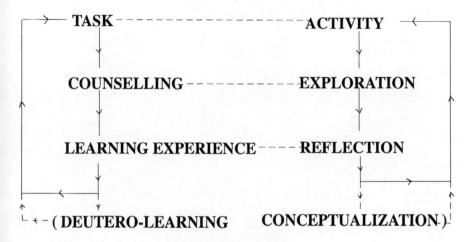

Figure 4.4 *The levels of learning*

individual/group interaction. Reflection is presented as equally active and is about the experience of learning; indeed, it is part of that experience, which students will take back into the next task. Conceptualization is not highlighted here because it may not occur; the authors equate it with the notion of deutero-learning (Argyris and Schon, 1978; Bateson, 1972). It may well be that this level of learning is only partial and perhaps only occurs for some students. It is possibly connected with the coming of some degree of wisdom. It may also have influenced the prevalent view that management cannot be taught to undergraduates. Almost certainly, its development is connected with learner autonomy and responsibility, and the authors hope that the establishment of a virtual environment where personal responsibility is maximized will encourage this development.

Figure 4.5 requires a brief explanation. The management game, research, individual study and discussion, projects, presentations and problem solving constituted the main learning activities for the group. Each required a different learning style and inevitably some activities appealed more than others, according to the preferred style of the individual.

The virtual organization concept allowed tutors and students alike to view the various modes of working within the group as sub-systems. This provided students with opportunities both for managing interaction and for exploring the systemic nature of learning.

The groups interacted in their virtual environment competitively, collaboratively, interactively and in parallel. Switching modes in this way allowed fuller exploration of working relationships, while simultaneously challenging some of the more simplistic notions of what it means to compete in a business market. Parallel learning (Hayes, 1993) allowed the groups to work alongside each other and share learning as and when they saw fit; more than that, it provided for the exploitation of the formalized system that students tacitly

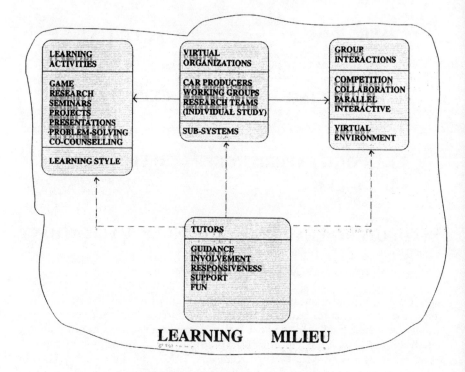

Figure 4.5 *Mapping the learning milieu*

accept is there in an educational establishment and which has its own requirements of conformity.

PROBLEMS AND ISSUES

Reflection and evaluation were not consistently handled by all groups, because of the demands that such activity made upon time and group effort. Given the nature of the role of the tutor, the extent to which the tutor could lead the reflective process was a matter of negotiation with the groups. It is not possible to give groups autonomy and then withdraw it, without a series of negative consequences. The tutor is faced with the decision of leaving groups to find their own way through their own issues. Learning does not take place at a consistent pace either within or between groups. This points up a moral dilemma around the issue of offering rescue. The guiding principle underpinning these decisions has to be to ensure that all groups are moving; the extent and direction of that movement must be primarily the concern of the group. Many groups handled the process effectively, but that effectiveness had to be defined in their own terms.

Differential degrees of empowerment were thus an inevitable consequence of the variations in reflection and learning. Some groups handled the flexibility and uncertainty better than others, although none failed.

Time and college pressures on a very small team will inevitably continue to create tensions, some of which are creative and others of which are more likely to be destructive. They afflict us all and to rehearse the arguments here would be to deviate from the purpose of this chapter.

Resistance to the learning process was largely to do with early uncertainties; the desire for a recognized and familiar structure was apparent, although the group had developed a high level of trust over the previous two years. Some of the more esoteric activities caused some reluctance, most notably those activities concerned with the development of creative thinking. Letting go sufficiently to allow right-brain thinking to occupy as prominent a position as left-brain thinking is not easy for many managers; students have the same reservations. Part of the difficulty is due to the presentation in other forums of these types of thinking as either/or; the tutors here were concerned to present them in a both/and context. Thus, what was unfamiliar and required risk was heightened by the ideological stand taken by the tutors.

Computer facilities and expertise were limited within the team and tremendous reliance was placed upon a member of the student group (and co-author of this chapter). He coordinated the inputs and outputs to enable an efficient and effective information system to operate between the groups. This required coordination of the groups, management of information and plain hard work, slogging away at the keyboard.

The richness and complexity of the process arguably had more effect upon the tutors than on the students. Personal learning for tutors was high, and the quality and depth of discussions in seminars was beyond the team's expectations. Certainly the commitment to continuing the course's development according to the principles established this year is strong. The opportunity to reflect and evaluate afterwards, through the concepts outlined here, has been invaluable.

REFLECTIONS

It is appropriate to reflect upon the process at this stage. Berger and Luckmann (1969) discussed the paradoxical process whereby people construct social order and yet regard it as a reality independent of themselves. Other writers have drawn attention to the fact that the reality of organizations is constructed by participants employing various shared rationalities and logics. The implication here has been in the nature of a warning of the danger of objectivizing a reality that has been constructed.

In learning situations, the constructed nature of the event has always been recognized and pointed up as a difficulty, in that it is not 'the real world'. By contrast, the authors were at pains to exploit the constructed nature of the events, notably the management game, but also all of the activities surrounding it. The aim was to exploit the very difficulties for gain that others had identified in the past. The fact is that every learning task in a sense constructs its own reality, to which students contribute very actively.

The idea was to push this a little further and create 'virtual organizations' out of each group and a virtual environment in which they operated. The experiences of being in that milieu were no less real or meaningful for the students than any other situation. By exploring and developing the fictional world thus created, it became the world that students could manipulate, partially control and interact with. In other words, the very limitations of experiential learning through constructed realities were exploited for their potential in developing student autonomy.

The virtual organization metaphor developed by Douglas (1993) was the starting point for the team, drawing upon the principles of virtual reality. This technological development refers to the experience of the world by participating in its simulation and becoming part of the illusion. It is based upon a graphic world which is inclusive, interactive and occurs in real time. A person becomes part of that world, can change it, and the changes occur as they are made (Aslam, 1993). Douglas extended the idea and coined the term 'the virtual organization' for that interactive space that exists between real organizations which are attempting to interact and collaborate, perhaps for the first time, in a highly uncertain environment. He recognizes the concept as offering potential for inter-organizational development. Thus, the paradox implied by Berger and Luckmann has become a recognizable entity – one hesitates to call it a reality – through a technological development. At the same time, it has offered a useful metaphor for exploring work between organizations and for exploring learning.

The Taoist concept of virtuality (te) refers to the inherent, organic potential of an organism and offers another insight into the processes thus described. The virtuality of the students is, we believe, to organize and manage, to communicate and make decisions, to interact with others and solve problems, to develop meanings of the world for themselves based upon shared meanings and on shared disagreements. If learning is a way of achieving meaning and thus identity, then the virtuality of the human being is to find that identity and become wholly human; learning thus involves the whole person. The whole person must, therefore, be involved in the teaching. In consequence, the total milieu has to be managed, as far as that is possible, and the creation of this virtual environment provides a place where these implicit possibilities can be explored – and individual identities developed.

> My path – the path of any me – is no path.
> Going a way once does not make a path.
> (Barry Stevens)

REFERENCES

Argyris, C (1957) *Personality and Organization*, Harper & Row, New York.
Argyris, C and Schon, D (1978) *Organizational Learning: a theory in action perspective*, Addison-Wesley, Reading, MA.

Aslam, S (1993) 'The Day of the Computer', unpublished dissertation.

Bateson, G (1972) *Steps Towards An Ecology Of Mind*, Aronson, Northvale.

Berger, P L and Luckmann, T (1969) *The Social Construction of Reality*, Penguin, Harmondsworth.

Douglas, R (1993) *Managing in Partnership*, Office for Public Management, London.

Hayes, J N (1993) 'The Journey of Systemic Thinking to Systemic Learning', unpublished dissertation.

Kolb, D A (1984) *Organizational Psychology: experiential approach to organizational behaviour*, Prentice-Hall, Englewood Cliffs, NJ.

McCarthy, M (1992) *Alternative Learning Strategies on a Degree Programme: some interim reflections*, EESAGA 1992, Praga Didacta.

Pedler, M, Burgoyne, J and Boydell, T (1991) *The Learning Company*, McGraw-Hill, London.

Revans, R (1982) *Action Learning*, Chartwell Bratt, Bromley.

Smails, D (1984) *Illusion and Reality*, J M Dent & Sons Ltd, London.

EXECUTIVE is a computer-based business simulation which models the Western Europe car market and is widely used for business and management training. It is available from April Training Executive Ltd, Tarvin Road, Frodsham, Cheshire WA6 6XN.
Tel: (0928) 735868; Fax: (0928) 735352.

ABOUT THE AUTHORS

R Choueke has an extensive background in marketing, and more recently teaching in HE as well as training and consultancy experience. His research interests are focused upon the application of the concept of the learning organization to small businesses. He is interested in the development of non-traditional approaches to teaching and learning with undergraduates.

M McCarthy has many years experience in education and management development. His interests include participative learning and the development of creativity. He has developed programmes in managing change focused upon the interaction between organizational and personal change and based upon a recursive model which utilizes the interaction of students for a group study.

ABOUT THE RESEARCHERS

S Aslam has recently graduated from Edge Hill, and is developing research interests in the application of virtual reality to management education and development. He is undertaking an MA in information systems.

N Hayes is undertaking research at Lancaster University in soft systems and its applications to learning. He is interested in the links between SSM, the learning organization and the virtual organization.

Address for correspondence: Edge Hill College, St Helen's Road, Ormskirk, Lancashire.

Chapter 5

A needs perspective on the induction process

Gordon Ellis

ABSTRACT

It has long been recognized that major changes in life may be difficult and stressful. Moving to a new organizational environment, in either an educational or a work context, is a major change. Newcomers may feel disoriented and confused. Some may become so worried that they suffer acute anxiety. All are likely to experience a degree of stress. The induction process offered to newcomers is therefore of critical importance in helping to overcome these potentially damaging effects of change. This chapter looks at the induction process by focusing on the needs felt by newcomers during the period of change. It attempts to identify the key needs which may have particular significance in the first few days in a new environment. It also makes practical suggestions by exploring ways in which those needs might most effectively be met. A number of games, exercises and other activities are suggested which may prove helpful.

INDUCTION, TRANSITION AND STRESS

Induction is the process of familiarization and socialization that follows a transition. Transitions are fundamental life changes. Induction most often follows the transition from

- home to nursery or school;
- school to further education;
- further to higher education;
- education to employment;
- one job to another.

In these situations induction serves two principal purposes. First, familiarization or orientation, which serves to introduce the newcomer to the organization, its structure, tasks and people. Second, socialization which, in global terms, will embrace the acquisition of skills and abilities, the adoption of appropriate role behaviours, and adjustment to the norms and values of the organization. For the newcomer, it is a process of change.

Change is often traumatic. Transitions are frequently stressful and place the newcomer in an unfamiliar environment, amongst unknown peers, and with uncertain expectations. Holmes and Rahe (1967) identified a wide range of life changes that cause stress. It is significant to note that even favourable, pleasant or desired changes may lead to stress. Stress, in this context, is the individual's reaction to the adjustment needed to cope with change.

Individuals may differ widely in their perceptions of such transitions. Some may view the change with trepidation, anxiety and worry. Others may view the change with eagerness, excitement and happiness. Work subsequent to that of Holmes and Rahe suggests that perception of the transition may be important in determining how an individual will adjust to change. For example, Sarason et al. (1978) found that physical and emotional problems resulting from change are more likely to occur where changes are perceived as bad, rather than good.

Regardless of individual perceptions, the process of induction must address a number of important issues. Any process that involves familiarization and socialization is inevitably complex. The fundamental requirement though is for the newcomer to make a good start. Making a good start is important to both the individual and to the organization. From the individual's viewpoint it is perhaps self-evident that settling-in quickly to a new environment is beneficial in, for example, overcoming the stresses of change and gaining advantage from new opportunities. From the organization's viewpoint there are also benefits in the newcomer making a good start. In the job context it is necessary to 'recoup' the high costs of recruitment and to get the newcomer to contribute to the success of the organization. In the educational context, cost may be less of a consideration but since courses tend to be only as successful as their participants then rapid integration is just as vital in education as in commercial contexts.

If making a good start is important, how can it best be achieved? The process of orientation and socialization is of such complexity that a range of valid approaches could be advanced to answer this question. It is suggested here that a very effective approach may be developed by adopting a clear focus on the newcomer's needs.

NEEDS AND INDUCTION

Needs have been extensively studied. These studies have often been in the context of motivation, for needs and drives are essentially two sides of the same coin. Maslow (1954) proposed his now-familiar hierarchy of needs, with a progression through needs satisfaction from the lowest (physiological) to the highest (self-actualization):

- physiological needs;
- security, or safety, needs;
- affiliation, or acceptance, needs;
- esteem needs;
- self-actualization needs.

Alderfer (1969) suggested a similar progressive approach to the satisfaction of needs, but with only three levels – existency, relationship, and growth. Alderfer differs from Maslow in a number of respects and argues that extra reward or satisfaction at lower levels may compensate for failure to progress. It is not clear that needs do work in this progressive manner. Hall and Nougaim (1968) found little evidence to support the theory of a hierarchy of needs. Instead it seems that the relative importance of needs is variable and dependent on situation and circumstances at a particular moment.

McClelland (1953) suggested that there are three motivating needs: power, affiliation, and achievement. However, he viewed needs in a less universal manner than Maslow and emphasized that needs are socially acquired and culturally variable. It is clear that needs satisfaction does occur predominantly in a social context. Presser et al. (1966) also stress the importance of the feeling of self as the point of reference for all one's behaviour.

Needs satisfaction and motivation are relevant considerations during induction. The success, or otherwise, of a newcomer's subsequent performance may depend on how well his or her individual needs have been addressed during the first few days in the organization. No single theory of needs or motivation has achieved universal applicability. There can be no doubt, however, that needs do exist and that needs will be felt keenly during any period of orientation and socialization.

Drawing from the knowledge of the various theories advanced it is perhaps possible to identify some specific needs of special significance during the period of induction. It is suggested that the following four needs are of particular importance:

- the need to belong;
- the need to know;
- the need for support;
- the need for skills.

PUTTING THEORY INTO PRACTICE

Organizational objectives and expediency during the induction period sometimes obstruct the focus on the needs of newcomers. This is unfortunate since, despite the complexity of orientation and socialization, induction is essentially concerned with first impressions. First impressions have a lasting impact and it is therefore in the organization's best interests to make a favourable impression. As Armstrong (1988) points out, recruitment is expensive and its cost would be largely wasted by creating a bad impression.

Induction, focused on the needs of newcomers, will form good first impressions. Furthermore, it will foster an atmosphere from which the newcomer – and, therefore, the organization – will gain most benefit. The approach described here is of greatest direct relevance to further and higher education but general principles are equally applicable to induction in other situations.

The need to belong, for affiliation and acceptance, has been generally recognized as a basic human need. Humans, as social animals, seek company and the approval of others. We tend to feel unhappy if lonely or rejected, and are distressed by isolation. We probably all know that a crowd of strangers can be a lonely place and that a sense of belonging and personal security is the only antidote to that loneliness.

Addressing the need to belong during the induction period requires time and activities to enable people (both students and staff) to get to know one another, to make new friends, and to form a sense of group identity. Increasingly, courses are becoming modular in structure. With modular structures the need to belong is even more important, but becomes more elusive. Course identity may easily be lost in modular schemes and students may feel 'homeless' in a module serving many different courses.

Time to break the ice and make personal introductions is valuable in fostering a sense of belonging. Many different forms of activity may be adopted to help in this task. Informal gatherings, of the 'wine and cheese' or 'tea party' type, are often suggested but tend, in practice, to further isolate introverts. More appropriate may be some of the wide range of games developed for ice-breaking.

On the choice of games van Ments (1978) warns of the dangers of using emotionally-charged or threatening games; it is advisable to heed this warning. Choice will ultimately be dictated by time available and personal preferences. An activity which has been found useful in effecting introductions and building group cohesiveness is to suggest to students that they compile a course members' directory giving some basic information about themselves. This may include names, ages, sex, interests and hobbies, personality or whatever information the students themselves decide. The completed directory may be photocopied and a copy given to each course member. More structured games may also be useful, providing they are non-threatening and enjoyable. A good example of this type is ISLAND ESCAPE by Crookall et al. (1988). (Incidentally, this game includes a profile sheet which might provide a suitable basis for compiling a directory of course members.)

The need to know is fundamental for the newcomer. Armstrong (1988) identifies the necessity for the newcomer to know what is expected of him or her and to provide the information to enable them to master their new environment. Students need a great deal of information during their first few days and face an informational jigsaw which must somehow be pieced together.

The potential range of information is enormous. Students need to know about staff and fellow students, about the course and options, about the university or college and its various facilities, about practical matters like accommodation and health, about the city or town, and so on. It is perhaps not surprising that students often suffer from too much information, rather than too little. Information overload is a very real danger.

Information may be gleaned by students in many ways. Handbooks, presentations – either in person or by video – and 'fairs' are perhaps the most common ways of giving information to students. Games and activities, though, may again play an important part in the process. Self-discovery activities, for example, may provide further opportunities to foster a sense of belonging while simultaneously enabling students to discover information themselves. The simplest form of self-discovery activity is the treasure hunt, in which groups of students are required to solve a range of clues (given overtly or in disguised form) in order to discover information about the course, university or college, the town and the surrounding area. This may be followed by an information 'swap shop' in which students exchange discoveries that they have found useful, exciting, boring, funny, frightening and so on.

During life it is inevitable that we will from time to time face difficulties and problems of one sort or another. These could be concerned with money, with work or study, with health, or with a host of other practical or personal issues. When faced with difficulties and problems it is reassuring and often comforting to be able to turn to others for help. We have a need for support. This need is quite closely related to the need to belong in the sense that it is concerned with feeling safe and secure. However, the need for support goes further and deeper than just belonging and being accepted.

The need for support through social and work networks has been widely recognized. Fensterheim and Baer (1976) suggest that satisfactory networks will possess four common characteristics:

- the provision of security;
- the inclusion of varying kinds of relationship, from close to superficial;
- gearing to the individual's specific needs;
- constant changes in composition.

Within the induction process it is important that the need for support is addressed. This may be tackled by asking students to think about their own network of contacts. Consider a range of situations (sharing good/bad news, handling a crisis, getting feedback, and so on), encouraging students to identify who they would turn to in each situation. Consider also whether the contacts are near at hand or far away. Ask students to think about ways of improving their personal network, by filling in gaps or adding 'near' contacts to supplement those further away.

The need for support may also be addressed through group activities. For example, teams of three or four may be asked to consider a problem scenario, advising on what action might be taken to solve the problem. All teams may tackle the same problem or, alternatively, different teams may be set different problems. Each team reports back to the whole class and further suggestions may be invited. As a follow-up to this activity, a directory of useful contacts, addresses and telephone numbers could be compiled.

The need for skills is essential to the successful accomplishment of many tasks. It is without doubt true that learning skills are vital if students are to gain maximum benefit from their chosen course. Within induction the emphasis need not be focused on traditional study skills, such as how to take lecture notes. Rather, the emphasis should be on increasing awareness and understanding of the learning process itself.

Learning is not a skill which is confined to formal educational contexts. It is a fundamental skill which enables us to adapt and to handle change throughout our entire lives. According to Naisbit and Aburdene (1986), learning how to learn is the most important skill to acquire now. We need to take responsibility for our own learning.

A variety of ways may be found to help students explore the learning process. One way to do this would be to ask students to focus on something they learnt in the past – mathematics, French, swimming, or whatever. Then, trying really hard to remember, the students should address a number of questions:

- What was it like to be the learner?
- What was good about learning?
- What was bad about learning?
- How were you able to get the best out of learning?
- What could you have done to spoil the learning?
- How does your learning happen?

The last question may have many different answers since individual learning may occur in many ways. Some may learn best by experimenting, others by watching and listening, or by reading or memorizing and so on. Some learn best in groups, others by working alone. Small group discussion on approaches to learning may follow individual consideration of the series of questions. Here the emphasis may be forward-looking, concentrating on how learning may best occur on the course about to begin.

CONCLUSION

The induction process is often traumatic. It is, however, a process which must be accepted and worked through since it cannot be avoided. Although it cannot be avoided, it is argued that induction may be made less traumatic, and hence more effective.

These improvements in the induction process stem from recognizing that during induction newcomers will have specific needs. If these needs are not satisfied then induction may be painful, prolonged and unsuccessful. If, however, these specific needs are properly addressed and satisfied then induction will be easier, quicker and much more successful.

The four specific needs of newcomers suggested here may or may not meet with universal acceptance and approval. Other observers and practitioners may wish to add to the list of specific needs or to change those suggested. It is felt, however, that the recognition of specific needs which can be addressed may be more crucial to success than the precise description of what those needs are. The essential element in planning a programme of induction is the attempt to address the needs of newcomers.

The practical approach to addressing needs which has been described relies heavily on experiential, student-centred exercises and activities. This approach, rather than a more instructional, didactic, approach is especialy well-suited to addressing needs during induction. The experiential approach is, in itself, and regardless of the purpose leading to its adoption, helpful in encouraging the discovery of information and knowledge. Additionally, because much experiential work involves group activities, the experiential approach automatically fosters a sense of belonging and encourages supportive relationships. No other approach appears to have these 'in-built' advantages in addressing the needs of newcomers so effectively or so effortlessly.

REFERENCES

Alderfer, C P (1969) 'An empirical test of a theory of human needs', *Organisational Behaviour and Human Performance*, 4, 142–75.

Armstrong, M (1988) *A Handbook of Human Resource Management*, Kogan Page, London.

Crookall, D, Oxford, R, Saunders, D and Coote, A (1988) *ISLAND ESCAPE, Perspectives on Gaming and Simulation*, 13, 151–6, Kogan Page, London.

Fensterheim, H and Baer, J (1976) *Don't Say 'Yes' When You Want to Say 'No'*, Futura/Macdonald, London.

Hall, D T and Nougaim, K (1968) 'An examination of Maslow's need hierarchy in an organizational setting', *Organizational Behaviour and Human Performance*, 3,1, 12–35.

Holmes, T H and Rahe, R H (1967) 'The social readjustment rating scale', *Journal of Psychosomatic Research*, 11, 213–18.

McClelland, D C (1953) *The Achievement Motive*, Appleton-Century-Crofts, New York.

Maslow, A H (1954) *Motivation and Personality*, Harper & Row, London.

Naisbit, J and Aburdene, P (1986) *Re-inventing the Corporation*, Macdonald, London.

Presser, H A, Boyd, G W D and Lea, R C G (1966) 'The social conditions for successful learning', in Oeser, A O (ed) *Teacher, Pupil and Task*, Tavistock Publications, London.

Sarason, I G, Johnson, J H and Siegel, J M (1978) 'Assessing the impact of life changes: development of the life experiences survey', *Journal of Consulting and Clinical Psychology*, 46, 932–46.

van Ments, M (1978) 'Breaking the ice: games to warm up a new group', *Perspectives on Academic Gaming & Simulation 1 and 2*, 15–20, Kogan Page, London.

ABOUT THE AUTHOR

Gordon Ellis is a senior lecturer in the Faculty of Business at the University of Luton. He has a long-standing interest in gaming and simulation. Published work includes various articles and the communication game, CLUEBUS-TERS! (Maxim Training Systems).

Address for correspondence: Faculty of Business, University of Luton, Park Square, Luton LU1 3JU.

SECTION 2: Induction, team-building and outdoor education

Chapter 6

Forty-eight warm-ups for group work

Jo Malseed

ABSTRACT

This chapter offers a valuable teaching resource to small-group tutors by providing a step-by-step guide to the use of warm-ups. It takes tutors through the nature, operation and benefits of warm-ups in small-group teaching, and goes on to describe the function and use of a collection of 48 low-, medium- and high-risk warm-ups.

Warm-ups are essential . . . . Working together as a group was slow to achieve, but it's now happening well. The warm-up exercises were indispensable. (First-year undergraduate on course based entirely on group work).

Warm-ups can make all the difference to the success of group learning activities, such as undergraduate and postgraduate seminars, training programmes and short courses. It is not unusual for group learning in, for instance, conventional higher education settings to be difficult for both students and tutors. Typically, some students spend much of their time silent with their heads bowed, trying not to attract the attention of the tutor. Others talk non-stop or are shy, bored or apparently unmotivated. At the same time, the tutor desperately tries to fill the silences, tactfully stop a student from dominating the group, reassure the others or gain their interest.

Careful use of warm-ups – as part of a package of participative learning methods – can help prevent this happening.

WHAT ARE WARM-UPS?

Warm-ups are games for more than one person, specially designed to use in group learning situations. They are generally employed at the beginning of a

This material was originally published by the Unit for Innovation in Higher Education (IHE), Lancaster University.

session, or before the first activity in a new phase of a course or training programme.

Warm-ups can be valuable not only at the beginning of, but also throughout, a course. They can fulfil a variety of functions; they can:

- help 'break the ice' in new groups, by allowing people to learn each others' names and something about each other;
- prepare groups for mixing and working together by encouraging, and presenting ways for group members to interact and participate;
- wake people up, both physically and mentally, which sharpens their concentration and helps them engage and work more effectively;
- help focus groups, both new and established, as preparation for activities to follow, and/or collaborative work;
- provide information for facilitators about, for instance, levels of ability and group dynamics, which can valuably inform subsequent planning;
- help people have fun and enjoy learning.

HOW TO USE WARM-UPS

Warm-ups should not be used indiscriminately. In order for them to be effective, it is most important that facilitators choose the ones most appropriate for their groups and desired outcomes.

Not all groups, or all group members, can stand the same levels of personal risk presented by warm-ups. For instance, groups of drama students may feel comfortable engaging in warm-ups which demand close physical contact, personal exposure, or looking 'silly'. However, groups of, say, conventional academics – who usually confine themselves to verbal interaction at work – or new groups, are more likely to find such activities too risky, intimidating or irrelevant at first, and feel safer with others which are less demanding and less threatening.

To help facilitators choose appropriate warm-ups, those presented here are allotted to three categories according to the degree of personal risk to participants which I feel they involve: low risk (section A); medium risk (section B); and high risk (section C).

I suggest that before embarking on any of these warm-ups, groups should be given clear instructions on what they have to do. This may mean a practice run, or at least asking if everyone understands what is expected of them. It helps if the facilitator has an idea of how the warm-up being used is supposed to run, and what the likely pitfalls and misunderstandings may be (those which I have encountered are indicated in the text). Ideally, this comes with first-hand experience of the warm-up, but failing that, it may help to go through the warm-up with colleagues or friends, or at least for facilitators to run through the steps beforehand in their heads. Each warm-up presented here is set out in a series of steps to help both with this preparation and with giving clear instructions.

Lastly, warm-ups are supposed to help groups feel comfortable and energized, not intimidated. To guard against participants feeling unnecessarily threatened, I suggest that facilitators point out that anyone can sit out of a warm-up at any time.

END NOTE: ISN'T IT RISKY FOR THE FACILITATOR?

It is quite common for facilitators to start using warm-ups at the beginning of a course, but lapse after a while, or to 'shy away' from them altogether. This is largely in response to the belief that groups will find them childish; that they are not appropriate for all groups; or that they serve no particular function other than helping people learn each others' names at the beginning of the course.

I must admit that I often think twice before using warm-ups with a new group, or before continuing with them with an established group, either because I forget and doubt their value or because I fear that some groups will not receive them favourably. However, the warm-ups presented here can be easily adapted to suit individual group needs and abilities, and I have successfully used them with a wide range of groups, including undergraduates, trainee tutors, youth theatre, and adults with learning difficulties and physical disabilities. It always surprises and heartens me how well they go down and how successful they are in serving their purpose, as the following comments from participants on a women's skills management course illustrate:

Really was 'fun'. You could feel the atmosphere change in the group.

Thoroughly enjoyable – a good ice-breaker. First of all I thought 'Not games, I hate games', but these were fun.

A good way of breaking the ice and getting to know each other.

Brilliant! Very effective and great fun. Made the rest of the course so much easier.

Excellent way of getting to know each other quickly and safely. Felt very comfortable with the group throughout the games and after.

It just leaves me to say that if you would like to go some way towards avoiding those difficult group learning situations shot through with apparent boredom, unconnectedness, distance, isolation, shyness, silence, apathy and limited learning, try introducing warm-ups.

LIST OF 48 WARM-UPS FOR GROUP WORK

To inform facilitator choice of warm-ups, I have briefly included here some indication of the possible value of each warm-up, in addition to that of being fun and raising energy levels, and encouraging group participation. Warm-ups can also be usefully employed to prepare groups for subsequent activities in a session, such as focusing on a partiular theme or drawing on particular skills. These benefits, of course, I cannot predict here. I take no credit for the design of any of the warm-ups presented here. They have been collected in various workshops and from colleagues over several years, the original sources unknown.

A. Low-risk warm-ups   **Page**

B. Medium-risk warm-ups

A. LOW-RISK WARM-UPS

A1. I am and I like
- The group sits/stands in a circle, facing inwards.
- Going around the circle everyone says their first name, together with something they like/do not like/both, or (for groups who can manage something more risky) something they would like the group to know about them.

NB It is important that the facilitator clarifies that no personal 'secrets' are disclosed, otherwise the warm-up becomes an encounter group.

A2. Name and throw
- The group sits in a circle, facing inwards.
- Going around the circle everyone says their first name.
- The group stands in a wide circle, facing inwards.
- One group member takes an easy-to-throw object, eg, a soft toy, calls out someone else's name, and throws the object to that person.
- That person thanks the thrower by name, then calls out someone else's name, and throws the object to him or her, and so on.
- The facilitator should point out that those throwing can check out names they may have forgotten before throwing, so that eventually everyone knows everyone else's name.

A3. 'Introductions' 1
- Divide the group into pairs.
- Give each pair time to introduce themselves to their partners in some detail, and explain that they will then reconvene and introduce their partners to the rest of the group.
- Reconvene and invite the pairs to introduce themselves.

NB This is a useful activity for small groups, such as ten people or less, but can be threatening for the final pairs in a larger group, as they have to wait a long time for their turn. It is recommended that this activity should be avoided in large groups, because with more than ten people it produces more information than members can take in.

A4. Introductions and three things

- The group mingles, and everyone has to introduce themselves to everyone else by saying their name and three short sentences about themselves, eg, 'My name's Jo. I have a black cat called Snowy. I cycle to work. And I laid my own lawn.' No one can change their three things: they have to tell the same three things to everyone.
- Although everyone must have the chance to meet everyone else, this exercise should be quick and involve no extra chatting.
- The group should be warned that they have to try and remember all this information.
- Repeat the exercise, but instead of giving their own names and three things to the people they meet, everyone has to recite the names and the three things of the people they meet back to them.
- At the end, the facilitator can call on the group to say the appropriate three things about each member.
NB In larger groups, the number of 'things' for each person can be reduced.

A5. Clap clap click click

- The group stands in a circle, facing inwards.
- Going around the circle, every one in turn says their first name out loud.
- The facilitator establishes a four-beat rhythm: clap, clap, click left-hand fingers, click right-hand fingers. The whole group takes up this rhythm.
- The facilitator say his or her name on the 'left click', and then the name of the person on his or her right on the 'right click'.
- This new person then does the same, passing the pattern on to the next person, and so on around the circle, during which the four-beat rhythm should not be broken.
- After the circle has been completed, the pattern can be passed randomly, and the beat increased.
NB If not all the group can click their fingers, change the instruction to patting left and right knees or shoulders.

A6. Magic box

- The group sits in a circle, facing inwards.
- Going around in a circle, each person has to imagine there is a magic box on his or her lap, and by miming indicate the size of the box and what is inside.
- The rest of the group have to guess what is inside the box.
- If the group cannot guess from the mime, the facilitator can allow questions with 'Yes' or 'No' answers.

A7. Hand squeeze passing

- The group sits or stands in a circle, holding hands.
- The facilitator squeezes the hand of the person on his or her right, and that person passes the squeeze to the next person, and so on around the circle back to the leader.

- This operation is timed, with the object of passing the squeeze around the circle as fast as possible.
- Repeat in the opposite direction.

A8. Birthday line-up
- The facilitator indicates that January is one end of the room, and December the other, and then asks the group to line themselves up in order of their birthdays.
- There is an optional rule: no verbal communication.
  Variation: the facilitator indicates that North is one end of the room, South the other, and East and West at either side, and then asks the group to arrange themselves according to where they live/were born.

A9. Making shapes
- The facilitator asks the group to make certain shapes, given by him or her, as a whole group by standing/sitting etc., together.
- An easy shape to start with is a circle. Others could include a triangle, hexagon, multiplication/division sign, question-mark.

A10. Change three things
- Divide the group into pairs.
- The partners in each pair stand facing each other.
- With one starting at the other's feet, and the other the other's head, the pairs study everything about their partner's appearance.
- The pairs turn around so that they have their backs to each other, and change three things each about their appearance.
- They turn back and have to spot which three things their partners have changed.
- Change partners and repeat, stipulating a greater number of changes.
  Variation: rather than using couples, pair groups of three or four participants at a time.

A11. String and ring
- The group sits/stands in a circle, facing inwards, with one person standing in the middle.
- The group holds a loop of string with a ring on it, and passes/pretends to pass the ring to each other.
- The person in the middle has to guess who has the ring.
- Change the person in the middle after every successful guess, or after a stipulated number of guesses (whichever comes first).

A12. Concentration circle
- The group stands in a circle, facing inwards.
- One person, A, makes eye contact with another person, B, and walks towards B, eventually taking B's place in the circle.
- In the meantime, B immediately makes eye contact with C, and walks towards C, eventually taking his or her place, and so on.
  NB Individuals must make eye contact with someone *before* they start walking towards them, and not *as* they walk towards them.

A13. Yurt circle

(This game derives from the design of a Mongolian nomad's tent where the roof pushes up against the walls in perfect equilibrium, keeping the structure standing. It works better with a minimum of 12.)

- The group stands in a circle, facing inwards, with an even number of people standing almost shoulder-to-shoulder and holding hands.
- Going around the circle, people are labelled alternately 'In' or 'Out', so that each 'In' is standing between two 'Outs' and *vice versa*.
- On the count of three, the 'Ins' lean towards the centre of the circle while the 'Outs' lean back, all keeping their feet stationary and supporting each other by their held hands.
- With practice, the group can lean further and further forwards and backwards, and also try switching back and forth in rhythm.

  NB It is worth giving a few participants the chance to observe the group from a distance, so for each Yurt Circle, give two people a rest and a chance to watch – from an elevated position if possible.

A14. Following

- The group walks around the room, and are instructed to follow someone, without being followed themselves.

  NB This is impossible, but until participants realize this, it can be fun and energizing to try!

A15. Psychology hands game

- The group kneels in a circle, facing inwards with their palms flat on the floor in front of them.
- Everyone should place their hands so that there is a hand of each of the people either side of them between their own.
- One person slaps one of his or her hands on the floor, followed by the person with the hand to his or her right, and so on around the circle, until someone slaps their hand on the floor twice in quick succession, in which case the direction is reversed.
- Anyone slapping their hand out of turn, or failing to slap, 'loses' the offending hand, until there is only one person left in the game.

B. MEDIUM-RISK WARM-UPS

B1. Constructions

- Establish groups of between three and six members.
- Using their own bodies, each group has to construct a still body statue/tableau/representation of an item given to them by the facilitator (eg, bathroom, record-player, cathedral, bridge, etc.).
- The facilitator sets a short time limit for this task, eg, two minutes.
- Each group then shows its statue to the other group(s), who have to guess what it is.

B2. Who stole the cookie?

- The group stands in a circle, facing inwards.
- Going around the circle, starting with No. 1, each person is given a number, which he/she must remember.
- This is a chanting game, which must keep to a rhythm established by the whole group clicking their fingers/clapping to a chant in the following way:
  No. 1: 'W*ho stole the co*okie from the co*okie j*ar? Number t*wo.'
  No. 2: 'Who *me?;
  No. 1: 'Yes y*ou.'
  No. 2: 'Not *me.'
  No. 1: 'Then w*ho?'
  No. 2: 'Number th*ree.'   * = claps, finger-clicks
  No. 3: 'Who *me?'
  No. 2: 'Yes y*ou.'
  No. 3: 'Not *me.'
  No. 2: 'Then w*ho?.'
  No. 3: 'Number f*our.'
  No. 4: 'Who *me?'
  and so on until the circle is completed.
- The chant can then be passed randomly.

B3. Fizz-buzz

- The group stands in a circle, and going around the circle counts from one upwards.
- Any multiple of five must be replaced by 'fizz' and any multiple of seven must be replaced by 'buzz', giving the sequence 'one, two, three four, fizz, six, buzz, eight, etc.'.
- After the number 22, anyone who misses a fizz or buzz, or makes a mistake, is eliminated from the game.

B4. Adverb game

- One member of the group leaves the room.
- The others decide upon an adverb.
- The person returns and asks up to three members of the group to perform a specified action each, in the way of the chosen adverb.
- The person then has to guess the adverb. Three guesses are allowed.
- Repeat with a new person leaving the room.

B5. Fruit bowl

- All group members, except one, sit on chairs in a circle facing inwards.
- The one without a chair stands in the middle of the circle, and labels everyone (including him or herself) alternately around the circle, either an 'apple' or a 'pear' (or any two fruits chosen by the group).
- The person in the middle then calles out 'apples', and all the 'apples' have to come into the middle of the circle, and then each find a chair – other than the one they have just left – and sit down.
- In the meantime, the original person in the middle has to try and find a chair and sit down.

- This should leave a new person in the middle, who repeats the operation by calling out either 'apples' or 'pears'.
- The person in the middle can also call out 'fruit bowl', which means that everyone has to get up, come into the middle, and then find a new chair.
  Variation: instead of fruit, group members can be labelled, for instance, farm animals and make appropriate movements and sounds. The person in the middle can also introduce adverbs, by calling out for instance, 'pigs, noisily'.
  NB This warm-up can be rough. I suggest that group members should be warned of this, and asked to be careful with each other. Alternatively, the facilitator can stipulate that people should move slowly, or take small steps.

B6. All those who
- All the group, except one, sit on chairs in a circle facing inwards.
- The one without a chair stands in the middle and makes a 'statement' starting with, 'All those who . . .', such as, 'All those who are wearing blue.'
- Those to whom the 'statement' applies have to leave their chairs, come into the middle of the circle, and then each find a chair – other than the one they have just left – and sit down.
- Meanwhile the original person in the middle has to try and find a chair and sit down.
- This should leave a new person in the middle, who then chooses another 'All those who . . .'.
  NB As for B5.

B7. Hands and feet statue
- Divide into groups of between three and eight members.
- The facilitator tells the groups to form body statues, stipulating the number of feet and hands which must be on the floor in each group, such as 'three feet and nine hands'.
- If this proves easy, reduce the number of feet and hands allowed.
  NB Facilitators may want to introduce safety rules, such as no standing on shoulders, etc.

B8. Clapping 1
- The group stands/sits in a circle.
- One person claps a short rhythm.
- The others join in, so the whole group is clapping the same rhythm.
- While the group is still clapping one person alters the rhythm, and the others have to copy the new pattern, without breaking the clapping, and so on.

B9. Clapping 2
- The group stands/sits in a circle.
- One person claps a rhythm.
- The next person in the circle copies that rhythm, and then adds one of his or her own.
- The next person copies the last rhythm, and then adds one of his or her own, and so on around the circle.

B10. Clapping 3
- The group stands/sits in a circle.
- Each person thinks of a word/phrase with several syllables.
- Going around the circle, each person in turn says his or her word, and claps the rhythm at the same time.
- Repeat, but this time each person continues saying and clapping their words, so that eventually everyone is saying and clapping together.
- Repeat, but without the words.

B11. Find the 'rat'
- The group sits on chairs, except one member who leaves the room.
- Those remaining have to hide a small object, eg, a soft toy, on one of them, eg, by sitting on it.
- The person outside comes back in and has to guess who has the object. He or she has a set number of guesses. The rest of the group have to try and mislead him or her.
- Repeat with another person outside the room.

B12. Do you like your neighbour?
[This can also supplement a name game.)
- The group sits on chairs in a circle, facing inwards, with one person standing in the middle.
- The person in the middle chooses one of the group and asks, '(Name), do you like your neighbour?'
- If the named person says 'Yes', then the two people sitting either side of him or her have to get up and swap places. In the meantime the person in the middle has to try and sit down.
- If the named person says 'No', the person in the middle asks, 'Who would you like?', and he or she replies by naming two other people in the group. Then the 'neighbours' and the two other named people have to get up and each find new places to sit.
- In the meantime, the person in the middle also has to try and sit down.
- This should leave a new person in the middle to repeat the whole exercise.
  NB It should be pointed out to participants that the warm-up is light-hearted, and that they should not take others' responses personally.

B13. Group humming
- The group lies on the floor with their heads touching, like spokes in a wheel.
- The facilitator instructs them to breathe in for the count of four, and then breathe out slowly, all humming the same note.
- Repeat until the group is concentrating fully.
- This activity can be 'rounded off' with a series of facial exercises led by the facilitator, such as patting the face, screwing up and relaxing the face, and opening the mouth wide and sticking out the tongue.

B14. Nose leading
- The group walks randomly around the room.

- The facilitator calls out a part of the body, eg, nose, chest, knees, etc., and the group have to walk with that part leading.
- Repeat with different parts of the body.
NB The facilitator can suggest that group members take it in turns to be observers, as the exercise can be funny to watch.

B15. Can Popeye have a corner?
(For a minimum of 12 people and a maximum of 18.)
- The group divides up with three to four members in each of the four corners of the room, and one standing in the middle.
- The person in the middle asks one of the corners 'Can Popeye have a corner?' The corner confers and then replies either 'Yes' or 'Try next door.' If 'Try next door', then the person asks another corner the same question.
- When one of the corners replies 'Yes', all the people in the corners immediately have to run individually to each of the other three corners, and end up in a corner with two or three others, none of whom they were with previously. In the meantime, the person in the middle has to run to a corner.
- The last person to find a corner goes into the middle, and repeats the exercise.
NB The facilitator should point out to the group that the warm-up depends on members keeping to the rules.

B16. Cat and mouse
(For a large group.)
- The group, except two, stands in a grid formation all facing the same way, each with their arms stretched out touching the two people either side of them, forming a series of 'avenues'.
- The remaining two are a 'cat' and a 'mouse', and the 'cat' chases the 'mouse' up and down the avenues.
- When the facilitator shouts 'left' or 'right', those forming the avenues have to turn 90 degrees to the left or right, changing the direction of the avenues.
- When the 'cat' catches the 'mouse', they swap places with two other people, and the game is repeated.

C. HIGH-RISK WARM-UPS

C1. Alternative musical chairs
(This is the same as conventional musical chairs, apart from one difference: the idea is to keep everyone in the game. This means that more than one person to a chair is allowed. As this game is culture-specific, it may be necessary to check whether the whole group knows the game, and to explain it in detail.)
- Set up two rows of chairs, back-to-back, so that there is a chair for every member of the group apart from one.
- The group walks/dances around the chairs to music.
- When the music is stopped, everyone sits down.
- Only when there are no hands and feet on the ground, can the music be started again, a chair removed, and the exercise repeated.

NB It may not be safe to continue until only one chair remains.

C2. Walking in different weathers

- The group members walk randomly around the room.
- The facilitator calls out different weathers (eg, windy, sunny, hailing, foggy), and the group members have to continue walking and react accordingly with their bodies.
  Variation: call out different mood adjectives, such as 'happy', 'sad'; or famous names.

C3. Medusa's raft

- The group forms a tight circle (if the group is large, form two or more circles), leaving one person outside the circle.
- Draw a chalk ring around the circle.
- The person outside the circle has to try and get inside, and the others have to try and stop him or her, without stepping outside the chalk ring.
- The game continues until the person outside gets in, or a member of the circle steps outside the ring.
- Reform, with a new person outside.
  Variation: as above, but with someone inside the circle, trying to get out.

C4. Elbow, fruit, hop

- The group members walk randomly around the room.
- The facilitator shouts 'Stop' and then calls out a part of the human body, eg, elbow; a category, eg, fruit; and a way of moving, eg, hopping.
- The group members immediately have to respond by simultaneously and repeatedly: moving that part of their body; shouting out something from that category, (eg, melon); and moving in the specified way.
- The facilitator then shouts 'Stop', and the group resumes walking randomly around the room.
- Repeat with other examples, eg, 'left ear, MPs, crawl'.

C5. 'Introductions' 2

- Divide the group into pairs.
- Ask each person to introduce him or herself to their partners by imitating the words and actions of someone in their everyday life, or from the media.
  NB Some groups may find it too risky to 'perform' in front of an audience, in which case all the pairs can work simultaneously.

C6. Applause

- One group member stands in front of the rest of the group and performs a short simple action to the group, eg, miming pouring and drinking a cup of tea.
- The group then applauds rapturously, and the 'performer' has to stand and take the applause and praise.
- Repeat with a new 'performer'.
  NB This may be difficult for some groups, and so should be used with care.

C7. Self, Cynthia, sandwich box

- The group stands at one side of the room and on a given signal walk forward and introduce themselves, all at the same time, to an imaginary person/audience until given the signal to stop.
- Repeat the exercise, but with everyone introducing themselves as a fictional or media character of their choice, for example 'Cynthia'.
- Repeat the exercise, but with everyone introducing themselves as an object, eg, a sandwich box.

C8. Problems

- Each group member thinks of a general personal problem, eg, acne.
- Everyone stands in a line at one side of the room.
- They all walk with small steps across the room making sure that they stay in a straight line, and simultaneously 'rehearse' explaining their problem to a friend, starting softly and getting louder, until they get to the other side of the room.
- Repeat, but saying just one word or phrase from the first stage over and over again.

C9. Ball tag

- One of the group is 'it', and is not allowed to move around the room.
- 'It' has to throw a soft ball at members of the group, who are allowed to move.
- When 'it' hits one of the others with the ball, he or she must shout out the name of whoever has been hit.
- This new person then becomes 'it', and the exercise is repeated.

C10. Mirroring

- The group stands in a circle, facing inwards.
- One person slowly moves his or her body from the waist up, and the others mirror the actions.
- The facilitator changes the person leading the actions by calling out someone else's name.
- This change of leader should become increasingly quicker.
  Variation: divide into pairs, with partners taking it in turns to mirror the actions of the other.

C.11 Masks

- The group stands/sits in a circle, facing inwards, with a minimum space of two feet between each person.
- One person makes a face, which the person to his or her right has to copy.
- When the new person has received the face, the first person can relax.
- The new person then has to make a new face or develop the old one, and pass it onto the person on his or her right, and so on around the circle.
  Variation: as above, but using postures or gestures instead of faces. Sounds can also be added.

C12. It's Tuesday

- The group stands in a circle, facing inwards.

- One person makes a simple statement, eg, 'It's Tuesday.'
- The person to his/her right has to overreact, in words and movement, to this statement.
- This new person then makes another simple statement, unrelated to the first, eg. 'I had a boiled egg this morning', and the person to his/her right has to overreact, and so on around the circle.
  NB This exercise is particularly valuable for 'clearing the mind', and encouraging spontaneity and new thought, rather than logical planning.

C13. What are you doing?
- The group stands in a circle, facing inwards.
- One person mimes an action, eg, playing a trumpet.
- The person to his or her right asks 'What are you doing?', and the person miming immediately has to tell a lie, eg, 'Riding a horse'.
- The original person stops miming, and the new person immediately mimes the new action – riding a horse. The one on his or her right asks, 'What are you doing?', and he or she has to lie, and so on around the circle.

C14. Voice machine
- The group stands in a circle, facing inwards.
- One person starts making a short 'engine-type' noise, eg, 'Clunk boing'.
- Going around the circle, the others join in with different noises, so that the whole group sounds like a machine.
- This can be tape-recorded and played back to the group.
  Variation: as above, with the addition of actions.

C15. Pile up
- The group sits on chairs in a circle, facing inwards.
- Each group member in turn poses a question to the whole group. The questions must be those which can be answered by 'Yes' or 'No', and must not be based on qualities which are visible (eg, 'Do you have blue eyes?' is not allowed).
- Whoever answers 'Yes' moves one chair to the right, and whoever answers 'No' stays in his or her seat.
- If someone moves to a chair which is occupied, he or she sits on the occupant's lap.
- The idea is to devise questions so that the whole group is eventually piled on the same chair.
  Variation: as above, but the group sits in a circle on the floor, and those answering 'Yes' sit in front of the person on the right, with the idea of the group eventually forming a queue of seated people.

C16. Circle trust game
(This game should be played with a group of seven or eight participants.)
- The group stands shoulder-to-shoulder in a circle, facing inwards, each with one foot set apart behind the other for stability, and with their hands held up at shoulder level.

- One person stands in the middle of the circle, with his or her feet firmly on the floor.
- The person in the middle leans to one side, is caught by the hands of the others, and then does nothing as he or she is passed (not pushed) backwards, forwards and sideways around the circle.
- The one in the middle should move as if the ankles are the only joint in his or her body. He or she may want to close his or her eyes.
- Repeat with someone else in the middle.
- As trust develops in the group, the circle can be widened.
  Variation: the group, minus one, stands and forms a cat's cradle with their arms and catches the remaining group member as he or she falls into the group, and carries him or her to another part of the room.

C17. Physical warm-up
- The group stands in a circle, facing inwards.
- The facilitator takes them through a physical warm-up of his or her choice, depending on the purpose of the exercise, eg, raising energy levels, or relaxation, etc.

ABOUT THE AUTHOR

Until recently, Jo Malseed was lecturer in the School of Independent Studies at Lancaster University, where she was course convenor and group tutor on an undergraduate course run entirely on group work. She has written and run training courses on alternatives to lectures and seminars, in particular small group approaches to teaching and learning. She is now a dramatherapist.

Address for correspondence: School of Independent Studies, Lonsdale College, University of Lancaster, Bailrigg, Lancaster LA1 4YN.

Chapter 7

ANIMAL SOUNDS:
a simple ice-breaker

Alan Jenkins and Simon Bearder

ABSTRACT

We outline a simple game in which students with eyes closed make the sounds of animals such as lions or leopards. The game ends with students in groups of three or four lions, leopards, etc, ready for the next activity. This has proved to be an effective ice-breaker to acculturate students to the bizarre behaviours they have to demonstrate in simulations such as BAFA BAFA.

Picture some 40–50 students wandering around a room with eyes closed and emitting such strange sounds as 'a repeated low pitched straining sound rather like someone sitting on the lavatory', or 'a sound like a saw cutting through a large log, relatively quiet and repeated several times'.

These particular sounds are arguably those of a lion and leopard. After some five to ten minutes, the game ideally concludes with students formed in clusters of three or four, each cluster being a particular animal and making their distinctive sound. Having done this the students are ready for more extended bizarre activities.

It has been particularly effective as an introductory ice-breaker to prepare students to fully involve themselves in simulations such as BAFA BAFA. One of us (Alan Jenkins) has long used BAFA BAFA as the central activity that opens a weekend field course for first-year students that is designed to build them into a cohesive group and introduce the way they will be taught (Jenkins *et al*, 1993). We have found BAFA BAFA ideally suitable for such purposes. It is a highly sociable activity while at the time time enabling much to be learnt from the experience.

However, like other powerful simulations it requires participants to act in strange ways and discard certain inhibitions. We have found it is far more effective if we start by playing certain warm up games.

ANIMALS SOUNDS was designed for that purpose. It is simple to play and takes approximately 10–15 minutes. We have used it with 30–50 participants but it could easily be adapted for more. Our experience is that it is simple to run, students quickly enter into the game, enjoy it and at the end are relaxed and ready to work on.

INSTRUCTIONS

Each student is given an envelope with the instructions set out in Appendix A and *one* of the animal sounds in Appendix B. Obviously you need to ensure that the number of animals matches the number of students. All one needs to do is to emphasize the basic rules, silently learn your sound, then keep your eyes closed. The game concludes when you think its aim has been achieved. It's not an activity that we debrief!

APPENDIX A

Do not tell anybody your animal! Your job is to learn the animal call, BUT UNTIL YOU ARE TOLD BY ME, TO MAKE NO SOUND.

Think of yourself as someone being trained in the method school of acting. You have to think yourself into the role of the animal – but the only way you are to convey the animal is through its call.

You will soon move around the room (with your eyes closed!) making your call. You are trying to meet two other animals of the same species as yourself, for example, if you are a chipmunk you are looking for two other chipmunks.

Once you think you are assembled as a group of three, put your arms around each other. Then each of you in turn repeats your call, *then* and only then quietly tell the others what species you are. If you are not three of the same species, close your eyes and move on (if two of you are of one species, move on together calling for your missing chipmunk). If you are now three chipmunks joined together, open your eyes and then keep making chipmunk noises until every animal groups is assembled.

SO NOW LEARN YOUR CALL SILENTLY. BUT WHEN I SAY SO . . . START CALLING!

Your animal is..............................

Its sound is like this......................

APPENDIX B

ANIMAL SOUNDS

1 LION – *ROAR* – A repeated low-pitched straining sound, rather like someone on the lavatory. Each series of 'roars' starts slowly and loud, gradually speeding up and trailing off in sound intensity. A total of about 10–12 roars in all and a long end series of soft grunts that can be likened to a distant steam train chugging along.

2 HYENA – *WHOOP* – A regularly repeated, drawn-out, mournful whooooooop, each one starting low-pitched and rising sharply at the end. A series of six to ten whoops is common. This sound is very loud and can carry for five miles or more.

3 WILDEBEEST – *SNORT* – A low-pitched, loud, nasal blowing sound repeated at irregular intervals. Can be made by blowing through closed teeth with the lips curled back, though this inevitably produces a certain amount of spray.

4 IMPALA – *RUTTING GRUNTS* – A very loud snorting series of pig-like grunts interspersed with loud blowing through the nose. Produced by low pitched guttural noise at the back of the throat and explosive rushes of air through the teeth.

5 BUSHBABY – *CRY* – Very like a cross new-born baby. A series of seven to ten loud cries repeated at regular, short intervals and trailing off at the very end of the series. The sound has also been likened to a crow caw that is repeated several times.

6 LEOPARD – *RASP* – A sound like a saw cutting through a large log. The low-pitched, back-and-forth, sawing rasp is relatively quiet and is repeated several times.

7 BABOON – *BARK* – An explosive 'YA-HOO' repeated at irregular intervals. This loud sound has heavy emphasis on the low-pitched 'YA' followed by what sounds like an intake of breath during the less-emphasized 'HOO' part.

8 GIBBON – *SONG* – A melodious series of brief HOOs building up in speed of repetition and length of each HOOO until, after about 10 to 15 such units they become very drawn out and highly modulated – sliding in pitch rather like a Swanee whistle.

9 JACKAL – *HOWL* – A high-pitched wailing howl, not unlike the coyotes of the movies. A series of drawn-out and high-pitched howls is usually given.

10 OSTRICH – *BOOM* – A number of very low-pitched, booming sounds that can be likened to 'WHOOOO-WHOOOOO'. The first WHOO has two syllables, with the emphasis on the second, and the second WHOOO is drawn out. The call is repeated irregularly.

11 MONGOOSE – A high-pitched, repetitive, chattering used to keep in contact with each other. Can be likened to a rapid keh-keh-keh . . . etc., given in a series while searching through the habitat.

12 MARSH FROG – Rather like a child's 'red-Indian' war cry. Made by rapidly vibrating a finger in the mouth while holding the lips rounded and giving a high-pitched call.

13 ELEPHANT – A very deep rumbling sound once thought to be the stomach rumbling, now known to be the audible part of a very low frequency repertoire mostly inaudible to us.

14 BUSH ROBIN – A very human-like whistling following a rather random pattern for some minutes at a time.

15 BUSH BUCK – A single sharp bark, not unlike a large dog, sometimes repeated after about 15 seconds in a series of four to five.

16 GIRAFFE – A very peculiar snort, hardly a call, more a strained expulsion of air. A cross between a sniff and a cough. Single snorts may be repeated at irregular intervals.

17 HOOPOE – A bird named after its call, 'HOO-HOO'. A doe-like, mournful two-tone call.

18 TREE HYRAX – A long and complex call made up of a series of knocks, picking up speed, very like a ping-pong ball dropping onto a table. When this finishes there is a series of screams starting fast and becoming slower and more drawn out until they fade off.

19 WILD DOG (Africa) – A mournful 'WHO-WHO' sound repeated several times. The first part of the call is lower-pitched (medium) than the second and is slightly longer.

REFERENCE

Jenkins, A, Gold, J R and Haigh, M (1993) 'Values in place: the use of a journalism simulation to explore environmental interpretation', in *The Simulation and Gaming Yearbook*, Percival, F, Lodge, S and Saunders, D (eds) Kogan Page, London.

ABOUT THE AUTHORS

Alan Jenkins long taught in the geography unit at Oxford Brookes University. He now works in its Educational Methods Unit.

Simon Bearder teaches physical anthropology at Oxford Brookes University and researches primate behaviour.

Address for correspondence: Alan Jenkins, Educational Methods Unit, Oxford Brookes University; Simon Bearder, Anthropology Unit, Oxford Brookes University, Oxford OX3 0BP.

Chapter 8

'Personal Development via the Outdoors'

Simon Read

ABSTRACT

'I now have a more confident and positive approach when faced with new challenges'
'I have learnt that most things are possible'

. . . reactions from participants on recent outdoor activity courses – overcoming personal fear, finding a new self-belief, a renewed self-confidence – *empowering individuals*. The purpose of this chapter is to illustrate how outdoor problem-solving tasks can be used to develop a range of skills of relevance to college or to the workplace. Particular focus will be placed on interpersonal skills such as teamwork and communication. The activities described in this chapter are available in a published form in *Personal Development via the Outdoors – the complete course and tutor guide* (see page 80). The activities are designed to be managed by staff who have no specialist background in outdoor sports, and can be run in the college grounds within a typical one-hour lesson.

RATIONALE

Why the outdoors? As well as being very enjoyable, outdoor problem-solving tasks are *real*, in the sense that participants experience the immediate and direct consequences of their actions. For example, the misreading of a compass may cause a group to become temporarily lost within a small area of woodland, with the real stress and conflict that are often associated with experiences of uncertainty and confusion. As such, outdoor tasks closely represent the stresses and tension which are typical of real life. Outdoor activities are memorable, and the lessons learned are successfully translated back to the challenges of college life or the workplace.

My experience is that the sensitive delivery of structured outdoor activities can be used to provide students and staff with fresh insight into their own abilities and how they are seen by others, creating a unique opportunity to develop and enhance personal and working relationships.

BTEC COMMON SKILLS AND GNVQ CORE SKILLS

Many colleges are using the kit to develop and assess the Business and Technology Education Council (BTEC) Common Skills or General National Vocational Qualifications (GNVQ) Core Skills. The Royal Forest of Dean College runs the course as a series of activity days at intervals during the year. BTEC National Coordinator, Andy Johns, commented that,

> As staff we do not possess technical skills in outdoor activities. Using specialists to provide abseiling or canoeing is simply beyond our budget. This would also mean that staff have no direct involvement in the course. The beauty of these activities is that skills in mountain leadership are certainly *not* required. As staff we greatly enjoy getting out of the classroom for a few days, while many students describe the activities as the most memorable part of the course.

Following each activity students assess their contribution towards achieving the task or in working with others, by the completion of skills checklists, which are based on BTEC Common Skills. Students are often able to extend this process of self-analysis to other aspects of their work, typically identifying those skills which they demonstrate in later assignment work.

KOLB

When introducing students to the idea of learning through outdoor activities, I find it very helpful to begin with a discussion of the experiential learning cycle model of David Kolb. Kolb suggests that learning is most effective and powerful when it is based on personal experience and incorporates reflection on that experience. Students are made aware of the structure of the activities, which is as follows:

- undertake activity;
- discuss group processes involved in the activity;
- identify those areas in which skills are currently lacking, or in which the group or individuals can perform more effectively in future;
- undertake a subsequent activity, to put into practice the learning points identified.

STEREOTYPED BEHAVIOUR

Outdoor exercises can be used very effectively to highlight issues of stereotyping. For example, it is fairly common to find one or more 'macho' males in a student group, who unthinkingly make the assumption that any task which is at all physical in nature is beyond the capabilities of the female members of the team. Conversely, some females may assume that the males are 'more capable' and leave them to get on with the task, not questioning the roles which have emerged. In teams where female members express resentment at their exclusion, the males are usually surprised to hear of the bitterness they have caused.

Students often find the action-centred learning model of John Adair helpful at this point. This focuses on the need to achieve the task, the need to maintain team spirit, and the importance of involving all individuals. The model can be used as a reference point during the discussion which follows each activity. For example, one or two male students may have achieved the task with complete success, but they may have done so independently, and without involving the other members of the group. The objectives of the task have been met, but at the expense of team morale and the feelings of other individuals. Any exclusion of female team members from the activity can also be looked upon in terms of the task itself. Task accomplishment is usually dependent upon the team making the best possible use of resources, in terms of equipment, time available, knowledge and people. If one or more team members is excluded from active involvement in the exercise, the ideas and expertise available to the team will be less.

Consider a group in which some males have enthusiastically rushed into action, failing to consult all the females at the planning stage. Some of the females start to complain bitterly amongst themselves at the lack of consultation, and at their exclusion from the task. Responsibility for getting involved is a shared responsibility. While the team as a whole (or the team leader at any point) should encourage the involvement of all team members, it is also incumbent upon each individual to take an active part. On some occasions the males may be unaware of their chauvinistic behaviour. On other occasions, females may be either unaware of or unwilling to confront stereotyped behaviour. They may also be reluctant to express to the group as a whole their feelings of frustration at being excluded. The reaction of those who are prohibited from an active role may vary from silent submission to angry confrontation. Alternatively, males may react to female complaints in either a dismissive manner or with a defensive reaction.

This can lead to a discussion of assertiveness, contrasting this with the aggressive and submissive behaviour being shown by team members. Female chauvinism may be addressed in a similar manner. One approach in subsequent activities is to pair up team members in complementary roles. For example, task-oriented people can be paired with skills communicators. Each pair then has a joint responsibility for carrying out a designated part of the task. This approach is likely to defuse a 'sex war' in which males and females are at loggerheads. The team can be encouraged to see the problem as an issue of team roles, which also falls along sex lines. The tutor can adapt subsequent activities to ensure that these cooperative relationships lead to immediate success.

TYPICAL EXERCISES

There follows a description of a range of outdoor problem-solving exercises which are available in a published form (for details, see below). The activities can be run without the need for high-cost specialist equipment. Most require only a few basic household items, available at low cost from a local hardware store. Each exercise can be run within a one to one and a half hour session, requiring the use only of a small lawn or carpark. The activities are designed to be completed by groups of five to eight members per team. They are suitable for use with students at secondary and tertiary level, and with supervisory-level staff within the workplace. They are most commonly used to develop interpersonal, team-building and leadership skills. The outlines given below describe just a few of the exercises in the kit.

In FIREBALL, participants construct 'a self-propelled device to carry a lit candle over six metres'. This, for example, may be done by making a 'hanging basket' from a plastic cup, and suspending this from a line of cotton, held at either end. The challenge is to avoid obvious solutions, such as using the plastic cups or cardboard cylinders provided, to make wheels, which is unlikely to lead to success. The exercise develops skills in communication, creativity and delegation.

In BARBECUE, participants make an improvised barbecue with which to cook lunch, and then give a sales presentation demonstrating the economy of their barbecue design. The activity develops skills in communication, creativity and delegation. The challenge is to make a barbecue with the basic equipment provided.

QUESTION TIME is designed to encourage participants to appreciate the dangers in making assumptions; to understand the value of open and closed questions; and to be able to phrase questions precisely. Participants act either as 'builders' or as 'questioners'. The builders and questioners form pairs, and then stand back-to-back. The builder constructs a simple structure and the questioner then builds an identical model – by questioning the builder on his or her design. The builder's replies are restricted to 'yes' or 'no'.

In CLUE-GO, participants undertake a form of treasure hunt in which their reward is a certificate of success, situated in a mystery location. This location is identified by answering a series of clues; by visiting various features in the vicinity; and by the use of reference books and general knowledge. The challenge is to coordinate the research undertaken by team members, who may at times be located in different parts of the area. The exercise develops skills in decision making, delegation, planning and control, encouraging team morale, and research and investigation.

The challenge in MINEFIELD is to communicate ideas clearly to all team members while under strict time pressure, and to plan and solve problems with the aid of lateral thinking. Particular focus is placed on objective-setting, creativity, planning and control. A bottle standing upright in a bucket simulates an unexploded bomb. Using limited materials, participants remove the 'bomb' from a 'cordoned off' area, without getting within two metres of the device itself.

In AIRCRASH, participants are faced with a simulated crash-landing, in which one survivor is injured and unable to walk. The task is to find the injured passenger, provide emergency first aid, build a stretcher, find and erect a tent, build a raft and negotiate a simulated cliff edge to take the passenger to safety.

The exercise addresses issues of objective-setting, communication, decision making, delegation, organization and cooperation between teams. Success relies on how effectively the team shares information with those who are working on other parts of the task.

FLIGHT RIDER is designed to examine how the evolving demands of the task affect team morale and motivation, to develop skills in communication and objective-setting, to encourage cooperation between teams, and to reveal how participants respond to a competitive environment. Participants form teams, with each team given the task of identifying a grid reference on a map. The team plans a route by road to this point, and is taken there by minibus. The team then walks to a 'search site', where the task is to find 'airmile vouchers' which entitle all teams to transport back to the centre. The challenge facing the team is to appreciate from the outset the objective of the task, and to adopt a systematic approach to the task, keeping to this plan when under pressure.

'PERSONAL DEVELOPMENT VIA THE OUTDOORS'

Personal Development via the Outdoors – the complete course and tutor guide contains a range of outdoor problem-solving exercises, some of which are described above, in addition to support material for tutors, providing advice on setting up and managing the activities. The *Tutor Development Programme* provides advice on leading the review session or discussion which follows each activity, relating learning back to college or the workplace. Further advice is given on integrating the exercises within the curriculum, including issues of assessment. The kit is published by Pinnacle Publications Limited, 8 Marine Gardens, Newland Street, Coleford, Gloucestershire GL16 8DD (telephone 0594–832895). The educational price of £295 includes a licence to photocopy the materials for on-going usage within the purchasing institution. Students who have completed the course have commented that, 'I'm no longer afraid of what people think of me – I enjoy moving others in the right direction'; and 'The fun we got from the activities did more than anything else to bring us together.'

ABOUT THE AUTHOR

Simon Read is a director of Pinnacle Publications Limited and is joint author of *Personal Development via the Outdoors – the complete course and tutor guide* along with Robert Larcombe and Frances Wade. He lectures at the Royal Forest of Dean College, Gloucestershire, where he is also BTEC National Certificate Coordinator. He has written articles and course materials published by *The Economics Association* and by the AEB-sponsored *Wessex Project*. He has an industrial background within management accountancy.

Chapter 9

Organizing an outdoor education programme: a guide for lecturers

Danny Saunders

ABSTRACT

A key feature of team-building programmes which use 'the outdoor classroom' is practical and physical problem solving associated with simulations and role play. Over the last three years the University of Glamorgan has organized numerous residential visits to the Dolygaer Outdoor Education Centre in the Brecon Beacons of Wales. This chapter reviews the many educational benefits of such activity, and acts as a guide for lecturers in other further and higher education institutions who will hopefully use their local outdoor education centres and organize similar events.

WHAT IS OUTDOOR EDUCATION?

Outdoor education is currently fashionable for many management training and staff development courses. They are usually run in conjunction with intensive classroom-based programmes, and serve to vary the learning experiences of participants as well as simply to entertain and interest people with something different and new. What is often overlooked is the long history of outdoor education – indeed since the 1930s Wales has been one of the main centres of excellence. The traditional and continuing focus has been on personal self-development through confronting challenges and dangers associated with 'the outdoor classroom'.

In its purest form, outdoor education is aimed at people who are not used to working with others, are not used to outdoor challenge, have no special outdoor skills, and who have not got that much confidence. It is perhaps a shame that the popular stereotype of outdoor education involves physical fitness and neo-military prowess, because this only serves to deter potential users who feel embarrassed about exposing a lack of ability in front of 'experts'.

There are many variations, ranging from an individual's mastering of an outdoor pursuit through to teamwork based on problem solving. The former refers to specific skills which are physically and technically demanding – examples include canoeing, wind-surfing, abseiling, climbing, orienteering and caving. The latter refers to the ability to work with other people and to organize teams effectively – examples include leadership, creativity, teambuilding, presentation skills, and listening. With our university's outdoor education programmes, both types of ability have been targeted, so that students learn about communication and outdoor pursuit skills but as an exercise in group learning.

A common question is, 'Why outdoors?' The advantage of outdoor education is that it is a refreshing change from the usual curricular experiences of our students. It provides an alternative context for learning about groupwork skills which are a central part of the higher education curriculum. To put this another way, it encourages learners to break away from traditional ways of doing things.

FINANCIAL CONSTRAINTS

Cost is the major initial consideration: these courses are not cheap. They demand the continual presence and supervision of qualified outdoor education instructors – usually one for every six participants. Added to this are catering and accommodation overheads plus use of equipment. If you use, as we have, a centre which has established formal links with a local educational authority it is possible to get reduced fees for people who are resident within the county. By way of illustration, in 1992 the average cost worked out at approximately £60 per head for two days and one night, inclusive of fees, accommodation, meals and the use of equipment.

In most cases, transport to and from the centre is shared. For example, with a group of 30 students the university might supply one minibus and the centre supplies another. The university pays for all photocopied materials.

IDENTIFYING THE PARTICIPANTS

Are there any people with special needs? This information will not exclude people, but instead helps the centre staff prepare for their participation.

In most cases, outdoor education courses can comfortably cope with a maximum of 30 participants although extra observers who do not actually participate in team activities are possible. Some centres can handle much larger groups but usually this requires extensive advance notice.

The most popular target groups are:

- first years;
- returning placement students;
- a mixture of students from different years/courses in order to develop peer tutoring;

- students who need a break from a rather intensely theoretical part of their studies;
- students with special needs.

It is also worth considering whether any students are already experts in outdoor education – somewhat surprisingly, we have found that many such individuals volunteer for our courses despite the fact that we advertise them as introductory. A useful tactic involves asking them to act either as observers or to give them 'facilitator' (rather than 'leader') roles within teams. Do not allow such students to supervise or instruct unless they are formally qualified, and the centre approves the arrangement.

Finally, it may be worthwhile targeting particular kinds of participants, for example, non-traditional, female and/or overseas students in order to 'balance' groups that may otherwise be dominated by (again, for example) male school-leavers.

TIMING

Obviously it is important that the outdoor event does not coincide with a particulary busy time of year for students, such as pending coursework deadlines or exams. But it is also important to select a time when all students can attend – not easy within modular schemes! This is why some outdoor education visits have been scheduled for weekends, but we advise that where this happens the following Monday should be clear of classes as students (and staff!) need time to recover.

Induction weeks have proved to be popular for outdoor education courses, as has the period between end of exams and the end of semester. Another convenient period seems to be during the transition between semesters, when many staff are busy with assessment but students have some free time.

CONTACTING THE CENTRE

Once written and/or telephone contact has been established with a centre of your choice, go to the centre along with any other staff who may be involved in the actual residential programme. This allows you to get a feel for the kind of activities involved, as well as to plan the details of the programme with the centre staff. You will be able to answer student queries with more confidence and detail – and enthusiasm! Specifically, you should agree the following:

- course programme (the centre staff will lead on this, but will genuinely be interested in knowing a little more about your students and their studies);
- transport arrangements and times;
- students with special needs and diets (the centres welcome such participation, but they need to know in advance what the needs are in order to make suitable preparations);

- sleeping arrangements (inside or outside – if outside whether in tents or 'rough' in bivouac bags);
- length of course (usually two nights and three days is more than sufficient, and we have run many successful courses lasting for one night and two days);
- equipment to be supplied by the centre;
- teaching rooms/facilities to be provided;
- photocopied materials to be used;
- input by academic staff in relation to centre instructors.

RECRUITING STUDENTS

We do not advise the recruitment of students who do not want to go. However, some visits have involved all students from a particular cohort during the induction period. The problem with using outdoor education as an ice-breaker is that unless everyone gets involved then it excludes people who do not attend. A useful compromise is to designate those reluctant to get involved in the actual activities to the role of 'observer', thereby still including them in the programme.

Fliers and handouts can also be used, an example of which is given in Figure 9.1. If you are over-subscribed it is worth creating an emergency waiting list and asking people to turn up at the departure point – usually two or three places fall vacant due to last minute drop-outs.

PREPARING STUDENTS

A few days before departure, it's worth holding a briefing session which explains the entire venture. This provides an ideal opportunity to tell everyone about transport, departure and return times as well as basic clothing and equipment advice. A torch is very useful, along with wearing loose and comfortable warm clothing (as well as a spare set of clothes which should be kept in a waterproof bag). While the centre provides kit, some walking gear can cause blisters, so if students have their own boots they should bring them along.

This session can also include video material of previous visits along with the identification of students with special needs, and the reassurance of students about the educational value of the exercise. Students will be relieved to know that while outdoor pursuits will be introduced, physical fitness is not a priority – instead teamwork, confidence-building, and communication skills are the focus. This also gives an opportunity to get students involved in assessing their own 'baselines' as regards abilities and skills. Questionnaire profiles such as the Honey and Mumford Learning Styles, or the Belbin Self-Perception Inventories can be most useful in allowing students to make 'before and after' comparisons.

D Saunders/Enterprise Unit/University of Glamorgan

OUTDOOR EDUCATION WEEKEND

We have some free places on our outdoor education weekend, at the Dolygaer Centre near Merthyr Tydfil. This involves various exercises in problem solving and team building, within a variety of outdoor settings (although accommodation is indoors). There will be opportunities to:

- orienteer
- canoe
- abseil
- cave

We ask teams to make brief presentations in order to practice communication skills and to reflect on how they performed as a group.

The weekend does not involve physical fitness, although we do need to be informed of any specific medical or dietary needs. On completion, participants receive a certificate as evidence of their experience.

You are advised to wear warm comfortable clothes and trainers; Dolygaer supply outdoor equipment and clothes, including walking boots. If you have specialist outdoor clothing of your own, you may choose not to rely on the Dolygaer resources.

You are also asked to bring a spare change of clothes, a towel, four pairs of socks, writing material and, if possible, a torch.

If interested, please see..

Figure 9.1 *A sample flier for advertising the outdoor education visit*

If you wanted to be more adventurous, this briefing session could include an early team-building workshop which allows you to observe students as they solve problems within groups. In this way these activities provide data for the selection of individuals and the 'balancing' of teams which are to operate throughout the outdoor course. The Belbin Profile has been especially useful in encouraging students to self and peer assess their team roles – figures 9.2 and 9.3 provide a summary based on the original typology.

Finally, the briefing session allows you to introduce some basic elements of careers guidance/consciousness-raising. The outdoor centre will issue a certificate, for inclusion with students' later cvs, but it is also worth emphasizing how mention of the outdoor education experience allows students to fill in difficult areas of the Standard Application Form (SAF) and to talk about personal and communication skills with more confidence and in more detail. Figure 9.4 provides a section from a SAF – it's worth handing this out in order to reinforce the relevance of the exercise to later job applications.

Please note: we do not recommend that you give full details of the programme at this stage – at first glance the schedule appears to be overly full

The eight Belbin categories	
Shaper	the task leader, full of energy, outgoing, emotional, impulsive, impatient, quick to challenge, looking for a pattern in discussion, wants action, competitive, intolerant of vagueness.
Investigator	relaxed, sociable, gregarious, positive, enthusiastic, goes outside group and gets information, diplomat, always exploring new possibilities, unoriginal, does not always finish off tasks
Company Person	the practical organizer, turns decisions into manageable tasks, logical, disciplined, trustworthy, upset by sudden change, efficient, inflexible, close to the team's point of balance
Finisher	worries about what might go wrong, eye for detail, checks and rechecks, has a sense of urgency and strength of character, intolerant of casual team members, likes to have order, meets deadlines, gets tied down by small details
Chair	presides over team, coordinates, concerned with objectives, an all-rounder without being outstanding in anything, disciplined, charisma with authority, trustworthy and not the jealous type, plays to people's strengths and establishes roles for them, talks easily and a good listener, sets the agenda, takes decisions after consultation
Plant	scatterer of seeds which others nourish until they bear fruit, original thinker, radical, imaginative and intelligent, no eye for detail, concentrates on overall objectives and issues, makes careless mistakes, critical, uninhibited, can go off on a tangent, sulks if ideas not listened to
Monitor	serious, unemotional, controlled, stops team from going off on tangents, criticizes for a reason and not just for the sake of it, slow but methodical and accurate, can understand large amounts of information, can be unpopular because the truth can hurt – is hardly ever wrong
Worker	mild, sensitive, an excellent listener, popular, someone who values friendship, helps others, can panic or freeze in times of crisis, uncritical, promotes team spirit, humorous, can get bogged down in detail, capable of doing unpopular or unexciting tasks

Figure 9.2 *The eight Belbin categories*

and busy and may deter people from participating, leading to last minute drop-out and wasted places (which you will probably have to pay for). Instead, it is worth outlining just a few of the activities.

YOUR NAME:..

DATE:..................................

EXERCISE:..

Self & Peer Rating

Categories	Self	Mem 1	Mem 2	Mem 3	Mem 4	Mem 5	Mem 6	Mem 7	Mem 8
Shaper									
Investigator									
Company Person									
Finisher									
Chair									
Plant									
Monitor									
Worker									

Figure 9.3 *Self- and peer assessment grid: teamwork*

HANDING OVER TO THE CENTRE INSTRUCTORS

On arrival at the outdoor education centre it is important for you to introduce the centre staff and to provide a very brief summary of the planning of the outdoor education course. You should also explain the importance of observer roles, some of which can be occupied by academic staff who are accompanying the students. These people provide feedback to groups as they debrief each activity, but are not allowed to actually help the groups as they solve the problems. You may be wondering why we do not advise lecturers to join the teams and participate like everyone else. The problem is that they often find it difficult to avoid becoming the 'authority figure' and 'leader' due to students' deference and expectations!

The centre staff will then take over. The purpose of outdoor education will be introduced as well as a short history of the centre. They will then describe their agenda, and set up the student teams. Sometimes this may have been

D Saunders/Enterprise Unit/University of Glamorgan

Describe any aspect of your course of particular interest to you
and/or relevance to your application

Activities and interests
Give details of your main extra curricular activities and interests to
date. What have you contributed and what have you got out of
them? Mention any posts of responsibility

Career Choice
Explain what attracts you about the type(s) of work for which you
are applying and offer evidence of your suitability

If you feel there is anything which has not been covered adequately
elsewhere on your application, please elaborate below

Figure 9.4 *Extracts from the standard application form (SAF) used by many graduate employers*

structured by yourself based on the prior 'balancing' of groups, but it is also permissible for the centre staff to randomly allocate people to teams.

THE PROGRAMME

After the above introductions, centre staff will then sort out accommodation and equipment arrangements. Usually you will all get 'kitted out' and then begin the first phase of activities. Programmes will vary from course to course and instructor to instructor. Here is an example of one schedule based on two days and one night involving four teams of six students:

DAY 1

Time	Activity
9.00	Minibuses collect students outside recreation and sports centre on the campus.
10.00	Arrive at centre. Coffee, introductions by lecturers and centre instructors. Aims and objectives.
10.30	Formation of teams based on Belbin Profiles, and kitting out.
11.00	Small team tasks on a carousel basis: four tasks of 30 minutes duration each.
13.00	Packed lunch.
13.30	Team presentations: each team to report back within this 30-minute period – time allocated includes 15 minutes preparation time and three-minute presentations per team to rest of course.
14.00	Planning for raft building exercise to include purchase of equipment by money accrued through the small team tasks within the carousel session. Each team to purchase equipment to build a raft and deliver plan of drawing to instructors for approval.
14.45	Collect equipment to consist of buoyancy aids, logs, planks, rope, paddles; actually build raft and get all team members across reservoir.
16.00	End of raft exercise; dismantle and return equipment to centre.
16.30	Tea, review and wash and change.
18.00	Dinner.
19.00	Core skills session. Each team to allocate group members to attend each of four demonstration/training events in preparation for the day 2 integrated activity:

A. Rope work
B. Canoe safety
C. Orienteering
D. Caving

20.00	'Night Owl' orienteering exercise as an introduction to 'Wizards Curse'. This information will be in sealed containers which will have a 'mythical' time lock and cannot be opened until after breakfast tomorrow.
21.30–23.00	Rehydration exercise.

DAY 2

8.00	Breakfast and kitting out.
9.00	Opening of sealed containers collected in 'Night Owl'.
9.30	Commencement of 'Wizards Curse'. This is an integrated circuit of activities which takes most of the day to complete. Teams complete tasks in canoeing, navigation, rock climbing, mountain rescue, abseiling, orienteering and caving. Cut-off time for this exercise is 13.30.
13.30	Return to centre and packed lunch, return of equipment and kit, cleaning up.

14.45	Team presentations: 20-minute preparation and 10-minute presentations per team.
15.45	Feedback from instructors, overview and summing up.
16.00	Tea and presentation of certificates.
16.10	Evaluation, completion of skills questionnaires and comparison with baselines established in briefing session.
16.30	Minibuses depart centre.
17.30	Arrive back at the university.

Day one is based on introducing students to a variety of activities and skills, while day two tries to integrate such learning within an overall programme.

Here are some descriptions of some of these activities and problems: this is where simulation and games become invaluable.

The carousel of small team tasks

Each group has a maximum of 30 minutes to solve a problem. This includes debriefing by observers and instructors, and at the end of the time period each team moves on to another problem located in another area. Thus if four teams are involved, they swap around four times until everyone has tried each problem. Examples include:

Barrels and planks:
Equipment: three barrels and two planks
Task: the team has to travel a distance of 40 feet over the ground by using the equipment provided and by following these guidelines:
- the starting point is from behind a line marked on the ground, and the task is finished when the group and equipment crosses the opposite line marked on the ground 40 feet away
- contact with the ground by team members is not allowed. If someone falls off they are out of the task (team loses 10 Dolygaers); if a hand or foot touches then it is a contact penalty (5 Dolygaers per instance)
- the planks are allowed to touch the ground when they are being moved. No team member is allowed on them while any part of the plank is in contact with the ground.

Successful completion of the task – 50 Dolygaers for spending on the Raft Exercise.

Blindfold Tent Erection
Equipment: two inner tents with poles, blindfolds
Task: the two tents have to be erected by the team within the time limit. These points have to be followed:
- all the team are blindfolded except for two sighted people
- the blindfolded people have to erect the tent
- the sighted people may give instructions, but they must not touch any of the equipment
- the sighted people may move around the area to give instructions.

Successful completion of the task – 50 Dolygaers for spending on the Raft Exercise.

The Raft Building Exercise

Still in the same teams, participants design a raft based on limited and few materials, typically two planks, six wooden poles, ten metres of rope, four large empty plastic barrels, and four paddles. They then use the Dolygaer currency they earned in the carousel task to purchase these materials and build a raft, subject to approval by instructors. At a given time all teams have to get all their members across a reservoir (usually about 100 metres); more than one journey is allowed. An interesting variation is to get one team to build another team's raft based on their approved design.

Night Owl Orienteering

Using maps, compasses and torches, teams have to search a forest and find and record markers which are rectangular aluminium plates on which are stamped numbers. The final list of numbers produced by these markers gives map grid references for the location of a sealed container. This container gives vital clues for the navigation part of the Wizards Curse circuit in Day 2.

Rehydration Exercise (optional)

A visit to the local pub for some refreshments and relaxation. Please note: a maximum of 90 minutes is advised, and no alcohol is to be taken back to the centre. Participants have a long day ahead of them, so no hangovers!

Wizards Curse

Teams now embark on a multi-activity exercise which involves finding and using clues, performing a sweep search, and rescuing someone (one of the centre instructors). That person pretends to have a broken leg, so they must be carried back to the centre. The only feasible way to do this involves teams working together and sharing their resources. During the course of the day participants will canoe and navigate on the reservoir, complete some rock climbing, abseil back down, orienteer and sweep search for the lost person, and follow safety and emergency aid procedures in bringing that person back to safety.

MAKING SENSE OF IT ALL

Not all centre instructors will be clued up on debriefing methods, often because they get so involved in helping groups master new skills, and in preserving the safety of everyone involved. It is very easy to get carried away with the details of learning about specific outdoor pursuits without tackling the underlying issues of personal development and confidence-building.

This is where the academic staff become important 'reminder agents' within the course, especially when it comes to making team presentations. In the above example of a two-day programme, two such presentation periods are scheduled. The first is just after the Carousel and the second is at the end of the second day. These provide valuable opportunities for teams to make comparisons between their earlier and later performances, and to evaluate what they have learned about themselves and one another. In most cases these presentations are entertaining and informative, and reveal dramatic insights into teamwork as well as the skills associated with the public speaking, itself a major fear and challenge for many students (indeed many prefer the abseiling to doing a presentation).

The initial briefing session can give students information about what makes a good presentation (Saunders, 1994), but the lecturers can also provide some suggestions about structuring content just before the students prepare themselves during the 15 or 20 minute fixed time periods. Such suggestions can include:

- give up to three examples of successful teamwork
- give up to three examples of poor teamwork
- the high point of the course was . .
- the low point of the course was . .
- the roles played by the team members were . . . (opportunity to include Belbin)
- the results of our team performance were as follows . . . (go through tasks in succession).

It is important for the observers to feed back their comments to the teams during the preparation phases for each presentation, and it is also worthwhile providing teams with overhead transparencies and pens for use with the OHP during presentations. Sometimes team presentations include 'sociograms' where drawings of communication channels and networks can be presented – again, the lecturer can introduce this kind of analysis before the start of the preparation periods. Figure 9.5 provides an example of a sociogram for one team.

During the final part of the programme, the instructors provide their views and insights about the entire programme, and there can then be a plenary session. This can be followed by completion of evaluation forms (see Figure 9.6 for an example) and a return to questionnaires used at the start of the course. This allows for comparison and the observation of change and development. A final activity includes actually drafting a statement for use with the SAF questions referred to during the introduction of the course.

A CHECKLIST

- set your budget
- identify participants

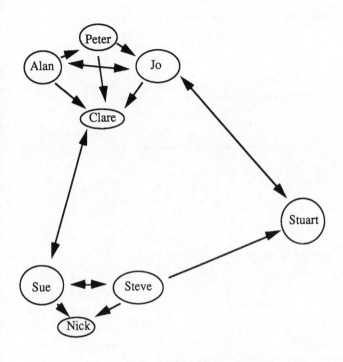

In the above example, two sub-groups have formed, with Stuart as both an outsider and an observer. Steve is looking to Stuart for advice, but Stuart has established more rapport with Jo as a representative of the larger sub-group.

Figure 9.5 *An example of a sociogram*

- identify a number of possible dates
- contact centre and arrange a planning meeting there
- when visiting them, bring other colleagues who will be involved
- outline participants' backgrounds to instructors
- agree final dates and schedules
- agree transport arrangements
- agree photocopying material
- agree teaching facilities and rooms needed (for example, overhead projectors, video)

Please circle the figure which represents your view on each scale.

Not at all enjoyable	1	2	3	4	5	6	7 Very enjoyable
Very boring	1	2	3	4	5	6	7 Very interesting
Taught me nothing	1	2	3	4	5	6	7 Taught me a lot
Totally irrelevant	1	2	3	4	5	6	7 Very relevant
Trivial	1	2	3	4	5	6	7 Very important
Purely theoretical	1	2	3	4	5	6	7 Very practical
Too easy	1	2	3	4	5	6	7 Too difficult
Very badly presented	1	2	3	4	5	6	7 Very well presented

Please add any comments you have, including suggestions for improvement:

Figure 9.6 *An example of an evaluation form*

- agree roles of academic staff (eg, observers, debriefing facilitators)
- identify items students and staff should bring with them
- advertise course back at college
- establish and notify centre of final numbers
- draw up a short waiting list if over-subscribed
- run briefing workshop
- establish self-assessed baselines if appropriate as well as team members
- notify everyone of transport times and venues
- go to centre and hand over to centre staff
- issue certificates
- evaluate and follow-up where possible.

ACCREDITATION

Many outdoor education centres offer specialist courses and programmes which lead to nationally recognized qualifications and training awards for outdoor pursuits introduced within such an introductory course. Some students complete such training on a regular basis throughout their stay at the college.

For some schemes and awards, the team-building and groupwork programme can be a recognized part of the curriculum, especially when core and common skills are being developed and then assessed.

REFERENCES

Safety in Outdoor Education, HMSO, London.

The Outdoor Source Book, Creative Reviewing, More than Activities, and *Silver Bulletts* are available from Adventure Education, 39 Brunswick Square, Penrith, Cumbria CA11 7LS.

The Mountain Craft and Leadership Handbook, Eric Langmuir; published by the Mountain Leadership Training Board of Great Britain and Northern Ireland. ISBN: 0-90-3908-75-1.

Personal Development via the Outdoors, Pinnacle Publications Ltd., 8 Marine Gardens, Newland Street, Coleford, Gloucestershire GL16 8DD.

Saunders, D (1994) 'Giving presentations', in Saunders, D (ed) *The Complete Student Handbook*, Blackwell, Oxford.

ABOUT THE AUTHOR

Danny Saunders is involved with many aspects of curriculum development and educational support, and has a background in social psychology. He has co-authored or edited several books on aspects of simulation and games and is currently designing a set of modules entitled 'Personal and Professional Development', to be offered to undergraduate students.

Address for correspondence: University of Glamorgan, Pontypridd CF37 1DL, Wales.

SECTION 3: Role play and cross-cultural negotiation

Chapter 10

Visions of Dutch corporate trainers on role playing

Geralien A Holsbrink-Engels

ABSTRACT

The purpose of this chapter is to draw together information on the use of role playing in corporate training, in particular interpersonal skill training. From the field of interpersonal skill training not much is known of the use of role playing. Many authors (Joyce and Weil, 1980; Nijkerk, 1988; Shaftel and Shaftel, 1967, 1982; Tistaert, 1987) only give (global) descriptions of this instructional method in an optimistic and positive way without empirical confirmation.

A written questionnaire was constructed from the literature in role playing. The questions refer to (1) background variables of trainers, (2) general characteristics (3) introduction and instruction, (4) running a role play session and (5) debriefing. The questionnaire was mailed to 201 corporate trainers.

This study attained a return of 87 per cent. Of the 175 respondents, only 68 questionnaires (34 per cent) were suitable for data processing. Reviewing the results of the study, we may state that role playing is a complex instructional method within which numerous aspects may vary.

In many outlines of interpersonal skill training programmes, role playing is used as an instructional method. This chapter concerns the use of the instructional method of role playing in corporate training. It focuses in detail on mapping out involved aspects which should be used to describe the use of role playing in corporate training.

In general, there are two motives for this explorative study, without employing an *a priori* explanatory model as to how the variables are related. The first motive refers to the diversity of viewpoints of most role playing theories combined with the lack of systematic empirical evidence for their assertions. From the field of interpersonal skill training not much is known of the use of role playing. Many authors (Joyce and Weil, 1980; Kessels and Smit,

1990; Nijkerk, 1988; Shaftel and Shaftel, 1967, 1982; Tistaert, 1987; Wanrooy, 1992) only give (global) descriptions of this instructional method in an optimistic and positive way without empirical confirmation. For example, they do not pay attention to problems a role playing strategy for trainers and trainees may have. Van Ments (1989) and Georges (1989) are exceptions. Their assertions are not empirically supported. Van Ments (1989) summarizes nine potential disadvantages of role-playing.

Georges (1989) severely criticizes interpersonal skill training. He states that the results of interpersonal skill training are vague and are seldom transferred into on-the-job behaviours. One of the weaknesses of standard skill training is role playing. According to Georges, playing a role a few times does not build skilful performance (p.44).

The second motive for this study relates to the fact that the description of role playing theories concerns in most cases regular education. Not much is known about the use of role playing in the domain of corporate training.

Before giving a more detailed review of the design, method and results of the study, it is desirable to give an indication of aspects involved in role playing on the basis of a literature review. The terminology that will be used to discuss this subject also has to be defined. A definition of the concepts involved will be given first.

In this study, role playing will be seen as an instructional method by which the trainees play a situation from reality. The situation concerns a complex (personal) interaction with a goal (Kessels and Smit, 1990). For instance, a doctor must give some bad news to a patient. The purpose of role playing is practising problem solving: a problem is delineated, solved and discussed (Joyce and Weil, 1980).

Interpersonal skill training will be broadly defined as training in which people deal with one another face-to-face (ie, their interpersonal skills; Guirdham, 1990).

A framework containing aspects involved in role playing has been developed by literature research and it will be used as a basis for the following empirical study. Role playing has been operationalized into many variables. Table 10.1 gives a sketch of role playing variables based on a literature review. In the following sections, the content of several variables will be discussed.

METHOD

Subjects

The population or target group used in the study is that of corporate trainers. Systematic inclusion and exclusion criteria are that the trainer must have (1) experience with behaviour change and behaviour modification training, (2) experience with role playing in (interpersonal skill) training, and (3) the trainer must have held his or her position for a minimum of one year.

In order to obtain an optimal coverage, different ways of tracing are used to find the members of the target-population. The corporate trainers (N = 406)

Table 10.1 *Specifications of variables in role playing based on a literature review*

Sub-phase in role play	Authors who mention the specific phase
1. Introduce	
objectives	Nijkerk (1988), Van Ments (1989)
	Van Ments (1989)
method and procedures (fish-bowl or multiple)	Joyce and Weil (1980), Van Ments (1989)
situation (background, context)	Joyce and Weil (1980), Nijkerk (1988), Van Ments (1989)
'props' or additional material like a telephone	Van Ments (1989)
arouse interest/motivation	Shaftel and Shaftel (1967), Joyce and Weil (1980), Tistaert (1987), Van Ments (1989)
warming up	Nijkerk (1988), Van Ments (1989)
2. Instruction	
choice of players	Tistaert (1987), Nijkerk (1988)
instruction of players	Shaftel and Shaftel (1967), Joyce and Weil (1980), Van Ments (1989)
instruction of observers	Shaftel and Shaftel (1967), Joyce and Weil (1980), Van Ments (1989)
	Shaftel and Shaftel (1967), Joyce and Weil (1980), Van Ments (1989)
3. Run session	
start of the actual role play (give a starting signal)	Shaftel and Shaftel (1967), Joyce and Weil (1980), Tistaert (1987), Nijkerk (1988), Van Ments (1989)
interruption	Van Ments (1989)
provide information	Van Ments (1989)
control time	Van Ments (1989)
stop the actual role play when it is justified	Van Ments (1989)
	Nijkerk (1988), Van Ments (1989)
4. Debriefing	
A. *Clear up role play*	Shaftel and Shaftel (1967), Tistaert (1978), Nijkerk (1988), Van Ments (1989)
1. ask main protagonist(s) for his/her reactions	Joyce and Weil (1980), Van Ments (1989)
2. ask subsidiary characters for their reactions	Van Ments (1989)
3. ask observers for observations	Van Ments (1989)
4. agree on what happened and final decisions reached	Van Ments (1989)
B. *Draw conclusions*	Joyce and Weil (1980), Van Ments (1989)
5. analyse causes of behaviour	Van Ments (1989)
6. draw conclusions about the way people behave	Van Ments (1989)
7. decide on what can be done to improve situation	Joyce and Weil (1980), Van Ments (1989)
8. re-run (amended) role play	Shaftel and Shaftel (1967), Joyce and Weil (1980), Tistaert (1987), Nijkerk (1988), Van Ments (1989)
9. Debrief repeated role play; step 5–7	Shaftel and Shaftel (1967), Joyce and Weil (1980), Tistaert (1987)
C. *Draw general conclusions and extrapolate*	Shaftel and Shaftel (1967), Joyce and Weil (1980), Tistaert (1987), Nijkerk (1988), Van Ments (1989)

are selected from the registers of the Dutch Association of Corporate Trainers (NVvO – Nederlandse Vereniging van Opleidingsfunctionarissen), from the registers of the Dutch Association for Management (NIVE – Nederlandse Vereniging voor Management) and from the registers of the Dutch Association of Training and Development Institutions (VETRON – Vereniging van Trainings- en Opleidingsinstituten in Nederland). A random sample of 201 of the 406 trainers was drawn to obtain for this study a representative sample of the population of corporate trainers. To draw this sample a program written in Pascal was used.

Materials

A written questionnaire consisting of 50 items was constructed to measure facts and attitudes toward the use of role playing in corporate training. Many variables, based on the literature review discussed above, are operationalized into five sections. The following sections have been distinguished:

- Background information of the trainer and characteristics of his or her work (14 questions).
- General questions about advantages and disadvantages of role playing and the preparations for role play (14 questions and statements).
- The introduction and instruction of role playing (six questions and statements about objectives, method and procedure, context, and warming up, choice and instruction of players, instruction of observers).
- Run role playing (nine questions and statements about the start of the actual role-play, interruption, provide information, control time and stop).
- Debriefing role playing (seven questions and statements about clear up role play, draw conclusion and draw general conclusions).

Two different structured response modes were used: checklist response and a scaled response (Tuckman, 1988). The gradations on a five point-scale are never, seldom, sometimes, often and always. Table 10.2 gives some examples of questions in the written questionnaire.

Procedure

A review of the literature in the area of role playing was undertaken to identify the variables to be measured. These variables served as a starting point for the construction of the questionnaire. In a pilot study, the questionnaire was tested by six experts for formulation and styling of the questions and statements. Revision has taken place on the results of the pilot study.

The initial mailing of questionnaires to the sample of 201 respondents included a cover letter, the questionnaire itself and a stamped, return-addressed envelope. In the cover letter the trainers were informed about the backgrounds, objective and means of the investigation and a request for cooperation. After a period of about three weeks had elapsed, a second mailing was undertaken to correspond with the 158 non-respondents. The second mailing included another letter soliciting cooperation, another questionnaire

Table 10.2 *Examples of questions in the written questionnaire*

Section	Question (checklist or scaled response)
1. Background information	Have or are you: Check one: (a) in salaried employment (b) in freelance employment (c) an owner/holder of an agency (d) otherwise, namely . . .
2. Advantages/disadvantages of role playing	In whatever degree do you see the next aspects as advantages of role playing in training? Trainees are enabled to analyse their own behaviour never---seldom---sometimes---often---always Role playing gives the opportunity to try out different behaviour never---seldom---sometimes---often---always Role playing changes attitudes never---seldom---sometimes---often---always
3. Instruction	In which way do you instruct the players: Check one: (a) oral/verbal (b) on paper (c) both (d) players receive no instruction
4. Run role playing	In which way are the next aspects reasons for your intervention? Players depart from their role never---seldom---sometimes---often---always Poor performance in role playing never---seldom---sometimes---often---always Repetition never---seldom---sometimes---often---always Emotional escalation never---seldom---sometimes---often---always
5. Debriefing	Who is the leader of the debriefing? Check one: (a) the trainer (b) the trainee (c) both (d) otherwise, namely . . .

Table 10.3 *Non-response, suitability and unsuitability of the sample*

Non-response and suitable response	Frequency	Percentage
Non-response	26	12.9
Suitable response	68	33.8
Reasons for unsuitability	*Frequency*	*Percentage*
Incomplete form	4	2.0
No longer in the employ of	39	19.4
Removal of the organization	2	1.0
No time for it	19	9.5
No or little use of role playing	9	4.5
Too late	8	3.9
Unclear reason given	19	9.5
Retired	3	1.5
Don't see the sense of it	3	1.5
Seriously ill	1	0.5
TOTAL	201	100.0

and another stamped return-addressed envelope in case the respondent could not find the original ones. Again after a period of three weeks when the second mailing had failed, additional mailings and about 100 telephone calls were employed to elevate the return. In this study a return of more than 75 per cent has been strived for.

In the data analysis, frequency and chi-square analysis are used. Five reliability checks for internal consistency (ie the Spearman-Brown Prophesy Formula, Nunnally, 1978) were made (four were significant for $r > .50$, $p < .001$ and one was significant for $r > .33$, $p < .01$).

RESULTS

In this section the results will be presented. First the response, drop-out and non-response will be discussed. In the rest of this section, the results obtained from sections two to five of the written questionnaire will be given in detail.

Response and non-response

This study aimed for a return of 75 per cent and achieved 87 per cent. After the first and second mailing and telephone calls, 26 trainers from the sample did not respond (non-respondents). Of the 175 respondents, only 68 questionnaires (34 per cent) were suitable for data processing. In Table 10.3 the reasons for unsuitability are given.

In order to give an idea of the background of the suitable part from the sample, some characteristics will be discussed here. There has been no explicit goal to have an equal number of respondents for each combination of background variables. The frequencies, percentages, mean, standard deviation and range pertaining to most of the characteristics are listed in Table 10.4.

Table 10.4 *Some characteristics of the sample*

	Frequency	Percentage	
Kind of training			
Communication	7	10.4	
Management	13	19.4	
Both	24	35.8	
Both and Other	16	23.9	
Other	7	10.4	
Gender			
Female	16	23.9	
Male	51	76.1	
Training target group			
Private sector	32	46.4	
Non-profit sector	4	5.7	
Both	33	47.8	
Employment			
Salaried	49	71.0	
Freelance	13	2.8	
Owner/Holder	24	18.8	
Other	16	7.2	
Educational level			
Intermediate vocational	4	5.9	
Higher vocational	18	26.9	
University	45	67.2	
	Mean	*Standard Deviation*	*Range*
Other characteristics			
Age	39.9	8.5	26–64
General work experience in years	9.5	6.7	1–24
Specific work experience	8.5	6.3	1–24
Average duration of training in shifts	6.6	4.0	2–27
Total training hours in a month	60.5	35.3	1–160

Kind of training. A major proportion of the trainers (60 per cent) cite communication and management training. A relatively large proportion (34 per cent) of the trainers cite other training. Training focused on self-presentation skills, personal development, outward bound, selling skills, team-building, commercial skills, marketing and technical skills come under that heading.

Gender. Most (76 per cent) of the trainers are male. A significant difference exists between gender and the age structure (chi-square = 14.05, df = 4, p = .007). The age of women is lower compared to that of men. In the sample 81 per cent of the women are younger than 40 years. Of the men, 39 per cent are younger than 40 years.

Target group. A major proportion of the trainers (94 per cent) work with trainees from the private sector. The participation level of males who *only* work in the private sector (57 per cent) is significantly higher than that of women (19 per cent, chi-square = 7.46, df = 2, p = .02).

Employment. Employment, in the context of the present study, is a variable which is not likely to be equally distributed over gender. Nearly all female trainers (93 per cent) have salaried employment against more than half of male trainers (64 per cent). The owners/holders of training cooperations are all male. It may be seen that generally the majority of the trainers (71 per cent) have salaried employment.

Educational level. The educational level does not differ significantly between other characteristics of the trainers' background (particularly age and gender). A majority of the trainers (67 per cent) are university trained, mostly in social sciences.

Other characteristics. The age of the sample in general lay around 40 years with a large range between 26 to 64 years. All adult age-groups are represented.

The general work experience (m = 9.5) in the sample is mostly one year longer than the specific work experience (m = 8.5). Specific work experience is defined as experience with interpersonal skill training. In the sample there is a large variation in work experience. The years of work experience differ from 1 to 24 years.

There is also a large variation by trainer in the average duration of training in sessions (m = 6.6) and the total training hours per month (m = 60.5).

Advantages and disadvantages of role playing

The second section of the written questionnaire consisting of 14 items about advantages and disadvantages of role playing and the preparation for role-play will be discussed here. In Table 10.5 the frequencies, percentages, mean, standard deviation and range pertaining to most of the variables of this section are given.

Advantages of role playing. The advantages of role playing are scored on the five-point scale. The gradation is never scored as one, seldom as two, sometimes as three, often as four and always as five. The mean or average score is computed by adding a list of the scores one to five and then dividing by the number of scores. Comparing the mean score on the advantages of role playing, it appears the largest advantage of role playing is the possibility of giving feedback on the behaviour of trainees (m = 4.5, 56 per cent answered 'always an advantage'). In second place is mentioned the advantage of analysing your own behaviour (m = 4.3, 35 per cent answered 'always') and in third place is the possibility to emphasize non-verbal behaviour and emotions (m = 4.0, 25 per cent answered 'always'). 'Attitude change' scores last.

Disadvantages of role playing. The pattern of mean scores shows relatively low scores (about 1 point) for disadvantages in comparison with the mean scores for advantages. Looking at the differences between the disadvantages, the dependence on the quality of trainer and trainee (m = 3.1) is mentioned as the major disadvantage of role playing. Second is the simplification of reality (m = 2.9) and third the large amount of time (m = 2.8). The control of the

Table 10.5 *Composition of some general variables of role playing*

	Mean	Standard Deviation
Advantages of role playing		
Feedback on behaviour	4.5	0.7
Analyse own behaviour	4.3	0.6
To emphasize non-verbal behaviour and emotions	4.0	0.8
Try out different behaviour	3.8	0.9
Better understanding/empathy	3.7	0.7
A good representation of reality	3.5	0.8
To discuss problems	3.3	0.8
Analyse group behaviour	3.1	0.8
Changes attitudes	3.0	0.7
Disadvantages of role playing		
Depends too much on the quality of trainer and trainee	3.1	1.0
Simplification of reality	2.9	0.8
Uses a large amount of time	2.8	1.1
Confusion about playing a role or playing oneself	2.5	0.9
Depends on what trainee already knows	2.4	0.9
May be seen as too entertaining or frivolous	2.2	0.8
Cost trainer too much devotion	2.0	0.9
Trainer loses control over what is learned and in which order	1.9	0.9
The trainer's role		
As provider of information	4.2	0.7
As facilitator	4.1	0.7
As time controller/planner	4.1	0.8
As motivator	3.9	0.9
As engenderer of energy	3.8	0.8
As corrector	3.3	0.8
As adjudicator	3.1	1.0
As therapist	2.4	1.1

	Frequency	Percentage
Objectives of training		
Improvement of interpersonal skills	44	64.7
Several options	18	26.5
Other	4	5.8
To obtain experience	1	1.5
To increase knowledge	1	1.5

Table 10.5 *continued*

	Mean	*Standard Deviation*	*Range*
Other general characteristics			
Average duration of role play (min.)	19.3	12.0	5–60
To demonstrate skills average frequencies trainer uses techniques:			
a. life role playing by trainees	3.9	0.9	
b. video	2.9	1.1	
c. idem by trainers	2.3	1.1	
Average number of role plays by session	1.9	1.2	1–9

trainer over what is learned and the order in which it is learned (m = 1.9) is seen as the smallest disadvantage.

The trainer's role. During the role playing the trainer has to perform a number of different functions. According to the sample the first and most vital function is to provide information (m = 4.2), the second function is to facilitate the role play session (m = 4.1), and to control time and plan the session (m = 4.1) is the third function mentioned. The function of therapist (m = 2.4) is seen as a (very) small proportion of the trainers' normal job although opinions differ.

Objectives of training. Among the trainers, the main objective of the training is to improve interpersonal skills (65 per cent). A quarter of the sample (27 per cent) does not want to give the priority to only one objective. They keep several options, like to exchange experience, to improve knowledge and insight in efficient behaviour, to increase behaviour alternatives, to remain in difficult situations and to increase awareness of own behaviour. Other (7.4 per cent) mentioned objectives are situation, person and skill dependent. No general statements are possible.

Other general characteristics. Per session the average number of role plays is two and the average duration is 19 minutes. Both averages have a large range. Some trainers run one role play in the morning or afternoon, others run nine role plays. The average duration of a role play differs from between 5 and 60 minutes.

The trainers were asked which 'techniques' they use to demonstrate an interpersonal skill: 26.5 per cent reported never and seldom, 47.1 per cent sometimes, 22.1 per cent often and 4.4 per cent always show a video (m = 2.9); 5.8 per cent never and seldom, 19.1 per cent sometimes, 51.5 per cent often and 23.5 per cent always let trainees play a demonstration role-play (m = 3.9); and 54.5 per cent never and seldom, 30.9 per cent sometimes, 13.2 per cent often and 1.5 per cent always play a demonstration role play by themselves (m = 2.3).

Table 10.6 *Composition of one variable of introduction and instruction of role playing*

	Frequency	Percentage
Instruction for observers		
Oral/Verbal	15	21.7
On paper	11	15.9
Both	38	55.1
No instruction	5	7.3

Introduction and instruction

The introduction and instruction of role playing was investigated in the third section of the written questionnaire consisting of six items. Table 10.6 shows the frequencies and percentages pertaining to one of the variables of this section.

Instruction for observers. In the most cases (55 per cent) the trainers instruct observers with an observer grid both orally and on paper. An observer grid is a structured framework with questions or attention points for observations. A number of behaviour categories are given low scores. Only 7 per cent of the trainers claim not to work with observations.

Running sessions

In order to gain insight into running the role play session, the fourth section of the written questionnaire consisting of ten items was developed. Table 10.7 presents the frequencies, percentages, means, standard deviations and ranges pertaining to some of the variables of this section.

Intervention. On the basis of the general question on whether the trainer intervenes during the role play, it appears that 60 per cent seldom or sometimes take action to stop role playing (9 per cent never, 34 per cent seldom, 26 per cent sometimes, 17 per cent often and 14 per cent always; m = 2.8).

By comparing the reasons for intervention, burlesquing (m = 3.2), emotional escalation (m = 3.0), departing from the role (m = 2.9) and repetition (m = 2.9) score the highest. Lack of empathy (m = 2.3) scores the lowest. All reasons for intervention tend to the left side of the scale which means that the largest percentages lay on the categories never, seldom and sometimes. These results agree with those of the previous general question.

The most used techniques for intervention are role-reversal (ie, the players who have been cast as protagonist and antagonist exchange their roles; m = 2.6) and the consultant group (ie, having a special home support group whose functions are to act as consultants and to advise the protagonist on how to proceed; m = 2.5). Many of them have been developed by Moreno (1953). The results tend to the left proportion of the scale.

Debriefing

Attempts have been made to explain details of debriefing in the fifth section of

Table 10.7 *Composition of some variables of running the role play session*

	Mean	Standard deviation
Intervention		
Intervention, general	2.8	0.8
Reasons for intervention		
a. Player deproportions from role	2.9	1.2
b. Burlesquing	3.2	1.5
c. Poor performance	2.5	1.0
d. Lack of insight	2.8	1.1
e. Lack of empathy	2.3	0.9
f. Repetition	2.9	1.1
g. Boredom	2.8	1.3
h. Emotional escalation	3.0	1.2
Techniques for intervention		
a. Role-reversal	2.6	1.1
b. Alter ego/Doubling	2.0	1.0
c. Mirroring	2.3	0.9
d. Role-example	2.3	1.0
e. Consultant group	2.5	1.1

Table 10.8 *Composition of some variables of debriefing*

	Mean	Standard Deviation	Range
Average duration of debriefing			
In minutes	27.6	14.7	5-55
Replay			
Frequency of replay	1.3	1.6	1-10
Average duration of replay in minutes	14.9	24.2	1-75

the written questionnaire consisting of seven items. The results are presented in Table 10.8.

Average duration of debriefing. The debriefing session often follows soon after the enactment itself. The average duration is 28 minutes. This average has a large range; some trainers debrief one session in 5 minutes, others debrief in 55 minutes.

Replay. A relatively large proportion of the trainers (39 per cent) never replay a role play. If the trainer let the role play be replayed, the average frequency is one (m = 1.3) and the average duration is 15 minutes. The standard deviation is very large (st. dev. = 24.2). This means that every trainer has his or her own style of conducting a replay session. There is not much consensus among the trainers.

CONCLUSION AND DISCUSSION

In the following section, an overall look at the findings of the study, its limitations and suggestions for further research will be discussed. Reviewing the results of the study, we may state that role playing is a complex instructional method within which numerous aspects may vary. There are several opinions about how to use role playing but for these there is not much empirical evidence and no instructional design theory. According to Reigeluth (1983), an instructional design theory consists of a set of prescriptions as to which model will optimize given desired instructional outcomes under given instructional conditions.

The advantages and disadvantages, as we have seen, substantially differ from what is found in the literature, where the role of attitudes has taken high priority (Joyce and Weil, 1980; Kessels and Smit, 1990; Van Ments, 1989) in contrast to the result of this study, where trainers appear to put attitudes in the last place in the advantages 'hierarchy'. The importance of behavioural feedback, as the trainers in this study indicate, is seldom emphasized in the role play literature. This may be due to the fact that the field of role playing is high-fashion (less 'soft') and/or the difficulties with demonstration and the measuring of attitude development and change.

In view of the optimistic and positive reports over role playing in the literature, not many authors write about the disadvantages. Van Ments (1989) is an exception. He gives a summary of potential disadvantages. The three main areas of role playing are (1) a consequential break down in the normal discipline of the classroom, (2) the trainer loses control over what is learned and (3) the use of a large amount of time, space and, sometimes, people. In the present study, the main areas 1 and 2 are placed in the last position. The third main area corresponds to the findings of this study.

Perhaps even more important are the list of objectives for training. An outstanding feature is that only one trainer (1.5 per cent) mentions the objective 'increasing of functioning in the work-place'. In instructional design theories, transfer is an important issue. The results of this study do not reflect this main topic. This may indicate a gap between science and practice.

An interesting finding is that for demonstration of the skill(s), the trainers only sometimes (m = 2.9) use a video-tape. It is probable that the trainers prefer more active instructional methods in which trainees experience their own behaviour. Other possible explanations may lie in the fact that trainers cast doubt on the learning outcomes by watching video (it is only nice to watch), or there are no suitable videos available, or the rental fee for the video is too high.

Another remarkable result, especially since it was less expected, is that 93 per cent of the trainers use and instruct observers. In the literature, authors indirectly mention the use of observation (Joyce and Weil, 1980; Kessels and Smit, 1990; Nijkerk, 1988; Wanrooy, 1992). Van Ments (1989) makes the remark that observers are useful in some role plays, essential in some, and not needed in others. The finding in this study is in contradiction to the literature.

The finding corresponds with an earlier finding of the study, namely the importance of feedback on behaviour (advantages). For good feedback, quality observations are indispensable.

The finding that the recurrence of intervention is generally low, may indicate that trainers rarely use intervention techniques. The reasons for this may lie in the considerable demands put upon the trainer by intervention. Towers (1969) says that the trainer must possess 'tact', 'receptivity', 'skill in communication', insight, imagination and flexibility in dealing with unexpected developments. Inexperienced trainers may find this difficult. It may also be caused by the advantage of keeping the role play going.

Some remarks can be made about the limitations and general reliability and validity of the present study. In this study the relationship is discussed between aspects of role playing, which are presented in a univariate way in the preceding pages. No attempt is made to answer the question: 'Do, and if so how do, the different aspects of role playing relate to each other?' The main reason for this limitation in the study is that a number of significant differences exist in the background variables in the sample. The sample was not matched for these variables. All the variables which were the subject of the study interact with the background variables in the sample. It is impossible to formulate reliable conclusions.

In being a systematic sample survey, the high response rate (87 per cent) but the unfortunately low suitable rate (34 per cent) contrasts with others. This presents a danger to the general reliability. This problem has also been caused by tracing the population. The addresses, especially those found in the register of de NVvO of 1988, have become obsolete. NVvO refused to participate with a new register because of internal reorganization.

The validity of the questionnaire which was used here is limited by three general considerations. First, to what extent might questions influence trainers to show themselves in a good light? Second, to what extent might questions influence trainers to attempt to anticipate what researchers want to hear? Third, to what extent might questions influence trainers that they may not know about themselves?

As is often the case, the findings of the present study lead to a range of new questions. Some suggestions for further research will be offered. In the first place, researchers should be aware that trainers may vary in a lot of characteristics. It is not easy to trace an homogeneous population. Further, more research into the instructional variables of role playing is desirable. Special attention should be given to the development of an instructional design theory. Further research should in particular concentrate on the instructional conditions that can lead to the desired instructional outcomes.

About the author

Geralien Holsbrink-Engels is an assistant professor of instruction technology at the University of Twente in the Netherlands. She is working on the project 'An instructional-design model for interpersonal skill training' in which role play occupies an important place.

Geralien Holsbrink-Engels is at the *University of Twente, Department of Education, Division of Instructional Technology, PO Box 217, 7500 AE Enschede, The Netherlands.*

Acknowledgement
Thanks are extended to Mariska Pikaart for her research assistance during the data collection.

REFERENCES

Ellington, H, Addinall, E and Percival, F (1981) *Games and Simulations in Science Education*, Kogan Page, London.

Georges, J C (1989) 'The hard reality of soft-skills training', *Personnel Journal* 4, 41–5.

Guirdham, M (1990) *Interpersonal Skills at Work*, Prentice-Hall, Englewood Cliffs, NJ.

Joyce, B R and Weil, M (1980) *Models of Teaching*, Prentice-Hall, Englewood Cliffs, NJ.

Kessels, J and Smit, C (1990) 'Rollenspel? Ik kijk wel (Role playing? I watch)', *Opleiding en Ontwikkeling*, 4, 9–15.

Moreno, J L (1953) *Who shall Survive? Foundations of sociometry, group psychotherapy, and sociodrama*, Beacon House, New York.

Nijkerk, K J (1988) 'Het rollenspel [Role playing]', in Kessels, J W M and Smit, C A (eds) *Handboek Opleiders in Organisaties* (Handbook for trainers in organizations), Kluwer Bedrijfswetenschappen, Deventer.

Nunnally, J C (1978) *Psychometric Theory*, McGraw-Hill, New York.

Reigeluth, C M (1983) *Instructional-Design Theories and Models: an overview of their current status*, Lawrence Erlbaum, Hillsdale, NJ.

Shaftel, F and Shaftel, G (1967) *Role-playing for Social Values*, Prentice-Hall, Englewood Cliffs, NJ.

Shaftel, F and Shaftel, G (1982) *Role-playing In the Curriculum*, Prentice-Hall, Englewood Cliffs, NJ.

Tistaert, G (1987) 'Rollenspel [Role playing], In het losbladig', *Onderwijskundig lexicon*, Samson, Alphen aan de Rijn.

Towers, J M (1969) *Role-playing for Supervisors*, Pergamon Press, Oxford.

Tuckman, B W (1988) *Conducting Educational Research*, Harcourt Brace Jovanovich, New York.

Van Ments, M (1989) *The Effective Use of Role Play: a handbook for teachers and trainers*, Kogan Page, London.

Wanrooy, M J (1992) 'Van rollenspel tot interactiedrama (From role playing to interaction drama)', *Opleiding en Ontwikkeling* 3, 28–3.

Chapter 11

Games on social skills: a cross-cultural course for Russian/English-speakers

Mikhail V Klarin

ABSTRACT

This chapter describes the author's experience working with English-language games on social skills (some of them designed by a British author) with native Russian-speakers belonging to a culture previously isolated from 'live', people-to-people international contact. The social/communication skills training course, based on a succession of gaming activities, is presented to advanced Russian students of English to go beyond the traditional framework of vocabulary and grammar patterns and develop more in-depth understanding/feeling/experience of a 'Western' communication manner.

The chapter presents an approach to combine a structured games repertoire with a design of 'dialogue threads', creating a personally meaningful social skills course for cross-cultural communication situations.

The author's work on communication skills training for advanced students of English had been the result of new social/cultural developments in Russia in the 1990s. The increase of cross-cultural contacts resulted in a growing number of people whose professional and personal interests were related to getting closer to people coming from other cultures (mostly English-speakers), both as employers and as business, social and personal partners. This readily made the case for in-depth understanding of English language communication going beyond the traditional framework of grammar patterns and vocabulary into the more sophisticated mechanics of a communication process with people belonging to a 'different world', having a different mentality and different communication manner.

Being a practising psychologist and a fluent English-speaker, the author made an attempt to use the experiential learning model (Kolb, 1984) together with psychological training experience to help people get to know the different ways of communicating on a genuinely personal level.

The foreign language being the only medium of communication in games throughout the training course gives a chance to step aside from the 'usual ways' acquired in life experience in the native tongue.

The perceived intent of gaming for the participants is 'trying a new way of learning', 'having more oral practice', 'having fun', etc. However, the games and gaming behaviour are only part of the course content, another part being the exchange of interpretations during debriefing, trainer's responses, leading to shifts of meanings as related to the process of and attitudes to communication.

THE GAMING EXPERIENCE

The major reason for using games as the main part of the course is that they provide rich experiential background for communication in the 'here and now' of the group and its analysis during debriefing.

Personality-centred approaches resulted in the choice of no-win-or-lose games. The games relevant for development of cross-cultural understanding can be described as self-competition games, challenging the participants with an unusual, new kind of rule-governed behaviour. Games of this kind can be also called gaming exercises. They have been partly borrowed from Tim Bond's inspiring collection of games (Bond, 1986), partly self-constructed. By their content, games belong to the situations of self-awareness, self-expression, self-presentation, interpersonal reaction (especially its positive/negative and trust/distrust dimension), use of language power in the perception of self and the world, and relativity of personal/communicative dispositions.

Accordingly, communication activities can be ascribed to the types of presentation games, judgement relativity games, self-expression games and positive skills try-on exercises. All of the games have a distinctly 'foreign' touch not only because of the overtly foreign language used throughout the course, but also due to the sharp contrast of their emotionally warm and spontaneous group climate with the more learning-directed, result-oriented atmosphere which still prevails in the use of games in Russia (Aransky and Klarin, 1987). Another contrast stems from the difference between the underlying mentality of personal choice, and positive self-image, with the more traditional closed way to respond to one's own needs and aspirations.

One important note should be made here: speaking about the 'native culture' of the participants I have in mind not the rich emotional, self-reflective and interpersonal experience belonging to Russian cultural heritage but rather the more simplified and rather impersonal everyday type(s) of popular communication cultures developed and spread in the Soviet/Russian society in recent decades. Moreover, one can find different sub-cultures within any large culture, so a cross-cultural stand is relevant not only on an international or inter-ethnic scale.

Presentation games like MY NEIGHBOUR IS . . . (Bond, 1986), MY GOOD/BAD POINTS and NEGATIVE REMARKS are used as starting points to build up (and for some of the players actually to discover!) positive self-communication patterns.

Self-expression games like AUCTION OF PET HATES (Bond, 1986) or LANGUAGE OF EMOTIONS (Klarin, unpublished) give high output of emotional energy that can be directed and used further. They also have the common quality of expressing feelings and/or attitudes in a rule-regulated way. Thus their content and course of activity is in contrast with the attitudes prevailing in the native culture of the players, who are more used to dealing with sudden uncontrolled outbursts of emotions, than to a controlled and self-reflective way of recognizing and describing feelings. The debriefing of these games gives rise to insights about the missed personal/cultural opportunities of both the 'language of emotions' and the language of self-expression.

Relativity games like TRUTH AND DECEPTION (Bond, 1986), GOOD OR BAD and GUESS WHO'S LYING (Klarin, unpublished) are lively and enjoyable games, enhancing the feelings of freedom in communication. They are followed by debriefing, stressing the relativity of personal judgements. This gives players the experience of flexibility in communication process.

THE PERSONAL/DEVELOPMENTAL MEANING OF GAMES: DIALOGUE THREADS

The content of the training course (including the actual games, their suggested interpretation, and trainer's responses) is based on two major threads of dialogue.

Direct experiential/emotional dialogue thread
Based on the 'here and now' of the group:
- intrapersonal (trainee encountering own experience)
- interpersonal (trainee encountering other trainees' and trainers' experiences and responses)

Indirect, meta-dialogue thread
Both experiential and quasi experiential: encounters of trainee's own culture/style of self-image construction, interaction patterns with 'foreign' mentality and manner of communication. The direct dialogue thread is designed along the following lines:
- Actualizing past personal emotional experience (building up personal involvement base), interpreting it in terms of 'the language of emotions'
- constructing self-image, interpreting self-image in terms of suggested/created 'self-concept language'
- experiencing the impact of the language patterns on one's own mentality
- increasing flexibility in the choice of communication mode (exercises with 'stressed relativity' meanings)
- development of skills in effective (active) listening
- practising positive supportive communication.

One of the vital goals in direct dialogue, besides understanding, is providing an array of positive communication experiences for players, thus creating a 'positive' learning environment (Thatcher, 1990, pp. 298–9).

Embedded within the more observable and direct thread of intra-

and interpersonal games-related dialogue, there is always the intertwining cross-cultural meta-dialogue introduced and supported by the trainer. The lines along which this dialogue is designed include the following:

- cultural differences in the expression of emotions
- self-presentation: 'home' and 'foreign' style
- mentality of responsibility and personal choice in Russian and 'Western' cultures
- differences of being positive (for example, why are 'they' always smiling 'like that'?)
- 'us' and 'them': discussing the ways of 'those foreigners'.

The results of this training match the intentions of building up the positive self-image and self-presentation potential in cross-cultural communication situations. This includes encouraging the mentality of personal initiative and responsibility, coming closer to the 'Western' manner of communication, feeling more at ease with 'foreigners', removing inner blocks to genuine understanding of (and cooperation with) people who come from another culture with different communication patterns. Being the designer of this programme, I definitely attribute the nature of both the process and the results to the combination of the *structured games repertoire* with the design of *dialogue threads* described in this chapter.

REFERENCES

Aransky, V S and Klarin, M V (1987) 'Modern teaching: the strategy of didactic game in the teaching process', *International Review of Education*, 33, 312–15.
Bond, T (1986) *Games for Social and Life Skills*, Hutchinson, London.
Kolb, D (1984) *Experiential Learning*, Prentice Hall, London.
Thatcher, D (1990) 'Experience as learning: implications for training and operation', *Simulation/Games for Learning*, 20, 3, 276–302.

ABOUT THE AUTHOR

Dr Mikhail V Klarin is the senior research fellow at the Institute of Theoretical Pedagogics and International Research in Education. He is also an associate professor of psychology, and is based at the Russian Academy of Education.

Address for correspondence: u(. admirala Makarova 37-1-4; 125212 Moscow, Russia.

Chapter 12

THE SUFFRAGETTES: a political game of civil unrest

Timothy McCoy Price

ABSTRACT

THE SUFFRAGETTES is a game designed to provoke debate about terrorism and anti-terrorist methods, including the role of the media, within a morally acceptable framework. It deals with the militant struggle for rights for women and the methods and techniques they were to use to further their political ends. It is primarily aimed at 14–16-year-old students as part of their studies.

INTRODUCTION

The role of the terrorist and counter-terrorist techniques, including the part played by the media, are an important part of today's society, yet rational debate in this area is fraught with difficulty. One person's 'terrorist' is another person's 'freedom-fighter'. Simulation and gaming techniques offer real utility in examining these subjects in order to demonstrate dilemmas and provoke debate, distanced from the grim realities of actual outrages.

The problem is that certain agencies and individuals view this subject, *in itself*, as one unsuitable for simulation or gaming. This game is an attempt to provoke the debate within the confines of a campaign not normally regarded as 'terrorist' in nature; it is a 'politically correct' terrorist game, if you like. It is therefore more likely to be acceptable under certain circumstances.

The game is also useful in highlighting issues that were indirectly relevant to the campaign, such as the techniques used by men in order to secure *their* rights previously; and in general education as to revealing what the average woman's situation was at that time.

INSTRUCTIONS

This game is intended to be used to provide a focus for attention into an unusual and neglected period of history. The suffragette movement teaches many lessons about civil unrest and political movements that are still relevant today.

The game should be played in the following manner:

- Split the players into two groups: the government, who should be *entirely* male: and the suffragettes, who should be *predominantly* female. If you have a lot of players you may consider making a few of the more mature players act as the members of the press.
- The players should be given copies of the background sheets, and the three principal players on each side, the personal briefing sheets. The remaining players are free to make their own point of view for each side, but you must stress that the three principals are the only players who can make decisions.
- The umpire, armed with the sheet listing the sort of incident that actually took place during the suffrage campaign, will move between the two groups resolving any conflicts that take place.
- It is important that the players taking the role of the government are given additional tasks to divert their attention from the suffrage question (and keep them under pressure!). The tasks that you may wish to give them, such as providing them with a simple, but historically relevant, multiple-choice question sheet (the answers of which can be looked up in an encyclopedia), should be capable of being quickly marked to provide a subjective judgement as to how well the government of the day is doing. Any spare players can do this for you while you are talking to the suffragette players.

In general, the government players are usually very reluctant to carry out forced feeding, and will often jump at the chance of changing the law so as to avoid having to do so (the Cat and Mouse Act). The suffragette players usually run rings around the government players, but are often unable to conceive that the real suffragettes actually used arson and bombings (albeit, carefully selected to avoid any casualties) to further their aims. The deliberate suicide of Emily Wilding Davison BA, is worthy of some discussion.

After a suitable period, you should get the two groups together, with any members of the press, to discuss how well they saw themselves as doing. You should then give some examples of what actually happened in the real campaign, and compare their actions to history.

BACKGROUND

During the nineteenth century, some women began to demand the right to vote in elections. In the recent past the focus for women's rights had concentrated on their rights in marriage. So, for example: up until 1870, a husband owned all his wife's earnings; until 1879, a husband was allowed to beat his wife; until 1882, a husband owned all his wife's belongings; and until 1891, a husband could lock his wife up. Women were now concerned that they should have a say in the running of the country. At that time the only woman who could do that was Queen Victoria.

At this time a number of women's sufferage societies were set up in the big cities. In Manchester, for example, Lydia Baker ran a sufferage group. The tactics were peaceful and limited to persuading MPs to support her, holding public meetings, sending petitions to parliament, and editing the *Women's Suffrage Journal*. In 1897, the various women's suffrage groups came together in the National Union of Women's Sufferage Societies (NUWSS).

Throughout these years a number of MPs had tried to pass acts which gave votes to at least some women. Most MPs, however, were against the idea, as were a number of women. Some women were granted the right to vote, but had to meet such stringent property and money conditions that the number who could qualify was negligible.

After some 50 years of trying, some younger suffragists were beginning to run out of patience with the peaceful methods. There had been violence before more men were granted the right to vote in 1832 and 1867. Perhaps it was time for a change in tactics.

In 1903 Emmeline Pankhurst formed the Women's Social and Political Union (WSPU). Support for the WSPU grew rapidly. Its approach was quite different to that of the more peaceable NUWSS. They picketed ministers' houses, demonstrated outside the homes of MPs, interrupted meetings, shouting and waving banners; they even chained themselves to the railings outside Number 10. For some of the actions they were arrested, refused to pay the fines, and went to prison.

The game starts in 1909, shortly after the latest bill on Women's Suffrage is 'talked out' of the current session of Parliament.

HISTORICAL BACKGROUND

1900 Boxer rebellion in China. Boer War starts. Count Zeppelin launches 420ft airship.
1901 Queen Victoria, 'the only women in politics', dies. Australia unified. Nobel Prizes first awarded.
1902 Boer War ends. Cecil Rhodes dies. Britain and Japan form an Alliance.
1903 The Wright Brothers' first heavier-than-air flight. Richard Gatling, of the 'Gatling Gun', dies.
1904 Russo-Japanese War. Plague in India. Entente Cordiale (Anglo-French settlement of colonial differences).
1905 Failed revolution in Russia. Cullinan diamond discovered (3,000 carats). Einstein formulates Special Theory of Relativity.
1906 Typhoid Mary found. US troops occupy Cuba (until 1909). Earthquake in San Francisco kills 700. HMS Dreadnought launched in Portsmouth.
1907 Rasputin enjoys great influence in Czarist court. Territorial Army created. Hague Peace Conference.
1908 Earthquake in Italy kills 76,000. Riots in Rome. Introduction of Old Age Pensions. Model 'T' Ford mass produced. Boy Scout movement founded by Baden-Powell.

ACTUAL EVENTS

The following events actually took place, at some time, during the suffragette campaign:

Mass meetings and demonstrations (eg, Hyde Park, the Albert Hall, etc.).

Marching on the prime minister, in order to obtain an interview in which to present their case.

Marching on parliament to present a petition.

Demonstrations and disruption of government political rallies (eg, Churchill).

Interrupting a meeting disguised as a telegraph messenger boy.

Chaining themselves to the railings. Chaining themselves to each other in groups.

Human letters (Miss McLellan and Miss Solomon) via the Post Office.

Hunger strikes.

Attempts to petition the king (in the Bill of Rights, prosecution for this is illegal).

Overseas support – America and France. Attempts at political status.

War on Windows – acts of vandalism on West End shops and MPs' homes.

Arson attacks (various unoccupied properties, timber yard, docks, etc).

The split between the militants (Pankhurst) and the moderates (Pethick-Lawrence).

General vandalism – railway carriages, bowling greens, golf courses, telephone lines, graffiti, street lamps smashed, etc.

Psychological operations – old ladies applying for gun licences, fake messages calling up army reserves and territorials, etc.

Bombings of an empty railway station, and an MP's home (when he was out).

Riots.

The Cat and Mouse Act, described as 'political suicide embodied in an Act of Parliament'.

Deliberate suicide – Emily Wilding Davison threw herself under the king's horse on 6 June 1913. The horse survived. She had sewn the WSPU colours into her petticoats so nobody could claim it was an accident.

Bodyguard of Women – jujitsu-trained women. On one occasion, frightened by the threat of the Bodyguard, a total of 102 police in 13 police cars, with motorcycle escorts (not counting those on crowd duties) were sent to arrest Mrs Pankhurst.

An axe attack on the Rokeby Venus in the National Gallery.

PERSONAL BRIEFINGS

HERBERT HENRY ASQUITH

You are Asquith, the 35th prime minister of Great Britain, and a Liberal. You are totally uninterested in the political nuisance that is the suffragette movement – 'Suffragettes! Let them Suffer!' is your motto.

You have experienced problems, however, in the recent campaign masterminded by that dreadful woman, Pankhurst. These women seem intent on challenging the government itself and, more dangerously, you personally. They disrupt the business of the government and distract attention from the more pressing and important matters at hand, such as the rise of German imperialism.

You have also had some problems where noted intellectuals, such as George Bernard Shaw and Keir Hardie, one of the founders of the emerging Labour movement, join forces to criticize the government. This can be politicaly dangerous when the likes of these are seen to be united against a Liberal government. You are, therefore, prepared to fob these women off with vague promises of introducing a Bill to address the idea of women's suffrage, at some time later.

There are a number of relevant facts:

- Some women have the right to vote, providing, of course, they meet some property and money requirements (you can't give every women the vote – or they will simply vote the way their husband directs; and what is the point of that?)
- The king, himself, supports the view that women must not be allowed to become martyrs, so any attempts at hunger strikes must be met with a very firm response.
- You are aware that some old legislation (such as the right to petition parliament) is open to misuse by these women, and it may be time to change the law. You have an absolute majority so, providing you are not too ham-fisted about it, you can do exactly what you want.

In the meantime, you have more important things to worry about, so just make sure the authorities keep Mrs Pankhurst away from you, and you will be happy.

WINSTON CHURCHILL

You are Winston Churchill, war hero, and Liberal member of parliament.

There a number of pressing matters that concern you at the moment, such as the alarming rise in German imperialist ambitions, coupled with a disturbing decline in political ability shown by Russia (the Russian navy has ceased to exist, after the war with Japan) and there is nobody, except Britain, prepared to curb German expansion.

You are well aware of the women's suffrage movement as you were singled out, during the 1905 campaign, by the suffragettes as their target (they lacked the resources to attack more than one prospective member of the Liberal Party). They proceeded to disrupt every single meeting you held and, although that did not prevent you being elected, you were returned with the smallest majority in the country.

This, along with the incredible skill and deviousness shown by these women, demonstrates that they are, perhaps, more of a problem than the Prime

Minister thinks they are. They are also a bunch of glassy-eyed fanatics. Why, after Mrs Pankhurst, herself, was arrested for a breach of the peace at one of your rallies, you, in a characteristically gallant gesture, attempted to pay her fine. She refused. You do have to admire her pluck, however, and she (and her daughters) are rather pretty – it is all most distracting.

You are also aware that you are a very junior MP, with a lot to learn, and with a healthy amount of ambition.

You must support the government as, after all, there are more important things to worry about than a bunch of crazy women (however attractive).

KEIR HARDIE

You are Keir Hardie, the founding father of the emerging Labour movement. You have devoted your life to championing the cause of the working man and woman, and the recent introduction of the National Old Age Pension, for those people of advanced age with no income greater than 10 shillings, is a great step in the right direction (even if it was a Liberal government that finally introduced it).

You have also been a passionate supporter of women's suffrage for a number of years. You have heard Mrs Pankhurst and her daughters speak, from time to time, and have always been impressed by their passion, energy, and commitment.

You are very worried, however, that they are being ignored by the government, when they do have a legitimate grievance. This may mean that faced with frustration at every turn, they will resort, like the men before them, to more extreme methods to get their voice heard. If that happens, it can only end in tragedy.

You will admit that there are a number of other matters that the government is rightly concerned about which, it may well be argued, require a higher priority to be placed upon them than the suffragettes. The principal of these is, of course, German expansionism.

The Government, in the meantime, enjoys a substantial majority so, unless it does something outrageous, it can do pretty much as it pleases.

You are also aware that too much attention to the suffrage question can be a disadvantage. While the subject is important, if you are seen to be ignoring important issues because of the suffragette question, you will lose credibility in many working-class areas. After all, many men and women do not support the idea of women's suffrage at all.

You will, therefore, support any and all legal methods of furthering the women's movement, but your sympathies lie more with the moderate NUWSS than with the radical WSPU. You can talk to the ladies of the WSPU at any time, if you wish to do so. Just ask the umpire.

EMMMELINE PANKHURST

You are Emmeline Pankhurst, the widow of the noted and well-respected Dr Richard Marsden Pankhurst, a staunch supporter of the women's suffrage movement. You have two devoted and beautiful daughters, Constance and Sylvia (who are active in the movement); and three other children, Harry, Adela and Henry.

The women's sufferage movement has been active for over 40 years, but has been lacking in any real popular base with the general population. Until now the movement has been ill-focused and mainly confined to a few noble-hearted intellectuals, achieving little after all these years.

Things have changed, however, since the huge publicity that went with your spell in prison after disrupting the Liberal candidate's (Sir Edward Grey) election rally. Since then the movement has gone from strength to strength, with thousands of women from all walks of life and all parts of the country joining the movement.

You are somewhat troubled, however, that despite all the popular support, you seem to be no nearer to persuading the government, and the perfidious Mr Asquith, to do anything concrete to change the unacceptable situation that exists concerning the rights of half the population. You have had empty promises of support from a number of members of parliament, but they have proved, with rare exceptions, to be utterly worthless.

You are convinced that more militant action is called for than the standard tactic of secreting a supporter into a political rally, and asking in a loud voice, 'Will the speaker give votes for women?', getting arrested, refusing the fine and going meekly to prison. There are a great number of options available to you: vandalism, disruption of public services, marching on parliament to present a petition, petitioning the king, arson, bombing, hunger-strikes, etc.

It is essential that the pressure and momentum of the movement must be sustained, and this can only be achieved by more militancy. What you need to do is decide, with your trusted friends, Lady Constance Lytton and Mrs Emmeline Pethick-Lawrence, on your next series of steps, that the Women's Social and Political Union (WSPU) is going to take. No surrender!

EMMELINE PETHICK-LAWRENCE

Your are Emmeline Pethick-Lawrence and have been a supporter of the National Union of Women's Sufferage Societies (NUWSS) (formed 1897) that was the first national group that pulled together the scattered different societies around the country. The women's sufferage movement has been making slow but steady progress in the last 40 years, but has now been galvanized into far greater prominence under the leadership of Emmeline Pankhurst in the newly-formed Women's Social and Political Union (WSPU).

You accept that the previous tactics of appealing for help from intellectuals and giving rallies around the country have been largely ineffectual, and that

Mrs Pankhurst's tactics of actually picketing the homes of members of parliament, disrupting political rallies, shouting and waving banners, have resulted in more support and publicity in two years than all the previous 40 put together. You are a bit worried, however, that it doesn't get out of hand.

You disapprove of some elements of the movement who advocate smashing windows and vandalizing railway carriages. Public opinion is fickle and we are, after all, women and must not alienate the less-militant elements in society.

You have been summoned to a 'council of war' by Emmeline Pankhurst, with Lady Constance Lytton, to discuss your tactics in the wake of yet another failure of the government, and that spineless jellyfish Asquith, to consider a Bill on women's suffrage.

You rather fear that Mrs Pankhurst is to advocate even more militant action than has so far been considered. You are very worried about this and, while you are sure that something must be done to keep the pressure on the government, you don't want things to go 'too far'.

You are constantly aware that a number of women are easily led, and fanatical about the cause, and there have been a number (fortunately few) of regrettable accidents resulting in serious injury or even death, to the ladies taking part. Lady Lytton is a frail flower, and you don't want anything to happen to her.

You have the support of Mrs Pankhurst's daughter, Christabel, in your moderate views, and the staunch support of your husband in all your work. It is absolutely vital, however, that whatever happens, there is no split in the movement, as this would be disastrous to the cause.

LADY CONSTANCE LYTTON

You are Lady Constance Lytton, the only daughter of Robert Lytton, diplomat, poet, Earl of Lytton, Viceroy of India, Ambassador to Paris (who died in 1891). You live with your mother in Knebworth, and have a small inheritance that looks after all your needs.

You have been a staunch supporter of the Women's Social and Political Union (WSPU) ever since you were involved in a prolonged argument with Mrs Emmeline Pethick-Lawrence at a rally, which you attended to obtain more information about prison, to support your interest in prison reform. You have gradually come around to accepting their point of view, faced with the appalling lack of interest displayed by the government. You accept the need for more militant action, but are a little wary of leading those less fortunate than yourself into prison.

You are aware that your background can give rise to as many problems as it can help the cause. You are frequently released as soon as your identity becomes known, whereas others remain in prison, and the police are reluctant to arrest you. You also regret that, since you have been a chronic invalid since infancy, you are physically frail, with a weak heart, and are unable to support the movement as fully as you would like. You do, however, support the movement with a passion, as you firmly believe that it offers the only hope for those women who are less fortunate than yourself – most of them.

You have been called together, with Mrs Emmeline Pethick-Lawrence, by Mrs Pankhurst in order to discuss tactics in the light of the failure of the government, once again, to consider a Bill introducing women's sufferage. No surrender!

Other games by the author with a 'terrorist' theme:

HIJACK.
SUMMER IN SOUTHEND.
GREENWAR.
EAT THE RICH.
LA REPUBLICA DE SAN SPLENDIDO.

ABOUT THE AUTHOR

Tim Price, born 1958, has been a government employee in the administration and support area, both in Great Britain and overseas, since 1979. He became interested in the use of simulation and gaming for both training and education early in his career, particularly in the study of conflict resolution and war games. He has developed a number of games for educational, recreational and training purposes in the past 15 years and is a member of Wargames Developments, an association devoted to the continued development of non-commercial wargames.

Address for correspondence: 46 Woodside Avenue, Beaconsfield, Bucks HP9 1JH.

Chapter 13

TRAFFIC IN BARABAKH: an introduction to role play

Claude Bourlés

ABSTRACT

TRAFFIC IN BARABAKH is a role-play game designed to introduce players with no previous experience to outdoor role-playing. The game does not require a high level of training from the facilitator, and can be played with a variable number of players.

The game may be played for leisure in a light-hearted frame of mind. It can also be used as a means to start discussions about contemporary civil war problems.

INTRODUCTION

Role play is one main area of gaming in the general practice of simulation gaming. We can recognize three sorts of role-play games:

■ business role play, used by trainers;
■ therapy role play (psychodrama) used by psychologists or psychotherapists; and
■ leisure role play played for fun by students (and sometimes their teachers and other older persons)

Teaching game science is perceived as pertinent by the staff, as some of the students may become trainers (and may have to use business role play), others may become therapists (and may have to use psychodrama). Sometimes, the students themselves practise leisure role play games.

TRAFFIC IN BARABAKH is an introductory game to role play. It was developed to introduce the students to role play in a light-hearted spirit. This game was played in the general frame of the course of game science. The title of the course is: 'Simulation des Problemes Contemporains' (Simulations of Contemporary Problems). Lots of such problems are surveyed during this course: terrorism, racism, totalitarianism, drug abuse, unemployment and, recently, ethnic cleansing.

Simulation gaming is an unconventional approach to these problems. It allows those involved to discover unknown points of view. It provides a lot of topics for discussion in the philosophy classroom, for example.

Some fallouts of the course are perceived by other teachers in their own courses or group activities. The need to introduce them to simulation gaming is aroused. The first edition of the game was a booklet including 34 characters; the new one will contain 100 characters.

As TRAFFIC IN BARABAKH was also played with success for fun, this game was chosen as an introduction to role play. It is a game and a scenario as well. The general idea of the scenario came from the recent years in Lebanon; the first draft was written during the trouble in Armenia, and it was completed during the war in Yugoslavia. Several people from such countries participated in some runs of the game. They generally agree upon the likeliness of the scenario.

The game design is mainly for leisure, but trainers familiar with business role play will recognize situations they can use with their groups. Some characters' briefings may also be used by psychologists.

PRESENTATION

This chapter is intended as an introduction to role playing games in general and to outdoors role playing games in particular.

The first medieval fantasy role playing game – that is, of course, Dungeons and Dragons, which was created in the United States – was introduced in France in the early 1980s. Since then, a great number of role playing games have been introduced in France. These games are quite varied and deal with a wide diversity of themes.

Role playing games used to be played in groups, around a game master, who, in principle, was the only person perfectly aware of the game's rules. Since then, new ways of playing have appeared.

For lack of partners sometimes, some people began to play alone with game books. Since the invention of personal computers, they have started to play with microcomputers. Others decided to play outdoors in greater numbers, for example in a castle they would have rented on this occasion or in other premises. This type of game is called an 'Outdoors role playing game'.

TRAFFIC is a scenario conceived for an outdoors role playing game. It only requires a short preparation from the umpire. If necessary the game might even be organized without an umpire.

In case some players insist on connecting this scenario to already-existing rules, they may consider it as a KILLER scenario.

SIGNIFICANT ADVICE

No brutality

TRAFFIC is not a 'physical' scenario. Neither fighting nor struggling is intended to be part of the game. Rather, TRAFFIC has been conceived for glib talkers and busybodies. It has already successfully been tested within uninitiated groups. Although TRAFFIC has been designed for beginners, people who are accustomed to role playing games will enjoy it a lot too.

The stake is not a very important one. Each character has an objective and the players who are wedded to such notions as triumph and defeat will be able to assess their degree of success.

BACKGROUND

BARABAKH is an imaginary country situated somewhere between central Europe and the near east, somewhere between the former Yugoslavia and Afghanistan, between the Caucasus and Yemen, without forgetting Armenia, Kurdistan, Lebanon and other places.

The Northern part of BARABAKH is inhabited by a majority of Ramenians who practise a Christian religion, and is kept under the authority of General Maounian, whereas the Southern part of BARABAKH is inhabited by a majority of Razeri, with Muslim beliefs, and is under General Omar's authority.

Some parts of the country are made up of mixed populations. Over the past few years, tension has been gradually increasing between the two major populations and has led to outrages, pogroms, and all sorts of crimes. The United Nations have initiated a peace conference for BARABAKH, which will take place at the International Hotel in a neutral, neighbouring country. Lots of characters are thus gathered together at the International Hotel and they do not all have very laudable motivations.

THE ROLES

There are over 34 roles to be played although they do not all have to be adopted: the number of players can therefore vary on each occasion. Eight examples of role briefs are provided in this chapter; readers are advised to contact the author for further information.

General Omar, Razeri politician

You are now standing in the Internaional Hotel's foyer. You are General Omar, chief of the Razeri militia. Part of the BARABAKH mountains is under your control. The other part of the mountains is under the control of your rival, General Maounian, chief of the Ramenian militia. Your partisans there grow hashish. The selling of drugs helps you in buying weapons.

You have officially come as a participant of a conference dealing with peace in BARABAKH, which has been organised by the United Nations delegate, Thor Sörensen. But you have unofficially entrusted one of your subordinates, Captain Abdul, with the selling of a substantial quantity of drugs amounting to several tons. You intend to use the money to buy new weapons. You need them indeed, for recent skirmishes with the opponent militia have led to a large utilization of military supplies. Another subordinate of yours, Colonel Rachid, is in charge of the transactions with arms dealers.

You intend to drag negotiations out until the weapons have been purchased. Only in the last resort will you accept coming to a compromise with horrible General Maounian.

General Maounian, Ramenian politician

You are now standing in the International Hotel's foyer. You are General Maounian, chief of the Ramenian militia. Part of the BARABAKH mountains is under your control. The other part of the mountains is under the control of your rival, General Omar, chief of the Razeri militia. Your partisans there grow hashish. The selling of drugs helps you in buying weapons.

You have officially come as a participant of a conference dealing with peace in BARABAKH, which has been organised by the United Nations delegate, Thor Sörensen. But you have unofficially entrusted one of your subordinates, Captain Maroukian, with the selling of a substantial quantity of drugs amounting to several tons. You intend to use the money to buy new weapons. You need them indeed, for recent skirmishes with the opponent militia have led to a large utilization of military supplies. Another subordinate of yours, Colonel Agrazian, is in charge of the transactions with arms dealers.

You intend to drag negotiations out until the weapons have been purchased. Only in the last resort will you accept coming to a compromise with horrible General Omar.

Constantin Gorytus, arms dealer

You are now standing in the International Hotel's foyer. You are Constantin Gorytus, a notorious arms dealer. You have an important deal in prospect: General Maounian, the well-known chief of the Ramenian militia, wants to buy weapons and military supplies from you. Thanks to politician Donald Fullerton, who is a sympathizer of the Ramenians, you have recently obtained a stock of weapons declared obsolete but still in good condition.

You have not met General Maounian yet, and you can therefore not recognize him. In the confusion arising from recent events, your usual intermediary has been the unfortunate victim of a stray bullet. You therefore have to find your partner on your own in the crowd in order to carry out the deal.

When you have achieved your business, you will have to find Captain Radovic to inform him about the consignees of the stock of weapons, which will be brought by barges sailing on the river Ranube which flows across BARABAKH.

You should remain careful, for you have been notified by your informers that, apparently, some Interpol policemen have heard about the whole matter.

Thor Sörensen, UN delegate

You are now standing in the International Hotel's foyer. Your name is Thor Sörensen and you are a delegate from the UN. You have been commissioned to organize a conference dealing with peace in BARABAKH. Your interlocutors are expected to be General Maounian, who is in control of the northern partof BARABAKH, and General Omar, who is in control of the southern part of BARABAKH.

You know that the two rivals have agreed to sit down around the same negotiation table only because they lack weapons and military supplies. There is no doubt that they intend to try and get supplied. As soon as they feel that they are in a position to do so, they will break off the negotiations. This is what is likely to happen if they manage to buy new weapons.

There is no doubt that beyond the scene transactions are being carried out with arms dealers. If you succeed in wrecking these transactions, the Peace Conference is likely to be a success . . .

Neither of the two protagonists will dare object openly to a ceasefire. Several journalists are staying at the hotel. If necessary, you know how to attract their attention in order to give the whole matter enough publicity.

Alfonso Ramirez, drugs dealer

You are now standing in the International Hotel's foyer. You are Alfonso Ramirez, an important hashish dealer. You import drugs from the Middle-East, where it is produced by General Maounian's partisans in the BAR-ABAKH mountains. General Maounian relies on the money made out of the selling of drugs to buy weapons.

You have not met General Maounian's delegate, and you can therefore not recognize him. In the confusion arising from recent events, your usual intermediary has been the unfortunate victim of a stray bullet. You therefore have to find your partner on your own in the crowd in order to carry out the deal.

You should remain careful, for you have been notified by your informers that, apparently, some members of the Narcotics Bureau and Interpol have heard about the whole matter.

When you have achieved your busines, you will have to find Captain Radovic to inform him about the consignees of the stock of weapons, which will be brought by barges sailing on the river Ranube which flows across BARABAKH.

However, you cannot remain too long in this hotel's hall, for a hired assassin is on your tracks. He has just arrived at the airport and he will be here in one hour.

Pamela Quickglance, investigator

You are now standing in the International Hotel's foyer. You are Pamela Quickglance, an investigator from the Narcotics Bureau. You are investigating substantial drug dealing, probably amounting to several hundred kilos. Succeeding in intercepting the freight would ensure your promotion.

Important politicians might get compromised in this matter, so you will have to act carefully, since a blunder would certainly be prejudicial to your promotion.

You have already been informed that notorious dealers such as Ben Tabrit or Alfonso Ramirez have come to complete the bargain. Unfortunately, the colleague who was to give you the photo which would have enabled you to identify the dealers has been the victim of a stray bullet. You will therefore have to look for the dealers and their accomplices on your own.

Other policemen are looking for the dealers. They could lend you a hand, but there is a risk that they will eventually double-cross you and turn your research to their own advantage.

One of the persons in charge of security at the hotel might help you in case you have a hard time. You have never met him before, but at least you know his name: Fred Fossrayer.

Conchita Cabezadevaca, journalist

You are now standing in the International Hotel's foyer. Your name is Conchita Cabezadevaca, and you are a journalist for the *Nouvelle del Mundo* newspaper. You are covering an important matter of drug traffic; that is, a substantial amount of hashish proceeding from the BARABAKH mountains. The money collected from selling these drugs would serve to finance the buying of weapons by either of the two militias which have put the state of BARABAKH to fire and sword. Succeeding in clearing up this matter would probably ensure your promotion.

Important politicians might get compromised in this matter, so you will have to act carefully since a blunder would certainly be prejudicial to your promotion.

You have already been informed that notorious arms dealers such as Alfonso Ramirez or Ben Tabrit have come to complete a profitable bargain. Unfortunately the colleague who was to give you the photo which 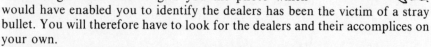 would have enabled you to identify the dealers has been the victim of a stray bullet. You will therefore have to look for the dealers and their accomplices on your own.

Other important reporters are also looking for the dealers. They could lend you a hand but there is a risk that they will eventually double-cross you, and turn your work to their own advantage.

Antoinette Longchemin, hotel manager

You are now standing in your hotel's foyer. Your name is Antoinette Longchemin, and you are the manager of the International Hotel. There is a great stir at the moment since the BARABAKH peace conference is to begin today.

There have already been several bomb alerts in the course of the past week. Each time you have conscientiously initiated evacuation orders and then systematically but vainly searched the premises. You have come to think that this could possibly result from the manager of a rival hotel, The Helton, manoeuvering to keep you away from the organization of the conference.

In order to be prepared for anything, you have hired a new detective together with a trainee detective, and you have also asked Superintendent Groussard and his SWAT team to come to your hotel; they are due to arrive at any moment.

The scenario

The map shown in Figure 13.1 helps participants to visualize the conflict within BARABAKH.

ABOUT THE AUTHOR

Claude Bourlés has taught biology, computer science and game science to students in psychology for years, at IPSA (Institut de Psychologie et Sciences sociales Appliques d'Angers).

Address for correspondence: GERSAFE, IPSA-UCO, BP 808, F 49008 Angers Cedex 08, France.

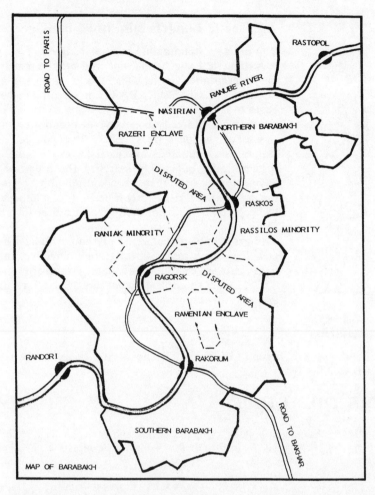

Figure 13.1 *Map of BARABAKH to be photocopied, enhanced and given to the first three characters*

Chapter 14

Simulating topical diplomatic negotiations

Paul W Meerts

ABSTRACT

This chapter deals with the use and usefulness of up-to-date role plays as tools to train people in international negotiations. The chapter explains how to create such role plays and how to apply them. By citing real-life experiences, possible pitfalls are illustrated. The chapter arrives at the conclusion that topical simulations are a very effective tool in teaching content and training skills in conjunction with each other and in a very short period of time.

The simulations are only time-consuming in so far as the trainer will have to follow the developments on which the simulations are based rather closely, because, if the games are not kept up-to-date, they will lose their effectiveness as learning devices.

One of the main tools in training (future) negotiators is the simulation exercise: a device to recreate reality as a means of learning by active participation in a game which represents a real-life problem. Three types (see Table 14.1) can be distinguished. First of all, the fully computerized simulation; second the simulation game (interplay of man and computer), and finally the interpersonal simulation (role play).

The latter variant can be divided into simulations meant to teach something about a specific topic, simulations providing a better insight into a certain process (eg, negotiation), and simulations providing both at the same time. The last form is a very cost-effective method of learning about a certain issue and could be further divided into three variants: simulations dealing with a purely imaginative or historical case, simulations about the reality of today or the near future, and a mixture of both. An example of the latter type is an imaginary case that will be dealt with by countries that exist in reality, or an existing problem being managed by imaginary states.

This chapter will concentrate on the relatively novel, topical simulation games as have been, and are still being, developed by The Netherlands Institute of International Relations, Clingendael in The Hague. Writing, designing and applying these simulation games are a few of the specialized activities of this institute. The simulations deal with current international problems and issues

Type	Orientation	Topicality
computerized	substance	historical/fictional
interpersonal	process	topical
mixed	mixed	mixed

Table 14.1 *Simulations*

which dominate the news. Advantages of this approach are that the participants already have some knowledge of the problem through media coverage so that relatively little background information on the subject needs to be provided. Another advantage of the topical approach is an enhanced motivation of the participants. Moreover, the players do not only deepen their insight into the negotiation process during their training, but into a specific issue in international politics as well. Possible disadvantages may be the necessity to keep the case up-to-date all the time, the danger of hurting the feelings of participants from the countries involved in a particular or parallel situation, and the risk of (temporarily) misinterpreting or miscalculating the situation or facts involved. Both the positive aspects and the possible risks will be dealt with in this chapter. We will come to see that the topical simulation games are to be preferred to the conventional simulation exercises when training (future) diplomats for (international) negotiation situations.

TOPICAL SIMULATIONS

As far as the issues are concerned 'topical simulation games' can basically be divided into two types: those which explain a regular negotiation process in a given organization, and those which make clear the dilemmas involved in overcoming a very polarized crisis situation.

Examples of the first type are the scenarios used to enhance an understanding of the negotiation process inside the institutions of the European Community on long-term issues, such as the development of a single European currency, a European army, and a coordinated European foreign policy. Questions such as 'Which rational and common interests are involved?' and 'How could they evolve in the coming decade?' play a central role in these kinds of scenarios and help to give outsiders an instrument to deal with the European Community and its member states.

Examples of the second type of conflict simulation, the crisis game, are scenarios on the crises in Yugoslavia, the Persian Gulf, Transcaucasia and the Baltic States. The form of this crisis management through negotiation is often the Security Council of the United Nations, but could include the Conference on Security and Cooperation in Europe, the North Atlantic Treaty Organization, or the Western European Union. While in the first type a better understanding of the standard procedures and processes is dominant, in the second type the (mis)management of conflict is the central issue.

With respect to the structure of the topical simulation, two models can be distinguished: the ongoing and the *ad hoc* type. The Clingendael Institute and its predecessors have developed since 1967 games that were meant to test the level of knowledge of participants after a full curriculum in diplomacy. They were of the ongoing topical simulation type. These games were prepared by extensive lectures on the relevant topics. Notes had to be made, position papers had to be written, statements had to be made, and the final document (the result of a night-long negotiation process) was assessed. As a whole this kind of simulation could be perceived as an examination and it was valued as such. The following had to be done in order to get good results:

- selection of relevant issues that would not have been resolved by the time the game was to take place (mostly in three months' time);
- writing of an overall scenario and individual instructions by the staff members on the basis of foreign policy documents, newspaper articles and interviews with policy-makers;
- introducing the game, lecturing on the topics, handing out of the instructions, handing out of basic literature on the issues;
- reading the position papers written by the participants, discussing them individually with the authors in order to correct mistakes;
- handing out the position papers, organizing the plenary session where the statements are made, followed by 'secret negotiations';
- discussing collectively the resulting final document, comparing it with real ones and perhaps organizing a mock press-conference.

Every staff member should specialize in one of the topics involved and an experienced diplomat should be invited to chair the plenaries and act as resource person during the evaluation after the game is over.

Another model had a less ongoing character. While the above-mentioned game is a continuous one, being made up-to-date for every new class but building upon the game of the foregoing group, the second model has a more *ad hoc* character. A scenario is written that can be used during a certain period and that will be replaced by a completely new one after the issue has passed into history. While in the first model the organization is fixed and the topics change, in the second variant both topics and context (organization) are replaced after some time. The duration of the game is limited to one or one and a half days. It can be used for groups without much knowledge of the issue and the context; no lectures are needed. The question of being right or wrong on the topics under discussion is as relevant as the question of negotiating in an effective way. As a whole the focus is on the process as well as on the matter under surveillance. This means that this kind of *ad hoc* diplomatic game is more suitable to train people in negotiation processes than the fore-mentioned ongoing model. Actually, it was developed for the purpose of preparing course members who took part in the ongoing game, for the processes they had to go through, but as years went by it developed into an autonomous device to be

	Issue	*Model*
continous	ongoing	ongoing
discontinuous	crisis	*ad hoc*

Table 14.2 *Topical simulations*

used inside and outside the institute in some 20 countries. We will concentrate further on the *ad hoc* model instead of the continuous variant as a tool in training negotiations, especially negotiations in a diplomatic and multilateral context (conference diplomacy).

FRAMEWORK

To use other people's simulations in training diplomats is of course possible, however not always advisable, especially when delicate political matters are the issue. The trainer can be confronted with criticism of the game, with people who try to manipulate it, and with people who get very emotional as the process goes on. It is recommended therefore that the trainer should write his or her own game, this having the advantage that he or she knows the context and details in depth, enhancing the legitimacy of the exercise, which is vital for a political game played by politicized people.

To write a useful, realistic and 'playable' scenario some points should be observed. First of all the selected topic(s) must be in the everyday news and at the same time the solution of the problem should not be very obvious. Preferably the life expectancy of the issue should be six to twelve months. There are exceptions to this, of course. The Clingendael Institute was asked by the Malaysian Diplomatic Academy to write a simulated United Nations conference on environment and development in order to prepare diplomats for the Rio de Janeiro meeting, two months later. Such a one-off simulation is only worthwhile if the financial returns are rather substantial. Another exception was a game called 'Crisis in Yugoslavia', written in 1984 and used up to 1989, *inter alia*, at the NATO Defence College in Rome. The case became more realistic every subsequent year but had to be stopped, not because the crisis in Yugoslavia was over, but as a consequence of the breakdown of the bloc structure in Europe. The case was based on the NATO – Warsaw Pact – neutral/non-aligned discrepancies and these ceased to exist, while the crisis itself became more and more violent. Consequently, the simulation was restructured to be used at the Diplomatic Academy of Germany in 1991 and could function further for some time. In both cases the Conference on Security and Cooperation in Europe formed the context. The fact that it took one year to rebuild the game doesn't mean that the writing of a simulation of this kind takes so much time, but it shows that the authors must wait until the transition period is over and further developments can again be foreseen to a reasonable extent.

Hence it is only possible to write a rather stable simulation if political analysis shows that developments can be predicted for the near future: usually between half to one year. At the same time, the investment of time is more worthwhile because the lifetime of the case will be reasonably long. Ideally the simulation should be used 10 to 20 times and after a revision it should be able to last for another number of training sessions as well.

This is also vital because of testing. The more often a game runs, the better it will become. It matures like wine. There are always mistakes, due to incomplete information, or miscalculations concerning the actual process. Sometimes some constructions don't work well because the participants find them too artificial or too complicated, or maybe too simple. Changes in the flow of the programme should be made then. New rounds of negotiations should be included or old ones must be skipped. The ideal international political simulation game should be rather simple as far as content is concerned (the participants must be able to play the game without much knowledge beforehand), but should become complicated because of the many opposing and cross-cutting interests involved. In the beginning the game is rather transparent and clearcut, but as players get further into their roles and more *au fait*, the process will get more complicated because of the multitude of actors and issues. This gradual development will guarantee the lasting interest of participants in the game: they will not be deterred nor bored.

An interesting aspect is sometimes the reaction of 'experts' in these matters. For example: Dutch Navy officers, participating year after year in the case 'Crisis in Yugoslavia', always remarked that it was highly unlikely that the West would send warships into the Adriatic in order to put pressure on Yugoslavia. In 1992 the West did exactly that. Many technical experts tend to concentrate on the situation as it was and is. They fail to see future developments that go against their experience with the real life situation. They will therefore tend to be critical of the game, even if this proves to be wrong, although proof may not come until years later. As the experts have a lot of legitimacy, the other players will tend to accept their criticism. This makes it an absolute necessity for trainers to be thoroughly acquainted with both the game and the real-life situation.

Sometimes criticism will stem from other sources. In 1992 a new simulation game was created concerning Transcaucasia, dealing with the Nagorny Karabakh question in the context of the Security Council and the Conference on Security and Cooperation in Europe. The game was used in a negotiation training for Eastern European Diplomats at the Diplomatic Academy in Vienna. As both Armenians and Azerbaijani were present, the simulation became very emotional. As the Transcaucasians were not ready to accept the possibility of a compromise yet, they criticized the game and left. The Slovenes and Croats present saw the relevance of the problem-solving simulation for their own situation and therefore went on and made the game a success. The best game to be selected for a group experiencing the crisis in reality should therefore work through a mirror: everybody knows that it is about their situation, but names and places should be different in order to neutralize the situation sufficiently to play the game.

CREATION

In order to update scenarios and instructions, information is needed. As it is of course impossible to know what the real instructions of governments to their diplomats will be, the script-writer will have to rely on newspapers, periodicals, speeches, final documents, resolutions and sometimes interviews (the use of resource persons is a very good tool to get information about topics and their long-term development). These activities require the use of a writer's intellectual side. We might call this side of writing and developing a game the 'scientific' side. But there's another aspect to it, which could be termed the 'art' side: a writer's intuition also plays a part. A writer has to select the right situation to be simulated, which has to be used for some time to come. He or she has to find a balance between various, often widely different, interests. The information needed should be sufficient for the game, and it must also be selected with a view to its playability factor. All this can only be done through intuition. Obviously, the writer's feeling for the area has to be supported by a good overall knowledge of (and insight into) the relationships between states and the workings of international organizations and conferences. It is therefore necessary to follow international developments as closely as possible, and to have done this over a fairly long period of time, preferably over many years. Only in this way is it possible to choose the right topic, the appropriate context, and to create realistic political positions. So, a good simulation game requires the interaction of both the intellectual and the intuitive side of a writer.

Two examples may illustrate the succesful outcome of such an interplay. In 1988 the Clingendael Institute wrote a case about a crisis in Transcaucasia, used in Prague, Bucharest and Riga to train diplomats from Central and Eastern Europe. At the time there was not a shred of evidence that a crisis would break out there. Another had been written about a *coup d'etat* in the Soviet Union and its effect on the Baltic States just one year before the *coup d'etat* actually took place.

A game should consist of the following:

- an overall scenario (one page);
- a programme (one page);
- a set of instructions (maximum one page for each role);
- additional information on:
  - the situation itself (a map, newspaper cuttings);
  - the organization to be simulated (procedures, etc.).

Depending on the kind of organization, the full script will contain, for example, some 12 (European Community), 15 (Security Council) to 52 (Conference on Security and Cooperation in Europe) briefs, plus two to ten additional pages on general information. An optimal game has 15 to 30 participants. If the group is too small, the process tends to become less interesting (not enough actors), if the group is too big, the distance between trainer and participants becomes too big (a good contact between trainer and trainee is vital for a succesful workshop).

The scenario should contain a paragraph on each of the following:

- the historical background;
- the political situation;
- recent developments;
- the organization to be simulated; and
- the goals of the meeting.

The central part is the third paragraph: this segment deals with a new development (not yet reality, but as realistically as possible) that causes the conference to be simulated to take place.

The programme for a day's activity could be planned as follows:

9.00   Introduction to conference diplomacy and to the case
10.00 Individual preparation/planning by participants
11.00 Plenary session: all countries intervene (statements)
12.00 Lunch
13.00 Caucus meetings: like-minded countries meet (three groups)
14.15 Plenary session: statements from caucus
14.30 Informal negotiations between caucus
16.00 Plenary session: decision making, debriefing of the game
17.00 Wrap-up

A variant is the 'condensed' exercise consisting only of a scenario providing the problems to be solved, the form to deal with it, and the countries that participate. In such a game the first stage of negotiating between individual countries can be left out. The second stage (negotiating between groups of countries after a preparatory phase) is the main part of the exercise. Participants will have to interpret their individual positions themselves, although some broad standpoints (pro, contra the question involved, or a position in between) will be given. This exercise can be used as a tool for showing the effects of negotiating in 'blocks' within a short period of time. A game like this, a simulated meeting of the Organization of African States dealing with a crisis in Djibouti, has been used in Addis Ababa to train Ethiopian diplomats.

APPLICATION

As the ultimate goal of the exercise is to enhance the insight into multilateral diplomacy, the topical simulation exercise can be applied in different circumstances. One way is to use it as a part of a wider course on international negotiation in order to highlight political and multilateral bargaining. In this instance other methods such as case study discussions, bilateral games, self-assessment exercises, will be used, the multilateral game being the last and overall game, the apotheosis. In other instances it will be part of a course on international relations in general, and functions as a major tool in the relations between states. It can be used at conferences on certain topics in order to show that simulations enhance the insight into particular topics (eg, crisis management, security relations, environment, political prognosis) more than the conventional lectures and workshops.

One may also apply the 'real time' simulation on its own as an *ad hoc* use for a group that wants to know more about processes and/or subjects. A simulation on widening and deepening the European Community has been used in countries like Switzerland, Austria and Sweden, the intention being to enhance the insight of diplomats into the process of multilateral negotiation within the European Community. It is expected that they will be better prepared for real negotiations in the context of the enlargement of the Community, because of the greater understanding which they have gained into the interests and cultural habits of the EC member states. Sometimes it is even possible to go further and to use the simulation as a problem-solving device for people who are directly involved in a certain situation. Perhaps one could even maintain that this would be a kind of political therapy, as in the case of the Transcaucasian game. It could be necessary, in such situations, to change the crisis circumstances in such a way that the country or region at stake is fictional (Clingendael wrote cases about countries like Turghanistan, Turgisia and Levantis in order to train diplomats from countries of the Commonwealth in places as far apart as Oxford and Hyderabad) while the organization and the participating countries used are real (for example the International Monetary Fund will have to decide on granting a loan to Turghanistan, the US being against this and Libya being in favour).

While being cautious about making huge generalizations about national stereotypes, it would seem that participants from different countries and cultures react in different ways to simulations like the above-mentioned ones. The experience of the author after several years of international training is that diplomats from Spain and Latin America have a tendency to negotiate in a very vigorous way, to become very excited in the process, without having much difficulty in dealing with politically sensitive matters. The emotional factor is the bargaining process itself, not the issues. In South and South East Asia the players are very patient, don't get carried away by the simulated negotiations, but are extremely sensitive to hot political issues. They will not (directly) deal with them; they will try to avoid the sensitive issue as much as possible. The Asians will do the utmost to avoid offending the other party.

In Africa the situation lies more in between these two 'extremes'. Trainees are ready to face burning political issues, but will do so in a diplomatic way, avoiding offending the other side unnecessarily. In Eastern Europe, however, course members can be very rude to each other but are hardly willing to take any risks as far as sensitive matters are concerned. Western Europeans are ready to take risks, to explore all possibilities; but while the Swedes were careful not to hurt the feelings of others, the Dutch and Germans didn't care too much. Notably different were the reactions in one group: West German men and East German women were willing to explore sensitive issues, whereas West German women and East German men tried to avoid them.

CONCLUDING REMARKS

Topical simulations are a useful means of increasing the value of negotiation seminars. The main advantage over 'static models' is the participants' greater emotional involvement and motivation. This aspect does, however, require a careful selection of the game to be used and close observation of the group, for the emotional sensitivity of a certain problem or issue may cause tensions within the group.

Various kinds of topical diplomatic simulations have been mentioned in this article: the 'continuous', the 'ad-hoc' simulation game, and the mixed variant. The 'continuous' game forms a fixed part of a curriculum and will be repeated time and time again, while being continuously adapted to reality. Its main function is to deepen insight into certain issues. The 'ad hoc' simulation game is very useful for the instruction of seminar participants on the subject matter as well as deepening their understanding of the negotiating process itself. Furthermore, games were mentioned that are a mixture of both topical and historical-fictional simulations, and simulations that are either completely historical or fictional (the conventional approach).

The advantages of the conventional approach are that there is no danger of hurting feelings, and that the game can be used regardless of time and circumstances. A negative point is that it may be regarded as being too abstract, too theoretical, which may lessen the participants' motivation. Unlike the topical simulation game, it doesn't teach the participants anything about current international issues which, in this case, has to be done in time-consuming lectures. The topical simulation game thus proves to be time-saving and therefore cost-efficient.

ABOUT THE AUTHOR

Paul W Meerts, political scientist, is deputy director of the Netherlands Institute of International Relations, 'Clingendael'. This institute does training and research and publishes the monthly *Internationale Spectator*. The training department provides courses for junior, mid-career and senior European diplomats. One of the topics is training in international negotiations. The simulations to be used are designed by the training staff itself. Paul Meerts specialized in diplomatic training, consulting diplomatic academies in Europe and Asia.

Address for correspondence: Netherlands Institute of International Relations, Clingendael 7, 2597 VH The Hague, The Netherlands.

SECTION 4: Applications to business and management

Chapter 15

THE HONEYCOMB PROBLEM: dealing with personal/group conflicts

Alan Cudworth

ABSTRACT

This chapter deals with the classical problem of personal success versus group gains. In most institutions, companies and industries, departments from time to time work in isolation, not knowing what overall strategy is planned by senior management, and this often leads to failure to maximize opportunities. Yet many companies use project management techniques which require good cooperation and communication between those professionals involved.

THE HONEYCOMB PROBLEM a game written by Clive Loveluck in MATREX illustrates these important principles and shows clearly that by cooperation and a willingness to work for the 'good of all', a greater level of reward can be achieved.

The problem of personal/group conflict is seen today in almost all professions. The senior managers of every large organization need to integrate the strengths, weaknesses and competences of all their employees for the perceived good of the organization. Often departments are operating without knowledge or concern for those in other departments within the same organization. This kind of situation often manifests itself in the construction industry, in particular in the area of project management.

Project management requires the cooperation of many parties, including client, consultants, contractors, sub-contractors and suppliers in order to become an effective technique. Personal preferences or needs may have to give way to team needs in order to ensure success for the client. Unfortunately this often brings conflict.

Pressures may be on individuals or their companies through:

■ senior management needing results – this may affect career visibility;
■ penalty for failure;

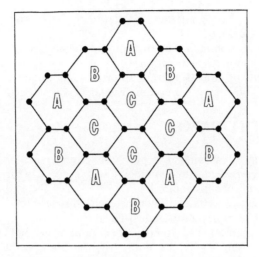

Figure 15.1 *Honeycomb exercise structure*

■ corner-cutting to achieve quick results or early completions.

Good teamwork allows staff from different functions to act together to achieve defined goals and react quickly in the light of unforeseen problems. Thus it is seen that an element of team-building in the early stages of a project is essential for management success.

Games and simulations can contribute to this learning by replicating the process in a simple format enabling the participants to function together effectively and perceive the benefits of close cooperation.

THE HONEYCOMB PROBLEM has been designed with exactly this in mind. It simulates the project management process and illustrates vividly the dichotomy between individual and team gains. THE HONEYCOMB PROBLEM is a simple but effective game to introduce the concepts of cooperation, communication and team-building within a project team or company.

The participants are divided into three groups A, B and C. The instructor introduces the game and gives each person a copy of the rules, allowing them time to read and understand them. After answering any question the game commences. The game progresses until stopped by the instructor or 'time' is called by one of the teams. In any event a minimum 30 minutes must elapse before the game finishes.

PARTICIPANTS' NOTES

You are going to be formed into three teams (A, B and C) and you will be allocated those hexagrams marked as such and represented on your team worksheets.

1. The requirement of the exercise is that each point of your hexagrams

must be occupied by a letter such that a six letter word will be formed when read *clockwise*.

The word may commence at any point in the hexagram but must always be read in a clockwise direction.

2. Where points of your hexagram are held in common with another team (or teams) you may use a common letter if you so decide.

RULES OF THE GAME

1. Each team has a £40 budget to purchase letters, which cost £1 each.
2. When the exercise time has elapsed you will receive £40 for each completed hexagram from our instructor.
3. You will receive a 'rebate' of 50p for each unused letter.
4. If the complete honeycomb is devised in such a way that each common point has a common letter, there will be a bonus of £500 for the group to be divided between the teams in any way that they see fit.
5. There will be an ample supply of worksheets available but you must tick the final version in the appropriate box.
6. You have 30 minutes to decide which letters you wish to purchase. No letters will be sold after that time although there is nothing to stop you exchanging or purchasing some from another team.
7. For any negotiations with another team you must appoint a 'negotiator' (who you may change at any time) and *only* three people may meet at any time in order to negotiate (ie, not more than one from any team).
8. The only exception to the last item is the final negotiation about the distribution of the bonus (if any).
9. The bonus is only paid if all common points have common letters.
10. The time limit will be set by the instructor but any team which has all hexagrams complete can call 'time' after 30 minutes and the game stops.
11. Should there be any doubts about the validity of any word the instructor should be consulted and his or her word is final.
12. The winning team will be the team that has the most cash at the end of the exercise, including the division of bonus, if any.

CONCLUSIONS

Project management is said by Brown (1992) to be the application of good management practices in a structured manner. The most obvious characteristic of project management is that there has to be a particular 'project' which distinguishes it from the routine activities of the company. Examples of the kind of project suitable for the application of project management techniques are the Channel Tunnel project, the Canary Wharf project, the Airbus project and staging a major event such as the Olympic Games. Project management usually requires the manager to operate within three distinct pressures – time,

A				
B				
C				
D				
E				
F				
G				
H				
I				
J				
K				
L				
M				
N				
O				
P				
Q				
R				
S				
T				
U				
V				
W				
X				
Y				
Z				
Total no				
Cost	× 1.00	× 1.00	× 1.00	× 1.00
Total Cost				

Figure 15.2 *Decision form for ordering letters*

Financial summary

Total cost of letters purchased   =
Expenditure to other
groups   =
                                          _____

Total expenditure   _____

Rebate for letters returned   =
Income from sales to other
groups   =
Income from completed
hexagrams   =
Share of bonus   =
                                          _____

Total income   _____

Excess of income over
expenditure   = income – expenditure
                         =   –   =

Total profit made by the
group

= _____

Figure 15.2 *Financial summary*

cost and quality – which inevitably requires a 'trade-off' or compromise between them to ensure success. In order to produce a successful plan for 'the project', the manager or management team will involve other professional consultants, contractors, sub-contractors, local and central government representatives and other interested local and national bodies. Each will be concerned with their own particular area of expertise or concern and it is the task of the project manager to bring together these people and make them feel part of 'a team'. If this can be achieved then there is more likelihood of the project being successful.

Project management is, of course, not the only area of professional life that requires teamwork to achieve success. Examples can be taken from the academic and business world in general and, I suspect, from each participant's own experience.

THE HONEYCOMB PROBLEM is a simple but effective exercise which illustrates clearly the value of teamwork as a contribution to achieving greater benefit for all. It has been designed as an introduction to project management but it is such a versatile exercise that it can be used in any situation where a trainer is involved in team-building. The exercise simplifies what, in real life, could be a very complicated task and allows the trainer to illustrate the classical problem faced by managers of how to deal with conflict between individuals which is preventing the optimum solution being achieved.

In introducing the exercise, the trainer could explain the scenario as three companies, or three departments within the same company, working together on a project. For both situations to be successful, good communication and effective organization are essential and if the parties can agree to work for the good of the whole then it can be shown that a greater level of success for all can be achieved. The game raises a number of important issues:

1. The need for cooperation in the planning process.
2. The need to develop good communication skills.
3. The need to develop good negotiating skills.
4. The development of leadership and decision-making skills.

1. The need for cooperation in the planning process

The planning process is an important stage in the development of the exercise. The trainer needs to get each group to evaluate their own performance during this stage and comment upon how they perceived the other groups performed. There is a need to consider how the problem was approached by each group – the level of communication between them and how the words and letters were chosen. The exercise allows the participants 'up to 30 minutes' to buy their letters; how was this perceived by the groups; did they buy accurately or speculatively? A major part of the de-briefing process will be to relate the planning process observed in the exercise with the life experiences of the participants, in particular, how any lessons learned during the exercise period could effectively be implemented in the participants' own work situation.

2. The need to develop good communication skills

Good communication skills are at the very heart of good management. Managers in all situations need to be able to communicate effectively with supervisors and subordinates alike, whether in writing or by word of mouth. The exercise encourages the development of these communication skills and the trainer should use part of the de-briefing time to consider the importance of clear expression, force of argument, diplomacy and body language within a management setting.

3. The need to develop good negotiating skills

An important feature of this particular exercise is effective negotiating. The trainer needs to discuss with each group how this was approached, how successful it was and highlight important features of successful negotiating.

The paper by Alan Coote (1990) should provide the trainer with interesting points to develop. The importance of honesty and trust within the group should also be developed and be reflected upon how it was shown in the exercise.

4. The development of leadership and decision-making skills

Although this exercise is not aimed specifically at leadership training, inevitably some form of leadership is displayed during the game. The trainer can explore the feelings of all participants to the decision process – how the negotiators were 'chosen', how effective they were and if a greater level of leadership was needed. Some participants may feel that they were neglected during the exercise period while others may be pleased not to have had the responsibility. The trainer might find that the negotiator's 'role' was rotated within the group, giving equal opportunity to all group members.

Finally

The success of this, and I suspect every other active exercise, simulation or game is directly linked to the de-briefing process. There are many issues and areas to explore in this exercise and the trainer needs to allow sufficient time for the participants to reflect upon them. The trainer might also ask, 'Who has won or who has made the most money?' If one team is able to say, 'We have', then one must ask if the exercise has achieved its objectives and if not – *why not*?

REFERENCES

Brown, M (1992) *Successful Project Management*, Hodder and Stoughton, Sevenoaks.
Coote, A (1990) *Twenty-one Techniques which People can use to Exert Influences in Formal and Semi-formal Meetings*, Polytechnic of Wales.

ABOUT THE AUTHOR

Alan Cudworth lectures in surveying at Nottingham Trent University and is a council member of SAGSET. He has lectured extensively throughout the world and is a visiting professor to the Danish Ministry of Foreign Affairs. Alan is the co-author of MATREX – a compendium of 30 training games and simulations, and co-producer of THE QUALITY CHALLENGE, an interactive board game on total quality management.

Address for correspondence: Department of Surveying, The Nottingham Trent University, Burton Street, Nottingham NG1 4BU.

Chapter 16

Student response to a competitive scenario: an unexpected finding

Howard Denton

ABSTRACT

A series of six, week-long, residential events for 17–18 year old pupils were run and observed at Loughborough University. These were based on the simulation of a commercial design scenario. Teams of students acted as design consultancies competing for a contract.

The simulations are described and some of the literature on competition discussed. The student response to the simulation is expanded on and this discussed in relation to the literature. Despite the overtly competitive structure offered, there was consistent evidence that students did not react competitively: there was considerable inter-team cooperation. There appeared to be a sub-cultural ideal of a cooperative management structure rather than more conventional hierarchical management.

Within many of our schools competition has been considered to be a negative influence on pupils' education (Wilson, 1988). This was based on the thesis that 'failure', resulting from competition, lowers the individual pupil's self-concept and is detrimental to educational growth. In some cases this approach has resulted in the abolishing of sports days, achievement prizes and so on. I accept that there is danger in pupils' self-concepts being damaged by failure. However, I have never accepted the thesis in its extreme form and consider that competition, if used sensitively, can promote work rate and possibly learning. Similarly I have felt that pupils should understand something of the competitive nature of industry and commerce so that they may adjust to it easily on leaving school. To 'protect' pupils from competition and then release them into such a world would be morally indefensible.

Theoretically simulation is an excellent vehicle for helping pupils develop experience and understanding in this area. It is active and teachers may use debriefings to discuss individuals' reactions to varying levels of competition. Strategies for coping can be developed from such work.

With these thoughts in mind I have designed and run a series of simulations which sought to simulate the type of competition and the pressures that may be generated in industrial settings. I had anticipated that the pupils would respond competitively; adopting a close intra-team focus while protecting their ideas from other teams and working harder than they would normally.

The work rate did grow over the course of the simulations to achieve a very high level as expected. In contrast, teams demonstrated cooperative rather than competitive attitudes at an inter-team level; this was not expected. This was manifested in continued inter-team cooperation and the cooperative management structures teams adopted despite the competitive scenario.

In order to explore these results it is proposed first to look briefly at the structure of the simulations; then some literature on competition will be reviewed; the response to competition in the simulations will be examined in more detail and then discussed in relation to the literature. Conclusions are then drawn.

THE STRUCTURE OF THE SIMULATIONS

The basic format was the same for all the simulations, though developments were made iteratively. The events were residential for one week and there was no timetable as such; the simulations ran in dedicated time. Pupils aged 17–18 years were put into teams on the basis of a mix of gender and ability. Participants in each team numbered from five to seven and they were told that they were simulating design consultancies. These teams then had to produce design proposals to a client's requirements. As the client had commissioned proposals from different teams these were in direct competition to gain the contract. The proposals had to be presented, by a given deadline, in the form of a display. At this point the teams became 'clients' and were able to evaluate depending on their own assessment of the proposals. They could not, of course, accept their own proposal. Pupils were briefed on this structure and knew they were to evaluate the work of the other teams. There were no laid down criteria against which to assess; however, each team was working to the same brief. A part of the simulation was to develop and clarify design specifications early in the process. Teams could then apply their own specification (which may differ from other teams) in evaluating other teams' proposals. The very point of the possible mismatch of team design specifications was a relevant point for subsequent debrief.

In this way it was possible to produce an order in which the 'clients' evaluated proposals and see which companies had been the most/least successful. Pupils were re-briefed each morning where the scenario was reinforced. At the end of each day a debriefing was held at team level and a final course debrief held on the last day. Debriefings opened up many opportunities for discussion on the nature of the response to competition, together with many other aspects of the simulations.

Teams were established on the principle that participants should not be peer groups and that they should be heterogeneous in terms of gender, culture and subject expertise. This was done to ensure that participants had to work at becoming a team rather than settling quickly due to existing social relationships. Similarly research on groupwork indicates a greater potential for social development from heterogeneous groups (Cowie and Rudduck, 1988).

Simulations were preceded by short warm-up exercises in the teams. Some of these were competitive, some non-competitive. The pupils were then briefed on the simulation and met in a team base to start considering the task. Possible team structures were outlined but teams were given autonomy to establish both structure and their approach to the task.

OBSERVATIONS FROM THE LITERATURE ON COMPETITION

There are two general positions on competition in education. The positivists maintain that competition aids personal development and provides a framework for qualities such as initiative, resourcefulness and independence to be developed. Some have claimed that competition can bring out new talents in individuals and that techniques such as handicapping can be used to enable all abilities to gain. The negativists consider that competition threatens cooperation and undermines personal and social relations. There is evidence to support both views but it is far from easy to extract simple 'truths'.

Miller and Davidson-Podgorny (1987) considered that competition increased task focus. Their work on team games tournaments indicated positive gains in knowledge-based learning. In these tournaments team members cooperatively learned material for a weeek prior to an inter-team competition. However, here the effects of competition are confused by the potential benefits of cooperative learning which need not be competitive.

Farran (1968) hypothesized that the use of competition, focused on knowledge-based learning in special schools, would assist in generating a higher pupil regard for that learning. Farran's work showed that individuals who competed appeared to learn more than those in 'inter-group' competition. This, to some extent, contradicts Miller and Davidson-Podgorny. These findings have been complicated by the use of simulation-games in the otherwise anti-academic atmosphere of these special schools; the novelty effect of the simulation may have had an effect. Nevertheless there is the indication that competition was, at least with individuals, providing a focusing function.

Stazinski (1988) confirmed this by providing evidence that individual competition in 'Biological Olympiads' enhanced pupil interest and subsequent achievement. In this case the competition was more conventional in that 'winners' were produced and followed over a period of three years. Unfortunately Stazinski only focused on the winners; it would have been interesting to have also had data on the response of all participants.

These pieces of work all looked at motivating academic learning through competition. None report any other forms of gain through competition. Similarly none used a broad task orientation such as was the case in my own work.

Wilson (1988, p. 27) considered that much educational practice was aimed at protecting pupils from the effects of competition such as 'humiliation . . . odious comparisons'. Yet competition is inevitable in society and the schools which are an integral part of society. The distinction which is probably more important is the way in which it is handled by staff. In sport, competition has been criticized for leading to excesses such as the 'professional foul'. Yet it is not competition as such which produces these effects but individuals' reactions to it. Competition is based on rewards, both intrinsic and extrinsic, and can be interpreted by focusing only on those aspects central to the reward. In sport this may become polarized into win or lose rather than the skill of playing the game. Yes, we do want goal scorers rather than skilful ball players but this is to interpret the situation simplistically: black and white. In fact, in the commercial world most companies perform with variable levels of success; it is rare for a company to be so successful that it dominates the market place and actually eliminates all competition. Within the approach adopted in my own work the simplistic 'winner and losers' situation which games and sports tend to generate was avoided for both psychological reasons and realism.

On a more specific level there are dangers to be recognized in adopting competition as a motivating factor. Hackman (1983) observed that 'group ethnocentrism' may develop and become dysfunctional. Similarly Hampden-Turner (1971) observed that competition may build *esprit de corps* but that interpersonal relations may degrade together with a fall in creative thinking and a rise in pressure to conform. Ravensdale (1978) considered that rising motivation may be a factor in improving learning but that there may be a point at which high levels of motivation become a handicap. This is similar to the Yerkes-Dodson hypothesis of arousal against performance, usually represented as an inverted U, as shown in Figure 16.1.

This indicates that competition may indeed be of value, but that staff need to be particularly careful for levels of arousal not to become counter-productive. This is more complex than it may sound. The response to competition-induced

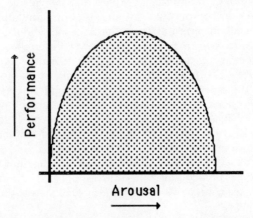

Figure 16.1 *The Yerkes-Dodson hypothesis of arousal against performance*

'arousal will be individual and probably dynamic. Acting within a team, as students were in these simulations, may mask the response of the individual from the observing staff. The dangers are obvious; staff must be particularly sensitive and be ready to act as the 'adaptive interventionist' (Roebuck, 1978) in order to support pupils who may have exceeded the optimum levels of arousal.

RESPONSE TO THE SIMULATIONS

Observation of the simulations under discussion showed that pupils demonstrated little competitive response at an inter-team level. The sharing of ideas between members of different teams was common, especially early in the simulations. While this sharing diminished later it was not eliminated. The diminution appeared to be due to the fact that the teams were, by then, very busy trying to meet the deadlines rather than developing any competitive spirit. Some of the sharing may have been between peer groups split by the team selection methods; the triangulated observational data did not differentiate.

It is interesting to note that, given the freedom to devise their own structure, the teams chose 'cooperative' models rather than more conventional leader-based structures. There was a positive antipathy towards the concept of leadership and an apparent sub-cultural ideal towards egalitarian cooperative models. Having said this it was apparent that some individuals did emerge as leaders, even though the teams themselves still felt they were operating a cooperative model. It was also apparent that it was the teams with reasonable leaders which performed the most effectively. They were more likely to respond positively and quickly to the simulation than other teams which spent more time in discussion without getting down to action. However, it may be hypothesized that such extended discussion may have generated enhanced learning while limiting the speed of response to the task.

In some of the early simulations the team bases were simply open tables and inter-team communications were easily possible. This does not accurately reflect the real world but was a part of the operational simplification of facilities required for the simulation. It was hypothesized that this inter-team communication was reducing intra-team focus and limiting the development of a competitive approach. In later simulations dividing screens 1.2 metres high were used to effect some degree of inter-team separation when participants were sitting down. This appeared to reduce inter-team communication to some degree but teams still appeared ready to share ideas when approached by individuals from other teams. The opportunities for communication had been reduced but there was not a direct relationship with competition.

In each simulation, as the final phases were reached, it was apparent that levels of endeavour had risen above those that teachers accompanying pupils would expect of them. Team participants encouraged each other and worked long hours and with sustained attention spans. There was evidence of pupils both feeling the pressure to succeed and wishing to do so individually There was, effectively, a competitive atmosphere but one aimed at meeting the deadlines. Even in the final phase of the simulations there were few examples of overt inter-team competition.

DISCUSSION

Living in a competitive society, in which pupils are exposed to team games both in and out of school and on the media, the above observations were surprising. Hampden-Turner (1971) observed that the therapy groups he based his research on in the USA naturally accepted competition. This contrasts with the results above. The culture and age of Hampden-Turner's 'T' group participants were very different from those in my work. Despite growing up in what is arguably a competitive society the pupils in these simulations did not immediately adopt competitive attitudes.

One hypothesis would be that pupils did not understand how commerce works and similarly the potential effects of their aiding a competing company. Another would be that friendship groupings from school were so strong that they transcended intra-team responsibilities within the simulation. This would probably be the case if the inter-team transfer of information and ideas were shown to be between friendship groups. Further work is necessary to establish if this was the case.

The indications are that pupils focused on the deadlines rather than the simulated commercial environment within which they worked. Perhaps this was because, within a complex simulation, the deadlines were the easier and most obvious focus. Lack of commercial experience made inter-team competiton a more difficult concept to grasp. A competitive scenario and structure had been set but pupils appeared not to be responding competitively.

Looking at the literature it appears that competition has more value in relation to knowledge-based learning when individuals competed rather than when teams competed, though this is based on limited research (Farran, 1968). The value of a competitive context for the team-based simulations described above appears diminished but not removed as debriefings opened many other valuable lines of discussion centred on competition in commercial contexts.

The observations on the teams adopting a cooperative structural ideal are interesting, especially when contrasted with the improved performance of those teams in which leaders emerged, even if unacknowledged. To develop an effective cooperative structure would probably take a great deal more time than was available in these simulations. Industrial research (Buchanan, 1989) into teamwork is indicating that autonomous teams can be far more productive than conventional methods of organization. These team systems emphasize partnership in which team members have much more responsibility. If we contrast this with my own findings it may be possible to hypothesize that cooperatively organized teams may be more effective than those with leaders if they have enough time and practice. A simple model of this may be as that shown in Figure 16.2.

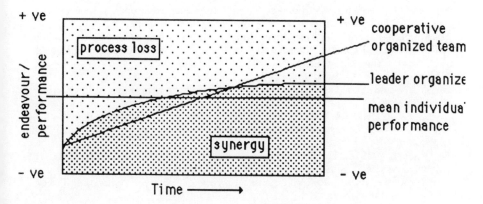

Figure 16.2 *A model of team outcome potential over time for cooperative and leader organized teams*

CONCLUSIONS

In conclusion my fieldwork indicates that within these simulations inter-team competition was minimal despite the intended competitive scenario. Motivation was most obviously generated by approaching deadlines. Nevertheless it was felt that there were potential benefits to the competitive scenario. At debriefings pupils and staff were able to explore possible reactions to competitive scenarios even though their own reactions had not been strong.

While the scenario of the simulation was overtly competitive the physical arrangements allowed a certain degree of inter-team communications. Peer-group and general social contacts appeared to have lowered any developing competitive reaction. The introduction of the low screens improved intra-team focus and cut down on inter-team communications and appears to go some way to confirming the above.

If a more overtly competitive reaction were considered desirable and were to be generated in future simulations of this type, it may be necessary to consider using teams with a greater degree of intra-team familiarity or existing peer groups. This may limit external communications and increase the competitive response. In contrast, such a policy would reduce the advantages of the heterogeneous teams in terms of promoting social, personal and group learning development.

REFERENCES

Buchanan, D A (1989) 'High performance: new boundaries of acceptability in worker control', in Sauter, Hurrell and Cooper (eds) *Job Control and Worker Health*, Chichester, John Wiley, pp. 255–68.

Cowie, H and Rudduck, J (1988) *Cooperative Group Work – an overview*, London, British Petroleum.

Farran, D C (1968) 'Competition and learning for under achievers', in Boocock, S and Schild, E (eds) *Simulation Games in Learning*, London, Sage.

Hackman, J R (1983) *A Normative Model of Work Team Effectiveness*, Technical Report No 2, Research Project on Group Effectiveness, Office of Naval Research. Code 442, Yale School of Organizational Management.

Hampden-Turner, C (1971) *Radical Man*, London, Duckworth.

Miller, N and Davidson-Podgorny, G (1987) 'Theoretical models of intergroup relations and the use of cooperative teams as an intervention for desegregated settings', in Hendrick, C (ed.) *Review of Personality and Social Psychology 9, Group Processes and Intergroup Relations*, Sage Publications, Newbury Park, California, pp. 41–67.

Ravensdale, T (1978) 'The dangers of competition', *SAGSET Journal*, 18, 3, 100–105.

Roebuck, M (1978) 'Simulation games and the teacher as an adaptive interventionist', in McAleese, R (ed.) *Perspectives on Academic Gaming and Simulation 3*, Kogan Page, London, pp. 102–108.

Stazinski, W (1988) 'Biological competitions and biological olympiads as a means of developing students' interest in biology', *International Journal of Science Education*, 10, 2, 171–7.

Wilson, J (1988) 'Competition', *Journal of Moral Education*, 18, 1, 26–31.

ABOUT THE AUTHOR

Howard Denton is a lecturer in design and technology where his primary interests lie in the training of design and technology teachers. He has recently been awarded a PhD for research in the area of groupwork in schools which included aspects of simulation.

Address for correspondence: Department of Design and Technology, Loughborough University of Technology, Loughborough, Leicestershire LE11 3TU.

Chapter 17

THE PARKING GARAGE SIMULATION

John F Lobuts and James Oldson

ABSTRACT

THE PARKING GARAGE SIMULATION is a one-hour exercise designed to illustrate the complexity of identifying an automobile with the manufacturer. Today's car is truly a global product developed from economic interdependencies. The exercise allows for testing what we know and provides a forum for learning.

PURPOSE

The purpose of this simulation is to raise levels of consciousness about the difficulty in identifying the true manufacturer of today's automobile. The simulation provides an opportunity for one to test one's skill and knowledge as they relate to automobiles and their manufacturer.

As the parking garage manager, the participant has the responsibility of admitting only American-made automobiles to the parking garage. Likewise, the participant's responsibility includes denial of parking privileges to all employees driving foreign-made automobiles.

Lastly, the simulation sets a stage for discussion of economic interdependency. The simulation illustrates the imperativeness of having sufficient knowledge before persons, groups, or organizations move toward trade barriers, tariffs or laws of protectionism.

Aims of the simulation

■ To understand the benefits of international competition in the context of the economic construct of 'comparative-advantage'.
■ To explore the economic outcomes with international competition and the strategy of win-lose.
■ To explore unproductive anxiety, emotionality and ethnocentrism often associated with international competition.

■ To explore the 75 per cent content rule in manufacturing within the US auto industry.

Group size

Twenty-five to thirty.

Time required

Approximately one hour.

Physical setting

One large class or meeting room capable of accommodating five or six work groups of five persons each.

Materials

A copy of the simulation for each participant.
Pen or pencil for each participant.

THE PARKING GARAGE SIMULATION

You have been appointed to serve as manager of the parking garage. You are responsible for admitting only American-made automobiles to the parking facilities. Likewise, your responsibility includes denial of parking privileges to employees driving foreign-made automobiles. Any car with less than 75 per cent domestic content will be denied.

Your decision (Please tick) Group decision (Please tick)

Auto Seeking Entrance Parking Facility	ADMIT	DENY	SCORE	ADMIT	DENY	SCORE
1. Corolla						
2. Dodge Stealth						
3. Ford Crown Victoria						
4. Ford Escort						
5. Ford Festiva						
6. Geo Prizm						
7. Honda (Accord)						
8. Mazda Navaho						
9. Mercury Grand Marquis						
10. Pontiac Lemans						
11. Range Rover						
12. Rolls Royce						

TOTAL: _____   **TOTAL:** _____

A. To score, place the number 1 by *each* correct answer and sum for the total

Your rating as an Auto Inspector-Rejector:
Number of correct answers:
11–12 Auto Expert
9–10 Auto Enthusiast
6–8 Auto Knowledge is Fair
Below 6. Need to Find Another Career or Buy Another Car

The PARKING GARAGE simulation scoring sheet

Rationale		*Correct Response*:
1. Corolla	75 per cent content, a Toyota built in Freemont, California, USA	Admit
2. Dodge Stealth	Chrysler Corp. product. A super sports car. The Stealth is a Mitsubishi 3000 GTVRH, uses Mitsubishi Engine.	Deny
3. Ford Crown Victoria	Ford Motor Company top of the line, produced in Canada, 27 per cent of parts come from Germany, Spain, Mexico, and Japan	Deny
4. Ford Escort	Made by Mazda	Deny
5. Ford Festiva	Made by Kia of Korea	Deny
6. Geo Prizm	Produced by the New United Motor Company, Freemont, California, USA with the Corolla.	Admit
7. Honda Accord	Manufactured and produced with 75 per cent content in Marysville, Ohio, USA	Admit
8. Mazda Navaho	Produced by Ford Motor Company, 75 per cent US content	Admit
9. Mercury Grand Marquis	Produced with less than 75 per cent US content	Deny
10. Pontiac Lemans	Great American name! Produced by Daewoo Motor Company of South Korea	Deny
11. Range Rover	The engine of a GMC design, but the car does not have 75 per cent US content.	Deny
12. Rolls Royce	The automatic transmission comes from GMC but the car does not have 75 per cent US content.	Deny

Process

1. The facilitator introduces the topic of international trade and the benefits attached thereto.
2. The facilitator leads a discussion on the strategy of dealing with conflict to include win-lose.
3. The facilitator explains the US Federal fuel rule and the 75 per cent content regulation.
4. The facilitator divides the participants into five-person groups and administers the simulation.
5. The facilitator conducts a discussion of the simulation and the management utility.

AN EPILOGUE

The economic interdependencies are comprehensible when discussed outside the framework of human emotionalities. However, so often in the complexity of political intervention we find a curious set of feedbacks and circularities. For example, in Japan there are political leaders who delight in disparaging the American labour force. Then too, in the United States of America we have those political leaders who are shouting, 'Buy American'. This creates an environment of win-lose, promoting a 'we' versus 'they' dynamic – 'We are right and they are wrong! We are good, they are bad!' This type of rhetoric is diametrically opposed to what is essential in a global market economy. The need for cooperation and collaboration is imperative for successful trading partnerships. There is an urgent need to rethink the win-lose paradigm designed for the management of athletic models and to develop modes of management paradigms that create environments which lead to win-win. It is so easy to get caught up in this state of emotional madness and entrapped in a very seductive call for protectionism. With the European Common Market evolving ever so rapidly, living in a global market economy becomes even more of a reality. There are a number of reasons why countries cannot afford to legislate roadblocks that imperil international competition. In our opinion the most prominent is the reckless endangerment and destruction of the 'comparative advantage' construct.

There is no question that the auto-industries are underpinnings to the industrialized West's economic development. Thus, when discussing automobiles in the United States, it's becoming more difficult to find an 'American' car. For example, the Plymouth Laser is a Mitsubishi Eclipse and vice versa. The Dodge Colt is also built by Mitsubishi. The Lotus is a General Motors Corporation product. The Ford Probe is really a Mazda MX-6 made by Mazda in Flat Rock, Michigan.

Failure to understand economic interdependency can be self-destructive. The call for protectionism, isolationism, tariffs and trade barriers manifests itself in a number of ways. In the summer of 1991, the International Brotherhood of Teamsters, a transportation workers' union with headquarters in Washington, DC, forbade employees from driving foreign-made automobiles into the union's parking garage. However, the Brotherhood soon learned the screening of cars based only on 'trade names' simply would not suffice.

The screening of cars is a complex process. One of the more prevalent reasons is the regulation attached to the Federal fuel rules. This regulation requires foreign auto-manufacturers producing cars in the United States to use 75 per cent of American-produced parts. This content requirement creates a paradox because many of the foreign cars produced in the United States are more 'American' in content than some of the products produced under the labels of the American manufacturers.

SOURCES CONSULTED

Brown, W (1992) 'Camry: apolitical value', *The Weekend Magazine, The Washington Post*, February 28, p. 54.
Harari, O (1991) 'Cars, customers and competition: lesson for American managers', *Management Review*, February, pp. 38–41.
Milloy, C (1991) 'Teamsters' impossible dream', *The Washington Post*, July 23, p. B,3.
Rosten, L (1965) 'The Myths by which We Live', the 20th National Conference on Higher Education, opening address, The Association for Higher Education, Chicago, Il., March.

ABOUT THE AUTHORS

John F Lobuts Jr is a professor of management science and James Oldson is an adjunct professor and doctoral fellow in the *School of Business and Public Management, George Washington University, Washington, DC 20052, USA*.

Chapter 18

Frame games in teaching economics

Clive Loveluck and Peter Nisbet

ABSTRACT

Economics is often regarded by students as a dry and analytical subject in which they find it difficult to become involved. The purpose of this frame game is to help overcome this potential obstacle to the teaching of economics by presenting a variety of situations in which the controlled introduction of new information generates commitment, discussion and insight.

A FRAME GAME

In the context of this chapter, a frame game can be defined as a game in which the structure and procedures remain constant but in which the content, that is subject matter and data, may be varied. Such games may be distinguished from normal business games because, in such games, the procedures such as decision making and organization tend to vary with the subject matter of the game. Thus a production-oriented game will have a different format and will involve different decision-making structures from those of a market-oriented game. This is understandable since the teaching purposes of the games are different. The design and use of games for the teaching of economics may, however, benefit from a different approach.

TEACHING ECONOMICS

There are many different taxonomies of the contents of economics, but for many undergraduate courses the subject matter is divided into three streams: microeconomics, macroeconomics and applied (or descriptive) economics. The first two involve teaching students a set of analytical tools, while the latter applies those tools to the contemporary world. Descriptive economics often appeals to students because it 'happens' on television, 'appears' in the news and is discussed by people with no economics training. Thus, a potential obstacle may be found to exist when trying to encourage students to study microeconomics and macroeconomics which are difficult, analytical and, in the early stages of their study, often appear to have no relevance to the excitements of the 'real' world of descriptive economics. In teaching the analytical side of economics, the emphasis is on the development of pertinent logical skills which are applicable generally and are independent of the area to which these tools are being applied. Thus, the concepts of opportunity costs, marginal costs and comparative costs are applicable generally but must be understood before students can understand descriptive economics in a 'professional' way. The frame game is applicable to these areas because the logical approach and procedures are constant even when the subject matter to which these are being applied may change.

PROCEDURES

The procedures involved in this game are very simple. Three sets of cards are prepared: red, green and blue. On each card of a particular set, different circumstances are described so that we may have red 1, red 2, red 3 and so on. The red cards are now distributed to each student, or group of students. Each group, or individual student (depending on the number of students in the class or the academic level of the students) is then asked a question. The answer to this question will depend upon the content of the card. Thus, red 1 may indicate that the inflation rate is 27 per cent, red 2 that the inflation rate is 1 per cent, and so on. The students may then be asked what they would do to change the rate of inflation. The green cards are then distributed in the same random manner. These cards may contain contrasting data about, for example, the level of wage rates. Thus, green 1 may indicate that the rate of nominal wage increase is 2 per cent, green 2 that the rate is 24 per cent, and so on. The students are now asked the same question regarding the policies they might adopt to change the rate of inflation. Clearly, their answers will depend on the precise mix of cards they have. Indeed, there are nine possible sets of circumstances which will determine their answers. The blue cards may contain additional information on unemployment rates, tax rates, etc. The content and number of cards is clearly at the discretion of the teacher, who will need to consider the number and level of students and the time available.

THE OPERATION OF THE GAME

The game operates by engaging the interest of the students. As the cards are distributed and students are asked questions, they find it interesting that each group is giving different answers. This is, of course, compounded as the game proceeds and as they have to explain, not only to the teacher but also to their colleagues, the derivation of their different answers. Clearly, there is nothing in the game which they could not have learned from their lecturer or from a textbook. The difference lies in the diversity in the responses and the group discussions which are generated: the lecturer becomes a game facilitator and, as such, has to respond to the students in a quite different style from that of the traditional lecturer.

Variations

In the game described above, students must provide answers which are then justified by argument. A powerful variant is to ask one group of students to work out what another group of students must have had on their cards in order to have answered the questions in the way that they did. This is equivalent to arguing from conclusion to data, instead of from data to conclusion. Similarly the game may be modified by increasing or decreasing the 'levels' of 'colours' of the cards.

CONCLUSION

This is a simple game structure which, as has already been explained, provides a 'frame' which can be applied to any analytical aspect of economics. It requires virtually no equipment and can be adapted for any level of economics teaching as well as being easily adjustable to available time. Specific examples have not been provided here since the object has been to explain the logic of the frame game structure. Further information and examples can be obtained from the authors.

ABOUT THE AUTHORS

Peter Nisbet is senior lecturer at the Cheltenham and Gloucester College of Higher Education. Clive Loveluck is an independent consultant, specializing in the development of games.

Address for correspondence: Bryndu, Sennybridge, Powys, LD3 8HN, UK.

Chapter 19

Using simulation to teach applied economics: 'ENVIRONMENTAL PLANNING IN MALUVI' and 'SOCIAL ACCOUNTING MATRICES'

John Nelson, William Bender and Linet Arthur

ABSTRACT

The Food Studies Group (FSG) has been developing materials to support training activities in economic policy analysis. A key challenge has been to design interactive exercises which deal with complex economic problems, without swamping participants with background information, or making the exercise too long and complicated.

This chapter describes two of the simulation exercises which have been developed, one to introduce some of the issues related to environmental economics, and the other to explain how a social accounting matrix works.

The environmental simulation takes place in an imaginary developing country, Maluvi. The issue focuses around government plans to provide a rough road infrastructure in forested areas. In this exercise, participants work in groups and are allocated the roles of resource extractors, agricultural unions, environmental pressure groups, or government planners. They are asked to choose different development proposals affecting an area of high biodiversity. The different groups then come together to discuss the conflicts that exist between their proposals, and the scope for incorporating economic criteria into their proposals.

The social accounting matrix exercise starts with a simulated economy based on three simple transactions between three volunteers. Participants calculate the GDP of the economy and create a social accounting matrix (SAM) for it. They then take part in a game based on a demand-driven economy. Participants are told the demand requirements and act the roles of manufacturers, service firms, urban households and rural households to produce the goods and services demanded. Once all the demand requirements have been met, the game comes to an end and participants are again asked to calculate the GDP and construct a SAM for this more complex economy. The debrief session draws out the key learning points in calculating a SAM. Finally, participants apply their skills to a real SAM and interpret the data to determine the effect of macroeconomic changes on the level of poverty for particular groups.

TRAINING SIMULATIONS AND ACTIVITIES TO TEACH ECONOMIC POLICY ANALYSIS

The simulation exercises described in this article, ENVIRONMENTAL PLANNING IN MALUVI and SOCIAL ACCOUNTING MATRICES, are part of a set of modular teaching materials on economic policy analysis. The Food Studies Group (FSG) is producing these 'learning by doing' materials in order to support training activities in sub-Saharan Africa, although they could easily be adapted for developing countries elsewhere in the world. The idea is that trainers can pick up selected exercises, role plays or simulations, and use them off-the-shelf, with a minimum of preparation. The training activities are supported by study notes, which cover essential theory. Intended participants are middle and senior level civil servants.

- *Application*: participants want information and skills that they can apply easily to their daily work. The material avoids being too theoretical and aims to have demonstrated practical applications.
- *Length*: courses may last from one day to one month. The modules are easily divisible, so that individual sections and exercises can be used on their own.
- *Preparation*: trainers need materials which can be used with a minimum of preparation. These modules contain all the necessary information and instructions for off-the-shelf use.
- *Flexibility*: trainers want to be able to use materials for a variety of courses. The modules have been designed so that trainers can 'mix and match' the materials in order to create their own courses or add to existing courses.

ENVIRONMENTAL PLANNING IN MALUVI

The goals of this simulation are:

- To allow trainees to explore the conflicts that exist between different interest groups over the use of natural resources for development purposes, and to test ways in which these different interests can be consolidated into a broader development plan.
- To demonstrate the role of economic theory in supporting decision-making on development proposals which affect environmental assets.

Background information

Participants are handed a sheet of background information which describes the demographic, environmental and economic pressures facing Maluvi. It also outlines the problem which forms the focus of the exercise.

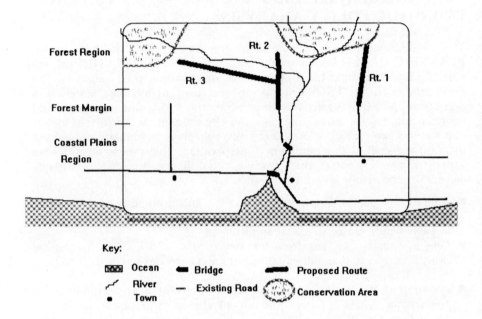

Figure 19.1 *Map of proposed routes 1, 2 and 3*

The problem

The government of Maluvi has been offered a loan from a multilateral institution to open up part of the forested zone to oil and mineral exploration (see map 1 of proposed route – route 1 in Figure 19.1). Increased revenues from oil and mineral exports would help the government regain control of the high foreign debt and open up new areas for agriculture, providing employment and opportunity for thousands of landless families, and growth to the national economy. But, the proposed route goes through the richest natural resource area of the forested zone and will destroy a range of biological resources.

The plan is a controversial one, and the government needs to negotiate with three key groups in order to smooth its way through congress. These three groups are:

- *Resource extractors*, whose goal is to promote a road building project into the forested zones.
- *Agricultural unions*, whose goal is to promote a road-building project into areas within the forest zone which have the highest agricultural potential.
- *Environmental groups*, whose goal is to conserve as much of the forested zone as possible, and to prevent all road-building projects.

A fourth group involved in the negotiations is the *government planners* themselves. They have been appointed by the current government and are therefore politically motivated. Their goals are to ensure that the government stays in power, and to increase economic growth.

Introduction to the simulation

After a short introduction to the background information, the participants are asked to brainstorm the tensions facing the four special interest groups. They are also asked to identify any problems that the country is likely to face in the near future. This ensures that they are familiar with all the different interest groups, and have an overall view of the constraints facing Maluvi.

Preparation for the simulation

The participants are divided into four groups, each of which represents one of the special interest groups described above. Each of the groups is given the task of preparing for a meeting between the groups, which the government has called to discuss the problem.

The groups are provided with an information sheet, giving a more detailed description of their goals and suggesting a possible development plan which stays within their terms of reference. For example, the resource extractors have developed an alternative route (route 2) for the road, because they think that the government route is likely to be strongly opposed on environmental grounds. The agricultural unions believe that route 1 will provide low gains for the agricultural sector, but that a different route (route 3), which follows the rich alluvial plain alongside one of the rivers, will be advantageous to them. The environmental group are opposed to all road building, so need to highlight the economic benefits of preserving the forest, or develop alternative, sustainable development projects. The government planners are asked to develop a list of objective criteria which they can use to judge the plans of the different interest groups.

Each of the groups is given a limited amount of economic information, which they can use to defend their own plan and to attack the plans of the other groups. They are also encouraged to think of how they could work with one or more of the other groups to strengthen their plan.

Simulated meeting

At the simulated meeting, the spokesperson for each of the different interest groups puts forward their proposals, while the government planners listen to their arguments. The spokesperson from the government planners is then asked to describe their criteria of judgement. The government planners are given 15 minutes, working on their own, to discuss the different proposals and select one of them, using their criteria of judgement.

Feedback

The feedback session focuses on

- the information needed to make decisions about proposals which affect the environment;
- the potential role of economic theory in helping planners to make such decisions.

The government planners identify the proposal which they have selected and explain why it was chosen. The trainer encourages the group to think of ways in which they could have strengthened their arguments (for example, by highlighting the economic costs and benefits of the different proposals), and how they might revise their approach in the future.

This simulation is designed to be used as the introduction to a training course which then teaches participants how to undertake the necessary economic analysis of environmental projects.

Using the simulation

Two factors seem to be key to the success of ENVIRONMENTAL PLAN-NING IN MALUVI. First, the trainer must be very clear about the task assigned to each group; otherwise, conservation-minded participants tend to develop their own radical plans for solving the environmental/conservation/development tension. In this case, the trainer may decide to act as a donor agency and put pressure on groups to choose among the proposals as outlined in the exercise.

The second issue, and perhaps the most important point arising from the exercise, is that most environmental pressure groups tend to emphasize the ethical argument when making their case, while the government planners tend to develop criteria which focus on more practical points related to economic and technical performance. Hence the groups encouraging development at the expense of environmental conservation (resource extractors and, to a lesser extent, agricultural unions) tend to fare better in achieving proposal approval.

These two issues seem to be the crux of many of the debates in developing countries between those trying to conserve environmental assets and those emphasising the need to sacrifice some environmental resources in order to sustain the development process. Hence, this exercise quickly opens up a wide arena for very fruitful discussions.

SOCIAL ACCOUNTING MATRICES (SAMs)

A social accounting matrix (SAM) is a comprehensive statistical presentation of the structure of an economy. This exercise is designed to help participants understand how an economy works, and how the entries in a SAM relate to the activities in an economy.

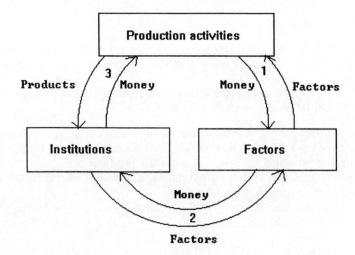

Figure 19.2 *The circular flow of goods, services, factors and money*

Background information for stage 1 of the exercise

It is easiest to understand a SAM from the context of the traditional presentation of national accounts:

AGGREGATE DEMAND	AGGREGATE SUPPLY	FACTOR INCOME
Consumption +	Agriculture +	Wages +
Investment +	Industry +	Own labour +
Government +	Services	Land rental +
Net exports		Interest +
		Profits

An economy is composed of a circular flow of goods, services, factors and money. It can be seen from Figure 19.2 that money flows around an economy in one direction, while there is an equivalent flow in the opposite direction of goods, services and factors.

A SAM summarizes the circular flow shown in Figure 19.2. It contains rows and columns for each of the three main actors in an economy:

■ factors of production (eg, unskilled labour, self-employed)
■ institutions (eg, households, local government)
■ production activities (eg, manufacturing, agriculture).

The basis of a SAM is a 3 × 3 grid, with rows representing receipts, and columns representing expenditures.

Stage 1

The trainer aims to give a simple demonstration of the circular flow of goods, services and factors, and the counterflow of money. Three volunteers are asked to do this:

Volunteer 1 is an urban labourer, with a card representing *one day of unskilled labour.*Volunteer 2 is a manufacturer and has a card representing *one chair.*
Volunteer 3 is a rural farmer, with a card representing *one basket of food* and *10 units of cash.*

The first transaction is the farmer purchasing a chair from the manufacturer for 10 units of cash. The second transaction is the manufacturer hiring one day of labour for 10 units of cash, in order to produce one chair. The third transaction is the hungry labourer purchasing a basket of food from the farmer for the 10 units of cash just earned.

Participants can see the circular flow of money in one direction, and the counterflow of goods (the chair and the food) and factors of production (unskilled labour).

They are asked to work in groups of three to calculate the GDP of the economy from this activity, and to complete the National Accounts table. The answer is given below:

AGGREGATE DEMAND	AGGREGATE SUPPLY	FACTOR INCOME
Consumption: **20**	Agriculture: **10**	Wages: **10**
Investment	Industry: **10**	Own labour: **10**
Government	Services	Land rental
Net exports		Interest
		Profits
GDP: **20**	GDP: **20**	GDP: **20**

Stage 2

Participants create a SAM for the economy. A sheet of background information helps them to identify factors, institutions and production activities. The trainer may complete one or two of the rows of the matrix to help participants; for example, looking at the first row in Table 19.1, column (6) shows that the labourer worked one day for the chair manufacturer (industry) and received 10 units of cash; in the second row, column (5) shows that the farmer (own labour) received 10 units from agricultural production (5).

The most difficult part of this exercise is understanding that the urban labourer is in fact two units conceptually:

■ a factor of production, the labourer; and
■ an institution, the urban household, which provides the labourer.

Furthermore, the farm represents three actors conceptually:

■ a factor of production: own labour;
■ an institution: the rural household; and
■ a production activity: agriculture.

Table 19.1 *Computed SAM for a three-person economy*

Receipts	Expenditure	Factors (1)	(2)	Institutions (3)	(4)	Production (5)	(6)	Total
Factors	Unskilled labour (1)						10	10
	Own labour (2)					10		10
Institutions	Urban HH (3)	10						10
	Rural HH (4)		10					10
Production	Agriculture (5)			10				10
	Industry (6)				10			10
Total		10	10	10	**10**	10	10	

Working in the same small groups as for Stage 1 of the exercise, the participants complete the SAM. The answer is shown in Table 19.1.

Stage 3

Once the participants have a basic understanding of SAMs, the game can be started. The participants are divided into four groups:

- *Service firms*, which produce haircuts.
- *Manufacturing firms*, which produce chairs.
- *Urban households*, which provide unskilled labour and consume goods and services.
- *Rural households*, which provide own labour and consume goods and services.

They are asked to satisfy certain demand requirements: urban households require two food baskets, 12 haircuts and six chairs; rural households require one food basket and one chair. They are told how many days of labour produces haircuts, chairs and food baskets, and each participant is handed a card with either a number of days of unskilled labour, or a number of days of farm labour, or an amount of money. The only exception is for participants in the manufacturing firm: they get nothing at the start of the game.

The trainer has cards representing haircuts, chairs and food baskets. Whenever one of the three types of production activities provides the proper amount of labour, the trainer gives the participant the appropriate number of finished products. Only firms of the appropriate type can produce goods or services, for example, only service firms can use unskilled labour to produce haircuts. Also, unskilled labour and farm labour cannot be substituted for each other.

The goal of all the participants is to satisfy the demand requirements of the urban and rural households. They can only do this by negotiating with each other to exchange labour for products, via the service firms and the manufacturing firms. Participants must keep a record of all their transactions during the game.

The game ends when all the demand requirements have been met. This is only possible after there has been considerable bartering.

As the game finishes, an urgent telex from the president arrives, requesting the Inter-Ministerial Committee of Esteemed Economists and Planners (ie the participants) to provide the GDP and SAM for the economy in order to meet urgent planning needs: a meeting with the International Monetary Fund has been arranged to take place in an hour's time. Participants have to work together to create the SAM within the time limit.

The game is debriefed after the SAM has been completed, and the key concepts necessary to create a SAM are reiterated.

Stage 4

Participants apply the skills they have learned to a real SAM, preferably for their own country or one with which they are familiar. They are asked to interpret the data provided, and to predict the impact of macroeconomic changes on the level of poverty for particular groups.

Using the simulation

Unlike a real economy, there is no objective function (eg, profit) for the actors in Stage 3 of the game. The goal is to complete the suggested transactions, and the participants will need to cooperate in order to do this. As in most games, participants respond to the game much as they respond to life. Some participants immediately try to make transactions, while others are cautious, hoard their assets and may prevent production from taking place. This is particularly true of the manufacturers, who must obtain credit from either labourers or purchasers of their products in order to make chairs. Some hesitant manufacturers do not participate in any transactions. Others produce all the products required for completion of the game.

In addition to teaching economic concepts, an experienced trainer can use both the game and the group construction of the SAM to examine individual and group dynamics, such as leadership, initiative and cooperation.

ABOUT THE AUTHORS

John Nelson is a research officer at FSG, who is interested mainly in training and environmental policy. William Bender is an associate economist at FSG, and a visiting assistant professor at the World Hunger Program, Brown University, who specializes in training and food security. Linet Arthur is a training officer at FSG, responsible for training strategy and course design.

Address for correspondence: FSG, International Development Centre, University of Oxford, 20–21 St Giles, Oxford OX1 3LA.

Chapter 20

How THE POWER STATION GAME was rescued from obsolescence: a case study

Henry Ellington

ABSTRACT

This is the third of three linked papers that describe how the author tackled the task of adopting existing games to fulfil new functions, or, in the case of the present paper, to enable a game to retain its credibility and relevance. It shows how THE POWER STATION GAME, an extended role playing simulation-game based on the planning of a new power station that was first published in 1975, was effectively rendered obsolete by the privatization of Britain's electricity generation industry that took place during the late 1980s, and how the game was subsequently completely rewritten in order to overcome this problem. The chapter describes the original exercise, explains why it became out of date, and then gives a detailed account of the way in which it was adapted to the modern world, showing how the opportunity was also taken to redesign the game package and make the exercise much more flexible and versatile than had previously been the case.

This is the third of three linked case studies in game adaptation – something that would-be users of a particular game or simulation often have to do if the exercise is to meet their specific needs. The first paper in the series (Ellington, 1990a) showed how POWER FOR ELASKAY, originally written as a structured lesson on alternative energy for use in British schools, was adapted for use with electrical engineering students in Singapore. The second (Ellington, 1990b) showed how TELECOM LINK, a highly sophisticated simulated design exercise developed for use with A-level physics students was converted into a much simpler, shorter exercise for use with GCSE/standard-grade pupils. This chapter shows how THE POWER STATION GAME (PSG), an extended simulation game primarily designed for A-level physics and engineering students, was completely re-written in order to rescue it from obsolescence.

The main body of the chapter is divided into four sections. The first gives a short history of PSG, describing how it was originally developed in the early 1970s, how it subsequently evolved, and how it became out of date because of the radical changes that took place in Britain's electricity generation industry during the late 1980s. The second describes how the problem of restoring the game's former relevance and credibility was tackled by making major changes to its scenario, the main one of which involved changing the setting from Britain to eastern Europe. The third describes how the opportunity was also taken to carry out a complete redesign of the game package. The fourth shows how this re-design enabled the new version of PSG to be made much more flexible and versatile in its range of applications than had been the case with the original exercise.

WHY PSG BECAME OBSOLETE

PSG was originally developed in Aberdeen during the early 1970s (Ellington and Langton, 1975). The original purpose of the team that developed the game was to produce an extended simulation exercise that could be used with physics and engineering students in the somewhat slack period between the end of the Scottish higher grade examinations at the end of March and the start of the summer holidays. The resulting exercise was based on the hypothesis that a Scottish electricity generating board wished to build a large new power station, the object of the game being to decide which type of station to build (coal-fired, oil-fired or nuclear) and where to site it.

After undergoing extensive field trials in secondary schools in the Aberdeen area (and two rewrites), PSG was published by the Institution of Electrical Engineers in 1975. The game rapidly achieved widespread use in schools, colleges and training establishments both in Britain and in many other parts of the world, and became one of the most successful and influential science-based educational games ever produced. The UK's Central Electricity Generating Board, for example, regularly used it as a training exercise for its young managers, and the Schools Liaison Service of the IEE used it as one of their main vehicles for promoting the electrical engineering profession throughout Britain (Ellington et al., 1984). The game was also incorporated (in simplified form) in the 'Science in Society' course that was developed by the UK's Association for Science Education during the late 1970s (Ellington et al., 1979). A number of foreign versions of the game were also produced, not all with the knowledge of the publishers; when the author attended an educational conference in Hungary in 1981, for example, he discovered a 'pirated' Hungarian version on display!

One of the problems with a highly-realistic simulation exercise like PSG is that the realism of the economic aspects of its scenario is rapidly eroded in times of high inflation. While the game was being developed between 1973 and 1975, for example, capital costs rose by more than a factor of six! Costs continued to rise during the remainder of the 1970s, and, as a result, the IEE published a revised version of the game in 1979. This took account not only of the rise in costs that had taken place since the game was first published in 1975, but also of the fact that the type of nuclear reactor used in the original game had now been abandoned.

In order to take account of the further cost increases that took place during the 1980s, a second revised version of PSG was published by the IEE in 1988. Shortly after the publication of this new edition of the game, however, a number of events occurred which effectively rendered the game obsolete. First, Britain's electricity generation industry was privatized, thus introducing the discipline of competition for the first time and making short-term market forces play a much more important role in the planning of new power stations than had been the case in the past. Second, this privatization led almost immediately to the effective freezing of plans to build a new generation of British nuclear power stations because of the resulting increase in the cost of nuclear electricity. Third, the newly-privatized generating companies also stopped building coal-fired and oil-fired power stations and changed almost completely to building combined gas-turbine/steam stations that burn natural gas from the North Sea. (This is a change that is based on short-term commercial rather than long-term strategic considerations, and is one that many commentators – the author included – believe Britain will come to regret.)

The result of all these radical changes in Britain's electricity generation industry was that the original scenario of PSG was rendered not merely out-of-date but manifestly ridiculous. Not only was Britain no longer building the three types of power station on which the scenario was based, but the key factor on which the game hinged – whether the proponents of the nuclear power station could convince the judges that its relative cost advantage over a coal-fired or oil-fired station was enough to overcome worries about its safety and environmental impact – had been negated at a stroke by the doubling of the price of nuclear electricity. It was therefore with great regret that the IEE (on the advice of the author) withdrew PSG from sale in 1990, and also embargoed its use by its own Schools Liaison Service.

THE BASIC PLAN FOR THE REVIVAL OF PSG

The withdrawal of PSG by the IEE caused howls of protest from many of the people who were using the game at the time – and had come to rely on it as a key teaching, training or promotional tool. As a result, crisis talks took place between Mrs Dianne Winfield, head of the IEE's Schools Liaison Service, and the author as to how the IEE's most successful exercise could be rescued from oblivion. At first, the author could not see a way to solve the problem, but events in another part of the world – the collapse and subsequent 'Westerniza-tion' of the Soviet empire – eventually came to his rescue by suggesting a possible means by which this could be done. He therefore proposed to the IEE that PSG should be completely rewritten round a new, Eastern-European scenario in which a newly-independent republic that had broken away from Russia invited tenders from three British consortia to build a new power station. Adopting such a scenario would get round all the problems that had rendered the British scenario obsolete, since it would be perfectly reasonable to suppose:

a) that such a newly-independent republic would want to enlist help from the West in modernizing its industrial infrastructure, and that British companies would wish to become involved in such modernization;

b) that the new republic had ample supplies of coal, oil and uranium, and therefore wished to build a coal-fired, oil-fired or a nuclear station;

c) that the new republic had no indigenous supplies of natural gas, and could therefore *not* build combined gas-turbine/steam stations of the type that Britain's newly-privatized generating companies are rapidly converting to;

d) that the strict commercial considerations that have effectively doubled the price that Britain's privatized generating companies would have to charge for nuclear electricity would not be applicable in an Eastern-European republic that retained central control over key strategic industries such as electricity generation;

e) that the new republic would be able to borrow the large amount of 'hard currency' needed to pay for the new station by raising an IMF loan backed by the sale on the open market of the various commodities (such as coal, oil and uranium) of which it produces far more than is needed to meet its own needs;

f) that the new republic had reformed its political and economic system and stabilized its currency, thus enabling realistic forecasts of future costs to be made.

A further advantage of such a scenario would be that the revised game would effectively be 'ring-fenced' from British cost inflation, since the currency used would be that of the new republic rather than the pound sterling. This would protect the game from the creeping obsolescence that is the inevitable fate of any simulation exercise whose economic scenario is based on realistic British prices. (Such a measure had proved extremely successful in the case of the conversion of POWER FOR ELASKAY to a Singaporean scenario.)

The IEE agreed to having PSG rewritten round a new scenario of the type outlined above, and the author undertook to carry out the work during the summer of 1992. It was also agreed that the author would carry out a radical redesign of the game package, enabling it to be supplied in the form of photocopy masters from which users could run off as many copies of the various items as they needed. The game would also be made much more flexible than the original exercise, so that it could be used with a much wider range of pupils and students.

HOW THE GAME PACKAGE WAS REDESIGNED

The original PSG package consisted of the following materials:

- A comprehensive *Teacher's Guide* providing detailed instructions on how to organize and run the game, together with specimen solutions to all the technical and economic calculations and to the siting problem;
- 18 copies of an 18-page *Introductory Booklet* on the electricity generation industry;
- three copies of a 28-page *Coal Station Booklet*, providing technical, economic and geographical data plus guidelines on how to carry out the technical calculations on the station (calculating the annual fuel consumption, cooling water requirements, etc.);
- three copies of a similar *Oil Station Booklet*;
- three copies of a similar *Nuclear Station Booklet*;
- three copies of a 26-page *Project Group Booklet*, providing guidelines on what to do in the later stages of the game, maps and geographical information about the area in which the new station was to be built, plus background information for use in the simulated public inquiry that brought the original version of PSG to a conclusion;
- a set of *role cards* for use in the public inquiry.

Over the years, this package of materials had served its purpose extremely well, enabling the original version of PSG – which consisted of seven clearly-defined stages (see Ellington and Langton, 1975) – to be run with great efficiency. It was, however, rather expensive to produce, and did not make it easy for users to run shorter or simplified versions of the game. It was therefore decided to carry out a radical restructuring of the game package, supplying all the student resource materials in the form of photocopy masters and designing the package in such a way that users could choose between a number of versions of the game of different lengths and levels of difficulty. It was also decided to incorporate student worksheets in the new package – something that had been absent in the original – and number the various items in order to facilitate cross-referencing. The form that the new package eventually took was as follows:

- a comprehensive *Organizer's Guide*, providing detailed instructions on how to run four different versions of the game with a class;
- S1: *Introductory Sheet*: a single-sided A4 sheet describing the new game scenario (see Figure 20.1);
- S2: *Coal Station Data Booklet*: a shorter (13-page) version of the original *Coal Station Booklet* containing all the technical and economic data needed by the participants;
- S3: *Guide to Technical Calculations on Coal Station*: a double-sided A4 sheet providing detailed guidance on how to carry out the *full* version of the technical calculations on a coal-fired station (essentially the same calculations as in the original game);
- S4: *Technical Calculations on Coal Station–Student Worksheet*: a single-sided A4 worksheet for use in conjunction with S3;
- S3(a) and S4(a): simplified versions of S3 and S4 designed for use in a shorter version of the full game for use with younger pupils [S4(a) is

basically the same as S4, but has roughly half the boxes filled in – see Figure 20.2.]

- **S5**: *Technical Calculations on Coal Station – Model Solutions*: the model completed version of both S4 *and* S4(a); intended for use by the organizer in checking the students' answers, or, if the technical calculations are to be missed out, as a student resource in its own right;
- **S6**: *Guide to Economic Calculations on Coal Station*: a single-sided A4 sheet;
- **S7**: *Economic Calculations on Coal Station – Student Worksheet*: a single-sided A4 sheet for use in conjunction with S6;
- **S8**: *Economic Calculations on Coal Station – Model Solutions*: a model completed version of S7;
- **S9**: *Guide to Siting of Coal Station*: a single-sided A4 sheet;
- **S10**: *Siting the Coal Station – Model Solution*: a single-sided A4 sheet showing a model solution to the problem of siting a coal-fired station, including a plan of the station;
- **S11–S19**: the corresponding materials for an oil-fired station;
- **S20–S28**: the corresponding materials for a nuclear power station (based on the pressurized-water reactor rather than the advanced gas-cooled reactor used in the 1979 and 1988 versions of PSG);
- **S29**: *Guidelines for Survey Sub-groups*: a common set of guidelines (a single-sided A4 sheet) for use by the 'survey sub-groups' in the three competing teams – the sub-groups that have the job of finding out as much as possible about the rival stations;
- **S30**: *How to Prepare and Present your Tender*: a common set of guidelines (a double-sided A4 sheet) for the three teams on how to prepare and present their tender;
- **S31**: *Map of Koravia*: a map of the hypothetical 'Republic of Koravia' on which the revised game is based, showing the positions of the eight possible sites for building a power station (a landscape A4 sheet);
- **S32–S39**: detailed maps of the eight sites (landscape A4 sheets);
- **S40**: *Geographical Data Sheet*: a single-sided A4 sheet providing supplementary information about Koravia (sizes of towns, river flow rates, outputs of coalfields, etc.);
- **S41**: *Plans of Station Plant for Use with Site Maps*: a single-sided A4 sheet giving scale plans of the different components of power station plant (main buildings, fuel stores, cooling systems).

Note that the new package contains no material for use in a simulated public inquiry, since it had been decided to drop that part of the original game. This was done partly because it had been found that most users stopped the game *before* the public inquiry (after the decision had been reached as to which type of station to build), and partly because it was felt that a British-style public inquiry would not readily transfer to an Eastern-European setting.

S1

The Power Station Game

Introductory Sheet

'The Power Station Game' is an extended role-playing simulation exercise based on the problem of designing a new power station. It is based on the assumption that the Republic of Koravia (formerly part of the Union of Soviet Socialist Republics) wishes to replace some of its ageing electricity generation plant with the help of the West. Since Koravia has now totally reformed its political system and economy, developing the latter into a 'market economy' along Western lines and achieving stability and 'convertibility' for its currency (the Koravian Rouble), it has managed to obtain the support of the International Monetary Fund for such a project. The IMF has undertaken to provide a 25-year loan to meet the entire capital cost of building the new 2000MW power station that Koravia wishes to build provided that Koravia guarantees to restrict its average annual inflation rate to a maximum of 10% over the period of repayment of the loan. Koravia has also undertaken to support the value of its currency by selling raw materials such as coal, oil and uranium (of which it has extremely large reserves) on the open market.

Because of its ample reserves of coal, oil and uranium, the Koravian Government has decided to build a power station that uses one of these fuels. (Koravia has no natural gas, so it cannot build 'combined' gas-turbine/steam stations of the type currently being built in Britain, and has no sites suitable for the large-scale exploitation of hydroelectric, tidal or wind power.) It has not yet decided which type of station to build, however, and has therefore invited tenders from three British consortia – one to build a coal-fired power station, one to build an oil-fired power station and one to build a nuclear power station. The three teams that will be taking part in 'The Power Station Game' will represent these three consortia, and will have the task of preparing and presenting tenders for their respective stations. You will be given detailed guidance on how to carry out the various stages of this work as the game proceeds.

The climax of 'The Power Station Game' will be a plenary session during which the three consortia will present their tenders to representatives of the Koravian Government and answer questions about their proposed schemes. The representatives of the Koravian Government will then decide which of the three consortia will win the contract to build the new power station.

Figure 20.1 *The introductory sheet of the revised PSG*

Technical Calculations on Coal Station – Student Worksheet	S4(a)
(a) *Calculation of annual fuel consumption of station*	
1. Peak electrical output of station (MW)	2000
2. Power needed to run station (MW)	68
3. Peak electrical output of generator transformers (MW)	
4. Percentage energy losses in transformers	0.72
5. Peak electrical output of generators (MW)	
6. Percentage energy losses in generators	1.41
7. Peak power output of turbines (MW)	
8. Overall thermodynamic efficiency of turbines (%)	47.5
9. Peak thermal output of boilers (MH)	
10. Percentage energy losses in boiler house	11.3
11. Peak thermal output from burning of coal (MW)	
12. Average load factor under which station has to operate (%)	74.4
13. Average thermal output from burning of coal (MW)	
14. Total energy produced from coal in 1 year (J)	
15. Amount of energy produced by burning 1 tonne of coal (J)	2.44×10^{10}
16. Amount of coal burned in 1 year (tonnes)	
(b) *Calculation of cooling water requirements of station*	
17. Peak heat removal rate from turbine condensers (MW)	
18. Heat removed by direct-cooling system per m³ of water used (J)	4.19×10^{7}
19. Peak water requirements of direct-cooling system (m³s⁻¹)	
20. Heat removed by wet cooling towers per m³ of water used (J)	1.13×10^{9}
21. Peak water requirements of wet cooling tower system (m³s⁻¹)	
22. Peak water requirements of dry cooling tower system (m³s⁻¹).	

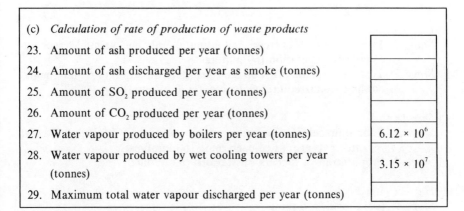

Figure 20.2 *One of the simplified technical worksheets used in the revised game*

THE DIFFERENT VERSIONS OF THE GAME THAT THE NEW PACKAGE MADE POSSIBLE

As we have seen, one of the reasons for restructuring the game package was to make the game *more flexible*, thus giving users the option of running either the full 'standard' version or a shortened, simplified or modified version that better met their specific needs. The revised 'Organizer's Guide' actually gives detailed guidelines on how to run four different versions of the game: the full version (requiring roughly eight hours); a shortened version of the full game designed for younger pupils (requiring roughly five hours); a simplified version of the game – omitting the technical calculations – for use with economics, modern studies or other non-technical students (again requiring roughly five hours); and a greatly simplified version of the game designed for use as a communication studies exercise (requiring roughly three hours). Details of these four different versions are given below.

The full (eight hour) version of PSG

This is primarily intended for use with sixth-form physics or engineering classes, or with science or engineering students at lower-tertiary level. It is designed for an optimum number of 18 participants (min. 12; max. 24) divided into three competing teams. It is recommended that it be run over one and a half days.

Structure of exercise

Day 1 (am)
Stage 1: Introduction to exercise, including a short background lesson on electricity generation (60 minutes)
Stage 2: Technical calculations on stations (determining fuel requirements, cooling water requirements, etc.) (120 minutes)

Day 1 (pm)
Stage 3: Economic calculations, siting work and 'survey' work carried out by three sub-groups of each team (60 minutes)
Stage 4: Preparation of tenders on stations (60 minutes)

Day 2 (am)
Stage 4: (continued) (60 minutes)
Stage 5: Presentation of tenders to 'Koravian Government'; judging (90 minutes)
Stage 6: Debriefing (30 minutes)

The shortened (five hour) version of the full game for younger pupils

This is primarily intended for use with fourth–fifth-form physics or engineering pupils. It is again designed for an optimum number of 18 participants (min. 12; max. 24) divided into three competing teams. It is recommended that it be run over one day.

Structure of exercise

Morning
Stage 1: Introduction to exercise (30 minutes)
Stage 2: Technical calculations (simplified versions) (60 minutes)
Stage 3: Economic calculations, siting work and survey work (60 minutes)
Stage 4: Preparation of tenders (30 minutes)

Afternoon
Stage 4: (continued) (30 minutes)
Stage 5: Presentation of tenders; judging (60 minutes)
Stage 6: Debriefing (30 minutes)

The simplified (five hour) version of the game for non-technical students

This is primarily intended for use with economics, modern studies or other non-technical students in the upper forms of secondary schools (S4–S6) or at lower-tertiary level. It is again intended for an optimum number of 18 participants (min. 12; max. 24) divided into three competing teams. It is recommended that it be run over one day.

Structure of exercise

Morning
Stage 1: Introduction to exercise (30 minutes)
Stage 2: Missed out – students given model answers to technical calculations
Stage 3: Economic calculations, siting work and survey work (90 minutes)
Stage 4: Preparation of tenders (60 minutes)

Afternoon
Stage 4: (continued) (30 minutes)
Stage 5: Presentation of tenders; judging (60 minutes)
Stage 6: Debriefing (30 minutes)

The greatly-simplified (three hour) communication studies version

This is primarily intended for use in helping senior pupils in secondary schools (S4 upwards) and tertiary-level students to develop their oral communication, presentation and team skills. It can be used with any number from 6 to 18 (optimum 12). It is recommended that it be run over a single morning or afternoon.

Structure of exercise

Stage 1: Introduction to exercise (20 minutes)
Stages 2 and 3: Missed out – students given model answers to technical and economic calculations and model solution to siting problem for their station.
Stage 4: Preparation of tenders (80 minutes)
Stage 5: Presentation of tenders; judging (60 minutes)
Stage 6: Debriefing (20 minutes)

CONCLUSION

This chapter shows how a long-established educational game that appeared to have reached the end of its useful life because its scenario had become hopelessly out of date was given a new lease of life by making radical changes to the game scenario. It also shows how it is possible to restructure a game package in such a way that the exercise becomes much more flexible and versatile in its range of use. The author hopes that the chapter encourages readers to carry out similar work themselves.

REFERENCES

Ellington, H I and Langton, N H (1975) 'The Power Station Game', *Physics Education*, Sept, 445–7.

Ellington, H I, Addinall, E, Percival, F and Lewis, J L (1979) 'Using simulations and case studies in the ASE's "Science in Society" project', in Megarry J (ed.) *Perspectives on Academic Gaming and Simulation 4*, Kogan Page, London, pp. 79–88.

Ellington, H I, Addinall, E and Percival, F (1984) *Case Studies in Game Design*, Kogan Page, London, ch. 7.

Ellington, H I (1990a) 'Converting "Power for Elaskay" into "Power for Pemang" – a case study', *Simulation/Games for Learning*, 20, 3, 314–28.

Ellington, H I (1990b) 'Converting "Telecom Link" into "Link-Up" – a case study', *Simulation/Games for Learning*, 20, 4, 418–28.

The revised version of PSG is available from The Institution of Electrical Engineers. For further information, contact: IEE Schools Liaison Service, Michael Faraday House, Six Hills Way, Stevenage, Herts SG1 2AY.

ABOUT THE AUTHOR

Henry Ellington graduated in natural philosophy from Aberdeen University in 1963 and obtained his Doctorate from the same University in 1969. Since 1973, he has been head of the Educational Development Unit at The Robert Gordon University, Aberdeen (formerly The Robert Gordon Institute of Technology), which awarded him a professorial title in 1990. He has been highly active in the simulation/gaming field throughout this time, having been involved in the development of over 50 games, simulations and case studies. He has also published over 100 papers in the field, and is co-author (with Eric Addinall and Fred Percival) of three books on gaming and simulation. He has served on the SAGSET Council for a total of nine years in two different spells, including being a member of the editorial board of *Simulation/Games for Learning*.

Address for correspondence: Educational Development Unit, The Robert Gordon University, Kepplestone Annexe, Queens Road, Aberdeen AB9 2PG. UK.

Chapter 21

The use of simulations in physiology teaching

Colin Chandler

ABSTRACT

Computer simulations provide an additional means of investigating physiological processes. While not replacing physiology experiments, students can explore quite complex phenomena in a structured and repeatable way. This may avoid the technical difficulties and expense involved in some experimentation. The example presented here is of a Squid Axon and is based on the Hodgkin Huxley model. The use of this model in teaching the basic properties of excitable membranes is illustrated. Reference is given to further sources of commercial or self-programmable physiology simulations.

Computer simulations are increasingly being used in the physiological teaching situation. They permit the exploration of physiological concepts in a controlled and repeatable environment. They may in some respects replace practical experiments but more often complement them. They allow the student a wider range of experience and can present a greater range of information on the computer screen than would be available in the experimental situation. This approach also avoids some of the issues and expense associated with animal experimentation.

The simulation described here considers the biophysical phenomena underlying the generation of the action potential. This process is fundamental to all communication in the nervous system, an understanding of which facilitates study of other aspects of neurophysiology.

ACTION POTENTIAL SIMULATION

The simulation of the Squid Axon is based on a model developed in the 1950s by Hodgkin and Huxley. This model uses a computation of the ionic flow through the nerve cell membrane to calculate the membrane potential. The model is based on experimental results obtained from the Squid giant axon.

Parameter	Value to be entered
Resting membrane potential	-70
Amplitude of stimulus 1	100
Duration of stimulus 1	0.4
Delay between stimuli	0
Amplitude of stimulus 2	0
Duration of stimulus 2	0

Table 21.1 *Example parameters which produce the simulation displayed in Figure 21.1*

While the time scale of events may be a little quicker in mammalian nerves, the general principle applies.

The simulation is used to explore some of the properties of the nerve cell membrane. The program allows the student to apply up to two electrical stimuli to the nerve cell membrane. These stimuli can be of variable duration, magnitude and delay. The display on the screen shows the membrane potential, the stimulus and the conductances of sodium (Na+) and potassium (K+) ions across the nerve cell membrane.

Students use the simulation to explore

1. The all or none nature of the action potential,
2. The refractory period following the action potential and
3. Temporal summation: i.e. the ability of two sub-threshold stimuli to add up and produce an action potential.

This exploration is guided by the use of a workbook in which the students are encouraged to record what they see on the screen and to interpret the changes in membrane potential with respect to the ionic conductances.

The student is prompted to enter a number of parameters; once these have been entered the simulation begins and the membrane potential, stimulus current and ionic conductances are displayed graphically in a matter of seconds on the screen. The student may then rerun the simulation with different parameters, export the data to a file for subsequent display and printing or exit from the simulation. The parameters in Table 21.1 would be used to generate a simulated action potential. The graphical output is illustrated in Figure 21.1.

The students would be asked to record a number of observations from the computer screen (Table 21.2)

Once the students have understood the basics of the action potential, other aspects can be explored such as the threshold current needed to generate an action potential, the effects of a second stimulus to illustrate the refractory period of nerve, the way in which two sub-threshold stimuli can add together to produce an action potential or the effect of an inhibitory (negative) stimulus. These together can allow the student to explore the concepts that have previously been introduced either in the lecture situation or in their own reading.

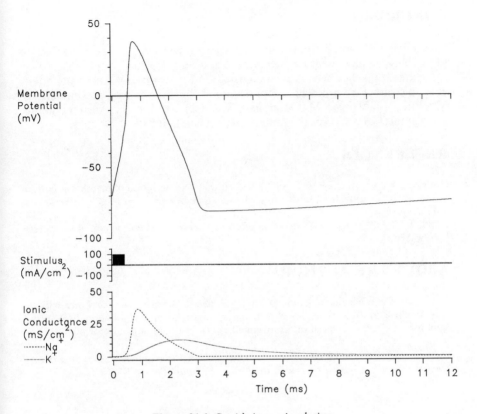

Figure 21.1 *Squid Axon simulation*

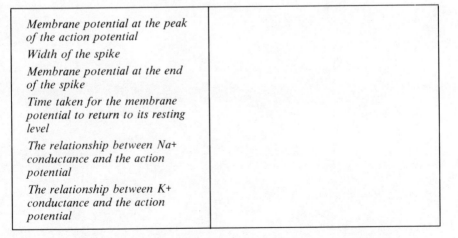

Membrane potential at the peak of the action potential	
Width of the spike	
Membrane potential at the end of the spike	
Time taken for the membrane potential to return to its resting level	
The relationship between Na+ conductance and the action potential	
The relationship between K+ conductance and the action potential	

Table 21.2 *Example of observations to be made from Figure 2.1*

CONCLUSION

Computer simulations may add another dimension to the teaching of physiology, complementing the more traditional teaching approaches. One specific example has been illustrated here but there are many other simulations available either commercially (for example the Mac family of simulations: MacPuff, MacDope, MacMan and MacPee), or for the keen computer programmer to program themselves (see Randall, 1987).

REFERENCES

Hodgkin, A L and Huxley, A F (1952) 'A quantitative description of membrane current and its application to conduction and excitation in nerve', *Journal of Physiology*, 117, 500–544.

Randall, J E (1987) *Microcomputers in physiological simulation*, 2nd edn, Raven Press, New York.

ABOUT THE AUTHOR

Dr Colin Chandler is a senior lecturer in health sciences at the University of Northumbria at Newcastle. As a neurophysiologist he uses simulation both in his teaching and in his research into movement control in neurological patients.

Address for correspondence: University of Northumbria at Newcastle, Institute of Health Sciences, Coach Lane Campus, Newcastle upon Tyne NE7 7XA.

Chapter 22

An evaluation study of THE CHEMISTRY GAME as a learning device

Usman Jibrin Muhamed

ABSTRACT

THE CHEMISTRY GAME mimicks a typical chemistry laboratory situation. Players who are senior secondary school science students (SS2) are required to identify, characterize and confirm samples hypothetically submitted by an indigenous mining company for analysis. Submissions are orally defended before other participants. Scientific observations are rewarded with marks and unscientific observers are referred to the 'library'.

Could the use of this game enhance cognitive gain in chemistry learners? Two random groups (32 SS2 Students each) consisting of an experimental group which played the game and a control group which did not were both pre-tested and post-tested with a validated researcher making cognitive tests. The student t-test carried out on the raw scores showed that the experimental group performed better than the control group ($P<0.05$). The use of THE CHEMISTRY GAME leads to significantly better learning results in qualitative analysis than the traditional approach alone. A full validation study of the content, gaming process and cognitive effectiveness is already in progress.

Educational gaming and simulation materials may easily tempt the uncritical user into associating their novelty with a supposed measure of effectiveness.

Objective evaluation evidence available to the potential users of academic games in Nigeria is scanty and the assessment of the merits of individual games has not been easy due to lack of feedback between the end users and the curriculum designers. It is therefore understandable why most buyers and users of academic games have no other alternative than to accept the claims made by the designers concerning the benefits. In most cases, such claims are either entirely unsupported or are extravagant generalizations made from limited evaluation evidence.

THE CHEMISTRY GAME is a science learning aid. It is designed to inject fun, motivation and competition into learning. It will excite the thought processes of players, improve their social skills, and above all consolidate their academic groundings. The design incorporates hearing, seeing and doing into the learning situation. Players may forget what they hear but they will at least remember what they see and know and what they have been able to do with their own hands.

THE CHEMISTRY GAME is recommended for senior secondary school science students. It can be introduced to the students by their chemistry tutor on completion of the scheme of work on qualitative analysis. Thereafter, it can be played during school club nights by members of the science club. It can also be used at home by science students on holiday.

MECHANICS

THE CHEMISTRY GAME is about the identification, characterization and confirmation of laboratory samples.

The starting point of the game is an assumption that an indigenous mining company without laboratory facilities has sent in a number of chemical substances suspected of containing certain metal ions and acid radicals for analysis. The object of the game is to confirm the presence of these ions. In doing so, the student (player) is expected to:

1. Carry out certain tests
2. Make reproducible observations
3. Make objective deductions.

THE GAME PACKAGE

The game is designed for two players and a referee. The package consists of:

- a game board
- introductory and 'how to play' leaflets
- 30 game cards made up of:
  10 chemistry master cards
  10 laboratory sample cards
  10 library cards
- 20 observation seeds
- 1 copy of a laboratory chemistry handbook
- sample copy of a score card

THE CHEMISTRY GAME is designed for the analysis of ten different laboratory samples. It can however be modified for the analysis of any number of samples.

THE GAME SCHEDULE

This can be divided into 4 stages:

Familiarization: at this stage, each player is given a copy of the introductory leaflet and 'how to play' leaflet. They are allowed 15 to 20 minutes to familiarize themselves with the characteristics and mechanics of the game under the supervision of their science tutor.

Sharing: the players are then issued with the game materials. The library cards and the sample cards are kept face-downwards on the gameboard. Each player is entitled to ten observation seeds and 5 sample cards. The referee keeps the Chemistry Master Cards (KEY).

Game format: the referee reshuffles the laboratory sample cards and places them face-downwards on the game board. A player is expected to pick a sample card from the pack of cards on the board, display it and make correct observations in all the nine test stations. The tests at the stations around the game board include a solubility test, the effect of heat, testing in NaOH solution, a flame test, etc. Observation is done by the placement of seeds against suggested options on the game board. Each player is required to confirm five laboratory samples to complete the game.

Oral defence: at the end of the game, each student player is expected to defend his/her submission before the other participants. The referee or chemistry master moderates this discussion. Five marks will be awarded by the referee for any correct observation. Wrong observations will not attract any mark or score: instead such an observer will be referred to the library for further research. The player with the highest score and the least number of visits to the library will be declared by the referee as the winner.

FIELD TESTS

A pilot study has been carried out on the effectiveness of THE CHEMISTRY GAME as a science learning tool.

Sample

The population for this study is the senior secondary school science students in Jos/South Local Government of Plateau State who offer chemistry. The sample consists of 64 senior secondary school year II students offering chemistry in the following schools:

Government Science Secondary School, Kuru,
Government Secondary School, Dadin Kowa,
Saint Joseph's College, Vom, and
Government Secondary School, Zawan.

The selection of the schools as well as that of the sample popualtion was done through a simple random sampling technique.

Experimental design

The design incorporates:

- a pre-test, administered on all the participants to determine their entry behaviour prior to the treatment (0_1)
- an experimental group which plays the game (E)
- a control group which does not play the game (C)
- a parallel post-test on both (C) and (E) to determine the effect of the learning outcome (0_2)

The participants were randomly assigned into the experimental group (E) and the control group (C). This design is represented below:

Group	Sample	Treatment	Test Instruments
E	32	Game	Pre-test (0_1) + Post-test (0_2)
C	32	–	Pre-test (0_1) + Post-test (0_2)

The random assignment of participants was designed to improve the equivalence between groups (E) and (C) and eliminate variance.

For this study it was hypothesized that:

a) the use by the experimental group of THE CHEMISTRY GAME enhances their achievement in qualitative chemical analysis;
b) the use by the experimental group of THE CHEMISTRY GAME has no effect on student achievement in qualitative chemical analysis.

The study was limited to the effectiveness of THE CHEMISTRY GAME in the cognitive domain. It is assumed that all schools in Nigeria are using the same examination and teaching syllabus for senior secondary school qualitative analysis. Based on these assumptions, the sample of the population used for this project was representative.

Measurement instrument

The apparatus essentially consists of a pre-test and a post-test. Both tests were researcher made and consisted of 25 multiple choice/alternative response/matching item types of cognitive tests each. The pre-test was based on the topics covered by the participants in normal classroom/laboratory work in the area of qualitative chemical analysis.

The post-test was a parallel test to the pre-test. The validity of both test instruments was determined by the curricular method and their combined reliability coefficient was found by the method of split halves and the Spearman Brown formula of conversion to be + 0.85.

Data analysis plan

The hypotheses were tested using the t-test of significant difference between

Mean score %			Mean gain	t-test calculated	t-test from table	decision df = 31; confidence level = 0.05
	Pre-test	Post-test				
Group (E)	45.4	54.0	8.5	7.63	2.042	Difference is significant and may be due to the treatment.
Control Group (C)	45.5	46.0	0.5	1.61	2.042	Difference is not significant and may be due to chance or experimental error

Table 22.1 *The group mean scores and t-test values*

mean scores of related samples. The tests were carried out using the students' raw scores obtained from the response to the pre-test and post-test instruments.

Findings

Table 22.1 shows the group mean scores and t-test values.

The statistics in Table 22.1 show that for the experimental group, the calculated value of the significance test (t = 7.63) is higher than the value (2.042) obtained from the statistical table at a confidence level of 0.05.

The difference in the mean scores between the pre-test and the post-test is significant and may have been caused by the use of THE CHEMISTRY GAME. The hypothesis that 'the use by the experimental group of THE CHEMISTRY GAME enhances their achievement in qualitative analysis' is therefore upheld.

For the control group, the calculated value of the significant test (t = 1.61) is lower than the value (t = 2.042) obtained from the statistical table at a confidence level of 0.05.

The difference in the mean scores between the pre-test and the post-tests is not significant and might be due to change or experimental error. The hypothesis that 'the use by the experimental group of THE CHEMISTRY GAME has no effect on student achievement in qualitative analysis' is therefore rejected.

A closer look at the pattern of students' responses to the post-tests also revealed that a majority of students in the experimental group performed better in stimuli requiring application of prior knowledge and interpretation of analytical data.

CONCLUSION

THE CHEMISTRY GAME has been field-tested in Nigeria and nationwide acceptability has been proved through the response from the end users (science students) and the targeted buyers (education authorities) in the different states covered by the survey.

It is also gratifying to note that the author won the National Agency for Science and Engineering Award in October, 1992 for the production of this game.

It is intended that THE CHEMISTRY GAME will be made available for use by all senior secondary schools offering science.

Acknowledgement

The author is grateful to the National Agency for Science and Engineering Infrastructure for the funding of this project.

ABOUT THE AUTHOR

Usman Jibrin Muhamed is a Nigerian science teacher and educational consultant. He is also completing some postgraduate research work in the department of curriculum studies and science at the University of Jos, Nigeria.

Address for correspondence: Consolidated Educational Aids, No. 110 Barkin Akawo Road, P.O. Box 6602, Jos, Nigeria.

Chapter 23

A computer simulation game for building

N M Bouchlaghem

ABSTRACT

THE BUILDING GAME is a simulation model introducing students to a real-life situation in building construction. They play the role of a contractor who is organizing the construction of the foundations and shell of a two-storey building.

This chapter presents a computerized version of the game, making it an even more efficient decision-making exercise leaving the tedious work to the computer. New features are introduced in the game giving the opportunity to the students to investigate different aspects which would influence the time and cost of building. The game has been tested on students and proved to be easy to use and attractive even to those with limited computer knowledge.

THE BUILDING GAME (Nowak, 1976) is a simulation exercise for building involving the planning of the construction process of the foundation and structure of a two-storey building. It has proved to be a very useful tool not only for architectural students but also for students in other building disciplines. It demonstrated not only the importance of early design decisions on the construction cost but also provided a very effective introduction to building site processes. The game presents to students a real-life situation where they have the responsibility to make decisions during the construction of the foundations and shell of a two-storey building.

The main components of the manual version of the game are: an illustrated network chart summarizing all the construction operations in a sequence, a mini bill giving the quantities of materials required to perform every operation, a selection of plant and labour with their output rates and an allocation chart where the results are recorded. The players go through the construction process selecting appropriate plant and labour for each operation, compiling the time necessary to complete it using the quantity of material and the plant/labour combination output rate and record the results on the allocation chart. When all the operations are completed the costs of all the resources used are calculated and added to the material cost to determine the overall contract cost.

It was thought that a computer version of THE BUILDING GAME would be even more useful in achieving the purpose of simulating construction processes. It would not only free the game from all arithmetic, leaving all the work concentrated on decision making, but also introduce new features which were not possible to apply in the original form of the game. The new features include the possibility of applying variations after the first attempt has been completed, and investigating aspects which can affect the construction process such as delays caused by certain weather conditions.

The following sections describe the different steps which led to the development of the computer game and a description of the program itself.

ANALYSIS OF THE MANUAL GAME AND DETERMINATION OF OBJECTIVES FOR THE COMPUTER VERSION

A thorough analysis of the features and use of the manual game was the first stage of the work. This led to general conclusions about its structure, the main difficulties in playing it and possible improvements.

The construction of the foundation and shell of even a simple building involves decisions about a wide range of plant and building operations. In the manual form of the game this process occupied a minimum of two academic days. This was mainly occupied not by the decisions involved but by the need for calculations and detailed entries to be made on the resource allocation chart after completion of an initial solution. After the first attempt was complete it was impractical to make variations to decisions in order to find an optimum solution because of the further calculations required.

Thus, although the game formed a valuable introduction to students of the nature of the work and responsibility of a contractor, the effect of varying design decisions, which were the objective of the game, could only be assessed from a comparison of the results of a group of students and no progressive exploration was possible.

A computer-based version would speed the operation of the game and enable variations to be explored very easily. None of the original objectives would be sacrificed. All the student interest would be retained and the tedious and error-prone arithmetic eliminated. In addition more detailed output demonstrating the underlying principles could be obtained.

The objectives of the computerized version of the game were, therefore, to provide attractive and readily understood displays of the nature of the processes involved; to make the decisions required clear; and to provide immediate facilities for change and for feedback, when required, of decisions made, progress, duration and cost of the proposed solutions.

In addition to the above items, which simply represent improvements in running the manual game, it was proposed at the outset of the work that additional features could be provided by the computer. These included comparison of productive and total times for both plant and labour, storage and comparison of past games, printed records of games and the ability to observe the effects of weather on the cost and duration of the work.

DEVELOPMENT OF THE COMPUTER GAME

The main objectives were to make the program easy to use and attractive to students, most of whom have limited computer knowledge. The programming stage was divided into two main parts: input control and computation, and screen displays.

Input control and computation

The input control was organized using input routines, providing facilities which would reject all inappropriate key strokes, control the nature and size of storing entries, control the entry of numbers to be within appropriate limits and enable the user to exit from inadvertent selections without losing previously input data.

In the computation process the duration of each operation is calculated and located in the construction sequence. The plant and labour costs durations for each type of operation are then computed and added up to determine the total cost and total duration of the contract.

Input displays

Screen displays were divided into two main types: operational displays which organize the input, and information displays which simply display information about the game. Colour coding has been employed to assist in the identification of trades. Operational displays include:

- The mini bill which shows the sequence of building operations and the quantities involved (Figure 23.1).
- Plant and labour selection screens which present the types of labour and plant available for the activity selected together with the amount of work to be accomplished. Any constraints upon choice are also displayed. A simple numerical entry enables selection to be made. Figure 23.2 shows a typical screen.

Information displays

- The network and isometric sketches: users of the progam can, at any time, make reference to a series of displays which show a network of the sequence of building operations (Figure 23.3) and diagrams showing the appearance of the work at any stage. Figure 23.4 gives a typical example.
- The allocation chart: this chart, which can be accessed at any time during the development of a game solution, shows the duration of work in the activities which have been selected together with the cost up to the stage of development shown and the overall duration of the work up to that stage. A colour coding system was used to differentiate types of operations (such as

MINI BILL A

Operations	Total qts	Operations	Total qts
Remove top soil and level site	200m^3	Reinforce 1st floor well beams	4No
		Erect formwork 1st fl well beams	4No
Excavate for foundations	35m^3	Concrete 1st floor well beams	3m^3
Excavate for column bases	10m^3	Strike formwork 1st fl w b	4No
Concrete foundations	10m^3	Reinforce 1st floor columns	4No
Reinforce column bases	4No	Erect formwork 1st floor columns	4No
Lay brickwork up to DPC	7500No	Concrete 1st floor columns	3m^3
Reinforce columns (First lift)	4No	Strike formwork 1st fl columns	4No
Erect formwork (First lift)	4No	Reinforce roof well beams	4No
Concrete columns (First lift)	1m^3	Erect formwork roof well beams	4No
Strike formwork clmns 1st Lift	4No	Concrete roof well beams	4.5m^3
Place compact blind hardcore	70m^3	Strike formwork roof well beams	4No
Reinforce ground floor	340m^2	Lay blockwork gr fl partitions	135m^2
Concrete ground floor slab	54m^3	Erect formwork roof edge beams	12No
Lay ground floor brickwork	24,000No	Reinforce roof edge beams	12No
Reinforce ground floor columns	4No	Concrete roof edge beams	6m^3
Erect formwork (gr fl columns)	4No	Strike formwork roof edge beams	12No
Concrete ground floor columns	1m^3	Erect formwork roof beams	16No
Strike formwork (gr fl columns)	4No	Reinforce roof beams	16No
Erect formwork (first floor)	300m^2	Concrete roof beams	8.5m^3
Reinforce first floor	300m^2	Strike formwork (roof beams)	4No
Concrete first floor slab	74m^3	Lay parapet brickwork	6000No
Strike first floor slab	300m^2	Lay blockwork 1st fl partitions	260No
Lay first floor brickwork	18,500No		

PRESS ENTER TO INPUT

F1 Help   F2 Allocation Chart   F3 Sketches   F4 Plant   F5 Networks

Figure 23.1 *Mini bill*

excavating, formwork, and steelwork). The top part of the chart is divided into weeks and days so durations are recorded using colour coded highlighting. The bottom part was reserved for costs and durations given in figures using the same colour coding. Also full-time and subcontraction costs are given for steelwork, formwork and bricklaying. The last line of the screen is a menu giving different options which could be performed at that stage (Figure 23.5).

ADDITIONAL FACILITIES MADE POSSIBLE BY COMPUTER USE

The computer version provides additional facilities to the manual one; these come into effect mainly after the first tentative solution has been completed. They are:

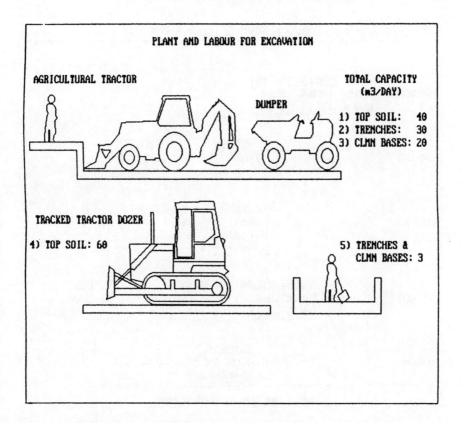

Figure 23.2 *Input display, plant and labour for excavation*

Possibility of variation of decisions

This facility allows the user to go back to any operation in the sequence and change the input already recorded. If an alteration is made to the input the program recalculates the new operation cost and readjusts the whole process according to that change. The user can make as many changes as needed for the sake of reducing the time and cost.

Weather analysis

The main new feature in the computerized version of the game is the weather analysis option which makes it possible to investigate the effect of weather elements on the duration and cost of the construction process. The program asks for a date for the start of the building work within a ten-year interval (January 1959 and December 1968) it then scans the temperature values from the ten-year data stored in the program and readjusts the whole process taking

ILLUSTRATED NETWORKS OF DESIGN A (STAGE 1)

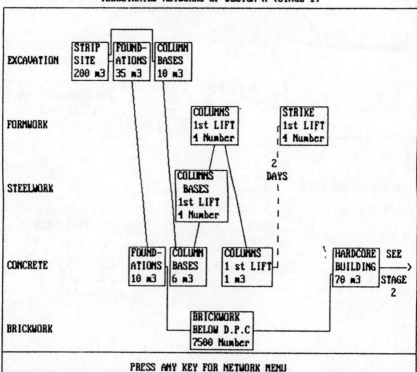

Figure 23.3 *Operations sequence*

into account the effect of temperatures on certain trades such as concreting and bricklaying.

Comparison of paid and productive time

In this option the program compares the time actually occupied in production and the time during which labour and plant costs must be paid. This is done for steelwork, formwork and bricklaying where the program displays a graph with two curves representing paid time and productive time. The X axis represents the time (from week one to the finish of the building process) and the Y axis gives the paid time and the productive time for each week of the process.

Comparison of total costs

In this graphical output the total costs of different games are plotted together on the same graph and enable comparisons to be made. The X axis gives the duration of the contract while the Y axis records the contract cost.

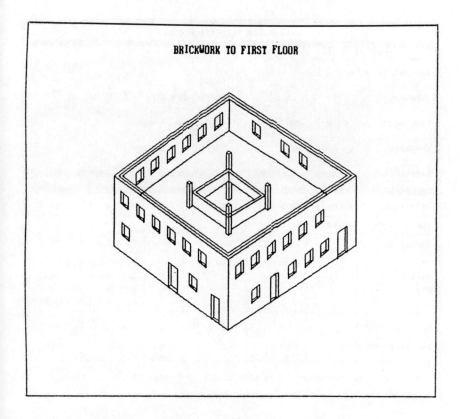

Figure 23.4 *3D diagram showing brickwork to first floor*

DESCRIPTION OF THE PROGRAM

The program is organized around three main screens: the main menu which is a utility menu, the mini bill around which the input is organized, and the allocation chart which displays the results.

The main menu

When the program is first started the main menu is displayed on the screen giving seven options:

- Introduction
- Start new game
- List jobs
- Display network
- Comparative chart

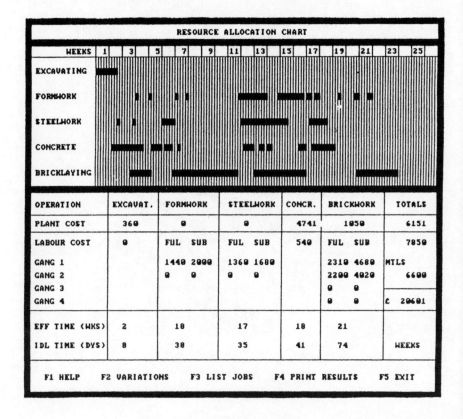

Figure 23.5 *Allocation chart*

■ Allocation chart
■ Quit.

The mini bills screen

When the 'start new game' option is selected from the main menu the program goes automatically to the mini bill screen (Figure 23.1) where the input can start. The input is organized in a sequence. Plant and labour are allocated to each operation individually till the completion of the construction process.

When an operation is highlighted, press the ENTER key and the appropriate plant and labour screen will be displayed. When the plant and labour are selected for that operation the program will go back to the mini bill screen and the next operation on the sequence is automatically highlighted. Other options in the mini bill screens include:

■ Displaying the isometric sketches which are drawings showing the main stages of the construction sequence.

- Checking all plant and labour available for each type of operation.
- Displaying the illustrated network which is a precedence diagram which also indicates certain operations that can be carried out in parallel. These are joined together by a diagonal line.

The allocation chart

The results can be checked at any stage in the allocation chart (Figure 23.5) which is displayed by pressing the F2 option from the mini bill screen. Options in the allocation chart include:

- *Saving the results*: the F3 option enables the saving of the results at any stage of the game (a partly played game can be saved and finished at a later stage) onto a specified file. Three options are available:
  - The first one is for saving a new job being played specifying a file name.
  - The second one is for calling a previous game from an existing file.
  - The third one displays all the jobs available in the directory.
- *Printing the results*: a hard copy of the allocation chart can be obtained at any stage of the game by pressing the F4 option (PRINT RESULTS) in the allocation chart. This will send the allocation chart to the printer.
- *Performing a weather analysis*: when this option is selected the program asks for a hypothetical starting date for the building process, scans the appropriate period of time within the ten years for which the temperature data is available then readjusts the whole process accordingly.
- *Graphical output*: this includes the comparison of productive and paid time for different groups of different trades, and the comparison of total costs from different games.

FIELD TRIALS

A number of field trials have been conducted to test the program with the help of students in various departments. A number of points emerged from each one leading to further improvement of the program. Those improvements were mainly related to the user friendliness of the program, making it more approachable to students with limited computer knowledge. The trials took place in three different departments.

- Department of Building Engineering, UMIST, Manchester,
- Department of Civil Engineering and Building, University of Glamorgan, Pontypridd,
- Department of Construction Management, South Bank University, London.

The results of the trials are summarized in charts comparing total costs from each student taking part in the trial. In every case during the field trials the game attracted the attention and interest of students who found it very useful and easy to use.

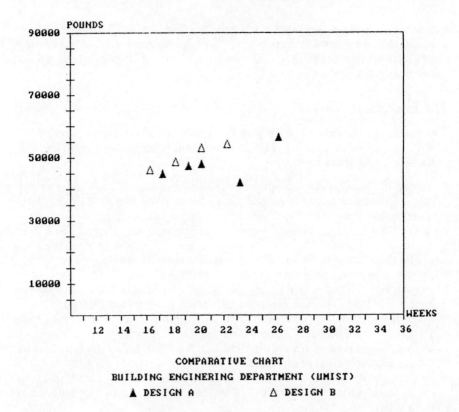

Figure 23.6 *Results of trials: UMIST*

CONCLUSIONS

The computer version of THE BUILDING GAME proved to be very attractive to students who demonstrated a keen interest during the field trials investigating the effect of alternatives in decisions at different stages of the building process on the final time and cost. It introduced some competitiveness among them to achieve the best result. Most students found it very easy to use, and even those with limited computer experience needed only few instructions to run the program.

The new features of the game introduce students to new concepts such as the effect of weather which would not have been possible without the use of the computer. Another important aspect was the comparison of productive and idle time for plant and labour. Such concepts were possible to implement in the computer version of the game, taking it to a higher level of understanding of building processes.

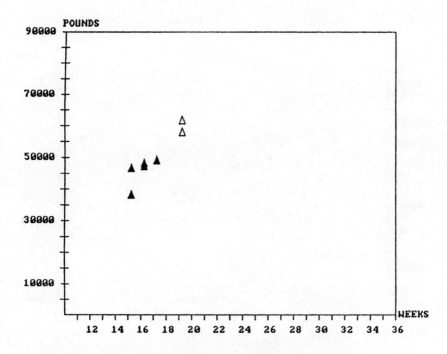

COMPARATIVE CHART
DEPARTMENT OF CIVIL ENGINEERING AND BUILDING
▲ DESIGN A   △ DESIGN B

Figure 23.7 *Results of trials: University of Glamorgan*

REFERENCE

Nowak, F (1976) *THE BRE BUILDING GAME*, Application Services Division, Building Research Establishment, Department of the Environment.

ABOUT THE AUTHOR

Dr N M Bouchlaghem lectures in civil engineering and building at the University of Glamorgan.

Address for correspondence: Department of Civil Engineering and Building, University of Glamorgan, Pontypridd, Mid-Glamorgan CF37 1DL.

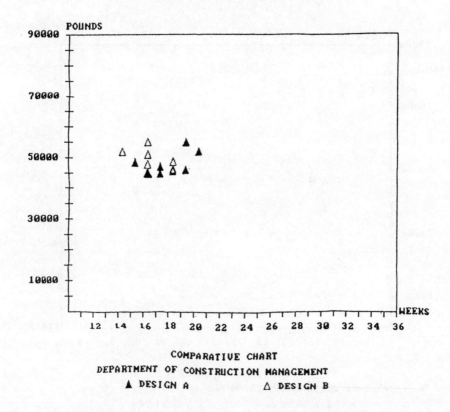

Figure 23.8 *Results of trials: South Bank University*

Chapter 24

Planes or bust: an OPT scheduling game

Laurence Legg

ABSTRACT

The purpose of this game is to introduce the optimized production technology (OPT) principles for scheduling in manufacturing systems. The 'product' is simply two pieces of folded paper stapled together in the general shape of an aeroplane. The process routes are similarly straightforward. The participants can quickly understand the requirements of the game; however, making a profit is not so straightforward. Upon completion of the game the participants can relate well to the drum/buffer/rope method and the OPT rules. These ideas and other issues are brought out in the discussion and analysis of the system. The time taken to brief the participants and run the game is about 40 minutes.

BACKGROUND

The game was initially designed as part of a two-day course for British Aerospace in materials management, hence the product being an aeroplane. It has subsequently been used with a wide variety of ages and ability levels, from schoolchildren aged 12 to 13 years through degree students to professionals in related areas. The schoolchildren usually run the game twice, the second run being where they implement the ideas brought out in the discussions after the first run, but other groups do not usually need reinforcement in this way and have other types of follow-up activities and exercises.

The group size can vary between eight and twelve, with nine or ten being preferred. Two or more groups can run simultaneously, but with more than two groups it is recommended that there is more than one tutor present. The game and partial discussion and analysis can be completed in an hour, but an hour and a half is preferable as this allows more freedom in the discussion stage. There is a wide variety of articles and books about OPT. The following books will provide the basic information needed to analyse the game and to generate discussion areas:

The Goal (1986) E M Goldratt and R E Fox, North River Press.

The Race (1986) E M Goldratt and R E Fox, North River Press.
Optimised Production Technology (1990) G Jones and M Roberts, IFS.
Production Management Systems (1988) J Brown, J Harken and J Shivnan, Addison-Wesley.
Theory of Constraints (1990) E M Goldratt, North River Press.

The equipment needed to run the game for one group is:

- Lots of A4 plain paper (recycled)
- 1 stapler plus staples
- 1 pair of scissors
- 1 ruler (30 cm.)
- 1 pencil
- 3 different coloured pens
- job cards
- machine cards

Spares of the above should be available in case the group wants to buy extra resources.

INITIAL BRIEFING

This should take about 10 minutes. Figure 24.1 is a network diagram of the process routes for the manufacture of a paper aeroplane (P). There are two spare parts, wings (P1) and fuselages (P2). The selling price is shown above each saleable product. This amount is only received when the product is moved into the finished goods store. The raw material, of which there is an unlimited supply, is A4 plain paper costing £30 per sheet, which is cut into three equal size strips worth £10 each. The operating expense for the system for the 15 minutes duration of the game is £2,000. The aim is to make as much money as possible from the system during a 15 minute run time.

The circles represent operations, with the estimated time in seconds per part given (in practice these are overestimates). Each operation requires one machine; initially there is only one machine available for each operation, and one person only can operate a machine. The members of the group are assumed to be multi-skilled and capable of performing any of the operations (including transfer of parts around the system). Note that as there is only one machine for each operation there can only be one person doing an operation at any one time, unless a second machine is bought, in which case two people are allowed to perform the operation. There is no limit to the number of people used in transporting parts around the system.

The 15 minute period is spent producing planes and spares but it should be pointed out that the machines are not dedicated to this particular product, and as such the system could be producing other products with different sequences. The purpose of this is to discourage a physical flow-line solution, but this type of solution would be financially penalized anyway as the machines would need to be moved from their initial positions.

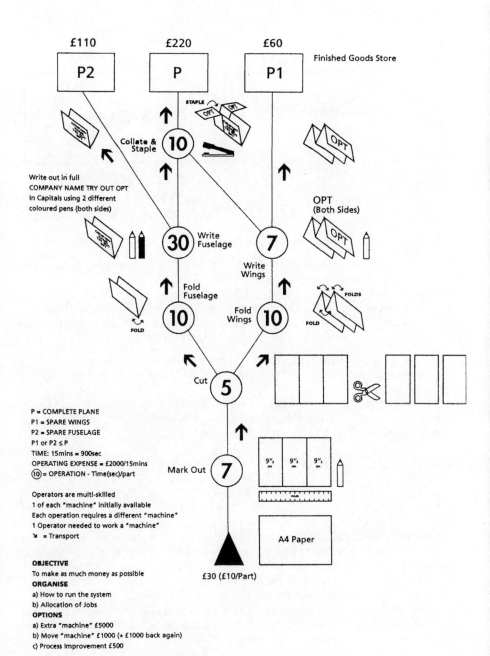

Figure 24.1 *Process routes*

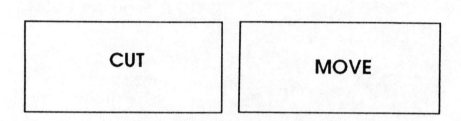

Figure 24.2 *Job card examples (full size)*

Before or during the game the group can decide to:

- Move a machine – costing £1000 plus a further £1000 at the end of the run to move back again.
- Buy an extra machine – costing £5000.
- Do a process improvement – costing £500. At this stage be vague about this option and say it is up to the group or individuals to be creative and think of 'better' ways of doing the various jobs. More about this later.

The only external constraint on the system is a marketing related one, where the number of spare wings or spare fuselages made cannot exceed the number of planes made.

No further instructions or help should be given at this stage, as it is up to the group to make their plans. All the information is summarized on Figure 24.1, which can be used to give this initial briefing.

GROUP DISCUSSION

This should take between 10 to 15 minutes.

Leave the group to formulate their plans and decide on the allocation of jobs. Job cards, as shown in Figure 24.2, can be provided to make this allocation easier. While the group is discussing, lay out the machine cards and their associated equipment around the room. This should be fairly random, but ensure that successive operations are not next to each other. A large space will be needed for the finished goods store. A large pile (about half a ream) of A4 paper (the raw material) is placed by the first operation (marking out). Listen to the group discussion, as often what is said can be incorporated into the end discussion stage. A few groups have produced excellent plans but then failed to implement them during the game!

Also put up the profit (loss) summary as shown in Figure 24.3, but do not include the work-in-process (WIP) line until the end of their 15 minute run.

At the end of this stage be clear whether the group wants to 'move', 'buy' or 'process improve' as this will need to be added to the profit (loss) summary.

£

	£
Sales of P (£220 ea.)	
Sales of P1 (£60 ea.)	
Sales of P2 (£110 ea.)	

Income from sales

Operating expense	2000
Move (£2000 ea.)	
Extra resource (£5000 ea.)	
Process improvement (£500 ea.)	500 (cut)
WIP (£10 ea.)	

Outgoings

Profit (loss)

Figure 24.3 *Profit (loss) summary*

RUNNING THE SYSTEM

This should take 15 to 20 minutes.

Allow a few minutes before starting the 15 minute run for individuals to get used to their jobs and to start filling the system with WIP. Remind the group they can 'move', 'buy' or 'process improve' at any time. Also inform the group that you are the divisional manufacturing director and will be checking on their performance during the run.

Once the few minutes are up, remove any completed planes or spares and start timing the 15 minute run. If asked 'how long is left,' be vague as their system of working should be controlling the WIP levels and output rate rather than attempting to empty the system of work during the last few minutes.

You will need to keep your eyes open for any process improvements, which are often done by individuals on a local work station basis. The common ones are cutting more than one sheet at a time and folding more than one strip at a time. These need to be recorded as shown in the example in Figure 24.3. In the follow-up discussion raise whether these were of benefit or not. In fact these two local 'efficiency gains' just increase the level of WIP in the system, though if used in the OPT way would lower the WIP marginally and it then becomes a matter of cost justification in terms of reduction of WIP versus the £500 spent, though there are other non-financial issues that can be raised.

Most groups want to buy an extra writing fuselage machine at some stage in the run. Agree to this or any other machine they may want to buy, and record on the profit (loss) summary. Note, though, that this is usually a crisis measure which is taken, and this again can lead to later discussion.

In your role as divisional manufacturing director you should urge the group and individuals to keep their labour and machine utilization high. Remark on idle machines and operators, and praise machines and operators for being continually busy. This can sometimes cause resentment; however, it can lead to later discussion on issues such as measures of performance; conflict between different departments; or whether optimizing sub-systems leads automatically to improvements in the system as a whole.

At the end of the 15 minute run, stop all activity and ensure that no completed planes or spares are moved into the finished goods store or that any strips of paper are 'lost'. All paper which has entered the system from the raw materials store needs to be counted up. This will include all the cut strips, any sheets which have been marked out, and any sheets which may have been moved to the cutting operation. The easiest way of counting is in terms of strips, as these are worth £10 each, so an uncut sheet is three strips. While this is being done, add in the WIP line on the profit (loss) summary.

ANALYSIS OF THE RUN

Enter all the amounts in the profit (loss) summary and calculate whether the group has made a profit or loss. Although this game has been run many times with a wide variety of ability levels, very few groups have come out with a profit.

ANALYSIS OF THE SYSTEM

For the purposes of this chapter the analysis of the system and discussion topics are separated, but in practice the two are usually integrated together. The level of analysis and discussion areas should be appropriate to the group and the outcomes you wish to achieve from the exercise.

The following analysis is in terms of the OPT principles, and can be directly linked to the OPT rules; see Figure 24.4

Identify the bottleneck (drum)

The bottleneck is the operation with the longest processing time, which is the writing fuselage machine at 30 seconds per strip. Hence, the output rate of parts is one every 30 seconds, and this is the drumbeat of the system.

The product mix

This is calculated on the return per unit of constraint (bottleneck), as shown in Table 24.1.

1. Balance flow not capacity
2. The level of utilization of a non-bottleneck is not determined by its own potential but by some other constraint in the system
3. Utilization and activation of a resource are not synonymous
4. An hour lost at a bottleneck is an hour lost for the total system
5. An hour saved at a non-bottleneck is just a mirage
6. Bottlenecks govern both throughput and inventories
7. The transfer batch may not, and many times should not, be equal to the process batch
8. The process batch should be variable not fixed
9. Schedules should be established by looking at all the constraints simultaneously. Lead times are the result of a schedule and cannot be predetermined.

MOTTO
The sum of the local optimums is not equal to the global optimum

Figure 24.4 *OPT rules*

Product mix	P only	P and P1	P and P2	P and P1 and P2
Selling Price	220	280	330	390
Raw material cost	20	30	30	40
Contribution	200	250	300	350
Seconds of bottleneck used	30	30	60	60
Return (£)/sec. of bottleneck	6.7	8.3	5	5.8

Table 24.1 *Product mix*

Hence, the product mix is to make P and P1 (planes and wings), with P = P1, and not to make any P2 (fuselages), provided that the making of wings does not affect the throughput of the bottleneck. This is checked by considering the longest operation in the wings-only process route, which is 10 seconds for 'fold wings'. Two wings will need to pass through this process, which leaves 10 seconds of excess capacity per 30 seconds from the drumbeat. It is therefore possible to match production of spare wings with production of planes.

Machine	time used/30 sec.	% utilization
Mark out	7	23
Cut	5	17
Fold fuselage	10	33
Fold wings	20	67
Write fuselage	30	100
Write wings	14	47
Collate and staple	10	33

Table 24.2 *Machine utilization*

Machine utilization

Knowing the product mix, the process loads of each machine can be calculated as in Table 24.2. Note that one sheet of A4 is completely used in making products, where two strips combine to make a plane and one strip to make a wing.

A pattern of working can be found which minimizes the number of multi-skilled operators required to run the system. An increase in the utilization of the non-bottleneck resources will lead to an increase in WIP (what price the process improvement in the cut machine?).

Quantity produced and profit for the system

The bottleneck can process 900/30 = 30 parts. So 30 planes can be made, and this is matched with 30 spare wings. Assuming no WIP at the end of the 15 minutes, the profit of the system is (30 × 220) + (30 × 60)–2000 = £6400.

Synchronizing material flow (time buffers and ropes)

This is achieved by using time buffers and logistical ropes for raw material release. Figure 24.5 shows the positioning of the time buffers, and approximate minimum level of parts to which the time buffer can fall which then signals release of raw materials. The approximate number of sheets to release is shown by the dotted lines (the ropes). Note that strips following the wings process route will split equally after *write OPT* operation.

Accurate figures can be calculated, and a Gantt chart produced detailing the timings, process batch quantities and transfer batch quantities for each machine. This could be given as part of a follow-up exercise, and compared with typical batch production methods.

Production strategy for the system

- The writing fuselage machine must never be idle.
- Finite forward scheduling from the bottleneck to the market.

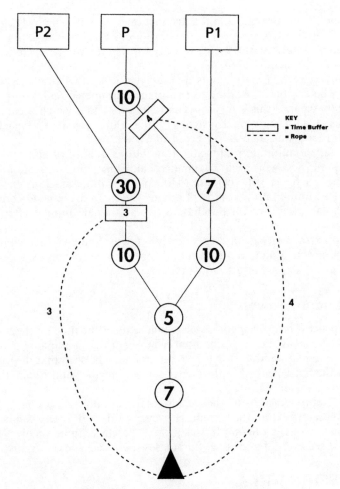

Figure 24.5 *Time buffers and ropes*

- The time buffers support the schedule of the bottleneck.
- The time buffers determine the level of WIP in the system.
- The release of raw materials is tied to the time buffers minimum allowable level.
- Backwards scheduling from the time buffers.
- Look for process improvements in the bottleneck.

CHANGES TO THE SYSTEM

Extra bottleneck resource

An extra writing fuselage machine reduces the operation time to 15 seconds; it will still be the bottleneck, and the product mix stays the same. The output of planes will double to 60; however, the output of spare wings will not double as there will no longer be sufficient capacity in the fold wings machine, unless a process improvement is used.

Continuing to take 30 seconds as the cycle time, two fuselages and three wings can be produced, leading to two planes completed and one spare wing. Thus in 900 seconds this is 60 planes and 30 spare wings which is equivalent to an increase from the original system of $(30 \times 200) = £6600$. The machine cost £5000, so there is an increase in profit of £1600.

Note that the minimum allowable time buffer quantities and raw material release quantities will need to change, and that the utilization of non-bottleneck machines will increase. The folding wings machine has become critical. Also note that the timing of buying the extra machine is significant in that the break-even time for purchase is two and a half minutes after the start of run.

If two extra writing fuselage machines are bought, this changes the bottleneck in the system and the analysis needs to be started over again. This could be given as part of a follow-up exercise.

Process improvements

The best process improvement is one which reduces the time on the bottleneck machine, and ideas such as using abbreviations for the company or organization's name are acceptable. The time reduction may be such that the machine is no longer the bottleneck; if so the analysis would begin again. Again, this could be a follow-up exercise.

Process improvements on other machines in the game will probably have led to an increase in WIP in the system. However, under OPT they can be used to reduce the size of the time buffers as process batches can be smaller. This can lead into discussion of statistical fluctuations with dependent events.

DISCUSSION AREAS

- Drum/buffer rope system
- Synchronized material flow
- OPT rules
- Measures of performance
- Continuous improvement (areas such as where to concentrate quality improvement, set-up reduction, maintenance, tool design)
- Comparison of OPT with Just-In-Time and Materials Requirements Planning
- Local optimization versus global optimization
- Interdepartmental conflict
- Team working
- Statistical fluctuations and dependent events
- Crisis management

■ Significance of WIP levels

ABOUT THE AUTHOR

Laurence Legg is a senior lecturer at the University of Central Lancashire, where he has worked since 1987. Prior to this appointment he has taught in schools and FE colleges. Since 1989 he has been a course tutor for the Open University on their postgraduate programme in manufacturing, and has acted as visiting lecturer to Dunchurch Learning Services, GEC management training college, on their Diploma in Manufacturing Management (DMM) course. In 1978 he graduated from Loughborough University of Technology in Engineering and Education, and in 1980 was awarded an MSc from the same University in design of production systems.

Address for correspondence: Department of Engineering and Product Design, University of Central Lancashire, Preston PR1 2HE.

SECTION 6: Computerized applications

Chapter 25

Inter-firm relationships and the use of marketing simulations

David Tonks and George Long

ABSTRACT

This chapter considers the use in marketing education of computer-based simulations to represent and demonstrate the reality of inter-firm relationships.

The underlying theme of the chapter, one which now occurs with some frequency in the literature, concerns the true effectiveness of learning through simulation. More specifically, the chapter questions the suitability of models of competition which are often implicit in marketing simulation software or which are superimposed in curriculum design. The chapter proposes that the use of marketing simulations, an educational device which generates high-involvement amongst both facilitators and participants, can lead to misrepresentation of the complexity of competition.

For illustration, the chapter also provides the results of an exploratory study into the emergence of inter-firm relationships amongst teams participating in one run of a marketing simulation exercise. These teams consisted of marketing major under-graduates at the University of Lancaster.

The chapter concludes by stressing the critical role of the simulation facilitator in providing suitable interventions to ensure that unrealistic models of inter-firm relation-ships are not inadvertently communicated to participants.

INTRODUCTION

Certain characteristics of management education in the 1990s can be expected to develop in the new millenium. The current interest in managerial com-petences and the associated shift of emphasis in curricula towards skill development will continue. Middleton and Long (1990) considered these issues in the context of marketing education and training. Associated with this, increasing recognition of the value of experiential learning is likely.

In parallel, information technology and use of the now ubiquitous PC will see further growth. The use of PCs in the general area of management education and the particular field of marketing education is well-established through familiar applications such as word-processing and presentation software, spreadsheet and database software, associated decision support packages and more specific offerings on marketing research and statistical analysis. Hirst (1991) provides a comprehensive review of the current state of play. These parallel lines converge where PCs are used to provide a simulated marketing environment in which teams analyse, plan, make decisions and 'compete' – usually on an interactive basis with other teams.

Lewis (1991) gives an overview of the use of computers in higher education and notes that evaluation of their effectiveness is 'virgin territory'. The authors have designed and run a variety of learning events which use marketing simulations as the core learning method with undergraduates and postgraduates at the University of Lancaster and also with managers on in-house training programmes. They are enthusiastic proponents of the method but also recognize some of the problems which can be encountered, including that of measuring true effectiveness.

Tonks and Wan (1991) considered the problems of measuring the effectiveness of simulations due to the intervention of 'hidden curricula'. This chapter is developed from Long and Tonks (1991) which looked at potential problems arising from the 'hidden rhetoric' of the conventional marketing simulation exercise. 'Hidden rhetoric' results from the assumptions of the simulation designer, the facilitators and the participants. It can work to distort the learning potential of the method by misrepresenting the complexity of inter-firm relationships through the provision of a powerful experiential reinforcement of particular and sometimes naive models of competition. Long and Tonks (1991) sought some remedies to such distortion on the assumption that inappropriate inter-firm relations can develop from the use of typical marketing simulations. This chapter extends that work.

MARKETING SIMULATIONS AND LEARNING OBJECTIVES

Involvement in simulation activity can have a variety of learning objectives. This can be linked to the various perspectives associated with the more general field of action learning. For example, McLaughlin and Thorpe (1993) suggested that action learning in management education can be seen as acquisition of a 'toolbox of techniques', as 'therapy' and as a 'philosophy'.

When considering and specifying learning objectives for marketing simulation work, the likes of Burgoyne and Stuart (1976) provide a classic starting point. This is recognized by Fripp (1993) who provides a list of possible competence outcomes derived from these and other authors. This list ranges from the lower-level skills of 'basic facts and knowledge' through to meta-level skills such as 'balanced learning habits'.

One common learning objective for marketing simulations is to provide understanding of the nature of 'competition' linked to the development of skills in coping with the competitive world. Such a learning objective will not be confined to, but is more likely to be encountered in, marketing simulations. This particular objective is made explicit during introductory sessions with marketing undergraduates taking the marketing simulation course at the University of Lancaster.

Simulation exercises are also recognized as being high-involvement learning activities so the following quote from Moutinho and Paton (1990) is not untypical:

> Competition increases motivation – simulation allows one group to compete against another group over a period of time. This interaction is very motivating for the students in learning the course material and applying it to the simulation.

At first sight, this quote may present few difficulties but underlying questions will concern the nature of the course material, the relationships which can emerge between participating groups and the process of applying knowledge to experience. Providing thorough responses to such questions may require close scrutiny of the effectiveness of marketing simulations in promoting learning about competition.

MARKETING SIMULATIONS AND MODELS OF COMPETITION

The marketing educator in the UK can now choose from amongst a wide range of marketing simulation software packages. The more popular include *MARKSTRAT 2*, *BRANDMAPS*, *MARKOPS* and *THE MARKETING GAME!*. Perry and Euler (1989) reviewed these and a number of other marketing simulations. Over the last five years, the authors have made extensive use of THE MARKETING GAME! authored by Mason and Perreault (1987) and it is this marketing simulation which is currently used with marketing undergraduates.

THE MARKETING GAME! provides a simulation of word-processing and desktop software marketing. At the strategic level, it places considerable emphasis on segmentation and positioning and these issues become the key strategic dimensions which determine the relationships between the 'firms'. All decisions made by the four firms in any one industry are interactive. The basic structure of *THE MARKETING GAME!* is similar to that of most marketing simulation software. The review by Perry and Euler (1989) concluded that THE MARKETING GAME! satisfies more action learning criteria when compared with other commonly available simulations.

Models of competition are assumed and built into marketing simulation software and accompanying documentation. In the case of THE MARKETING GAME! and in common with most other marketing simulation exercises, the assumed model is one of oligopoly or imperfect competition where a small number of teams compete against each other as suppliers in a world where other actors in the network of relationships are reduced to ciphers.

The student manual for THE MARKETING GAME! includes the following sentence:

To develop effective strategies, a marketing manager must analyze available opportunities, understand and select target markets, and develop a marketing mix that will give the firm an advantage over competitors.

Practical constraints in software design mean that it is difficult if not impossible to include in full all the strategic, tactical and network considerations faced by the typical marketing manager. However, while any one design may go some way towards recognizing the various network relationships, the emphasis in marketing simulation software design is often on rivalry between competing teams. Furthermore, through curriculum design and the inclinations of participants, the emergence of a combative world can become the norm.

One major issue is therefore the suitability of such a model of competition given the needs of the participants, the intended learning objectives and the reality which the simulation experience is supposed to represent. The inherent model built into the software and the documentation may be seen as appropriate with respect to all these criteria. More likely is a recognition that there are limitations and that in adopting the simulation, some adaptation will be required to tease out those lessons which are considered to be important but perhaps not immediately apparent.

MARKETING SIMULATIONS AND CURRICULUM DESIGN

Evans and Sculli (1984) were concerned with the effectiveness of business games and their research suggested the following conclusion:

The degree of competition in the game influences the game's effectiveness; a highly competitive environment detracts from the game's value as a teaching aid.

Clearly, there are potential problems here with curriculum design if the learning objectives specify understanding and coping with competition. The role of the course facilitator and the nature of his or her involvement in the simulation process become critical in determining the learning outcomes. This conclusion drawn by Evans and Sculli suggests two related problems.

First, the mode of competition assumed in the simulation design or superimposed intentionally or otherwise by the curriculum will create or reinforce perceptions of the nature of competition. Second, participants who do not or cannot stand back from the competitive game element will recognize few of the more substantial lessons that can be drawn.

A classic example that covers both of these problems would be where individual or team assessment is based on or includes reference to the results of the simulated firms using conventional measures such as profit, contribution, market share and so on. Such an assessment procedure provides incentives for rivalry and can discourage what has been termed 'deep-level' learning.

When designing curricula, initial questions will concern what the simulation should achieve and how it should be achieved. There is also the related problem of measuring the degree of success or failure.

APPARENT LEARNING OUTCOMES

The time, effort and perhaps anxiety required to move beyond the comfort of apparent learning outcomes should not be underestimated. In the normal course of events and in most educational environments there is rarely the luxury of being able to resource an evaluation in depth. Trying to evaluate the outcomes of simulation work beyond the level of 'happiness sheets' is fraught with the kinds of problems addressed by Tonks and Wan (1991).

Course evaluation data on the use of THE MARKETING GAME! with undergraduates runs back several years. The unanimity of the data over time means that it is sufficient to consider the evaluation of events run in 1991.

The Students' Union at Lancaster produces an 'alternative prospectus' which concluded its review of the marketing simulation course with the following comment: 'Advice to students: good course that is hard work, yet good fun to do if you get a good group . . .. The majority of students said "do it"'.

More formal departmental evaluations in 1991 strongly support these sentiments. The three statements eliciting the highest degree of agreement were that the course, '. . . is an interesting and worthwhile scheme of study', 'Ranks highly amongst other courses taken' and '. . . is likely to prove vocationally useful'. Responses to open-ended questions concerning the 'best things' about the course included, 'fun, challenge, teamwork, learning, application of theory and practical nature'.

Rather than continue with such quotes it can perhaps simply be noted that these comments are typical of those reported by Moutinho (1988), Moutinho and Paton (1990) and more generally in the literature. Given that literature, these data have high face validity. Marketing simulations enjoy significant apparent success. The danger is that the face validity of apparent learning outcomes acts as a strong barrier to change. Caution must be exercised to ensure that measuring excitement and involvement is not confused with measuring useful learning.

What is of interest in the above data is the strong agreement amongst participants on the general effectiveness of simulations. Shortcomings identified by undergraduates can be grouped into two categories. The first focuses on inherent characteristics of the learning process mentioning time pressures, the volume of work and the use of group assessment. The second was not related directly to the course design and covered areas such as over-competitiveness and stress. Echoing these fears, the alternative prospectus warned, '. . . over-competitive, watch as your friends stab you in the back'.

These comments suggest a tendency for participants in a marketing simulation exercise to adopt a confrontational mode of behaviour with respect to
other teams even though there is no encouragement from the facilitators to do
so and, in the case of THE MARKETING GAME!, no particular requirement
in the simulation model to operate in this way.

It is to a discussion of this issue, the element of competition in marketing
simulations, that the rest of this chapter now moves.

METAPHORS IN MANAGEMENT

Language gives order to the world, so even the choice of vocabulary transmits,
and can legitimize, interpretations. Similarly, but usually with greater force,
the use of metaphors can provide single or multiple concepts of reality.

The use of metaphors in management and in attempts to understand
management is widespread. They can serve a number of purposes but
fundamental to all is the function of providing a framework for reality.
Metaphors drawn from biology, marriage, the world of sport and from warfare
have all gained substantial currency. Easton and Araujo (1991) provide an
assessment of the use of metaphors, mainly in the context of network analysis.
Mason (1991) summarizes the role of metaphors as follows:

> metaphors and the language that accompanies them are important not only
> as a means of expressing and communicating about an observation, but, in
> addition, . . . the metaphor itself is a fundamental determinant of how the
> world is viewed. It describes what is observed, which aspects are given
> attention, and which aspects are ignored.

Critical to the use of metaphors in management thinking and management
education is the extent to which a balanced rather than a simply colourful view
of reality is obtained. Metaphors work to convey or reinforce meaning and can
become models, hypotheses and theories.

Disciplines as disparate as military strategy, economics and social psychology have contributed to the creation of alternative models of inter-firm
relationships. The military metaphor has been explored at some length in the
marketing literature since Kotler and Singh (1981) mined the work of Von
Clausewitz and others. The essence of this model is that military ideas provide
an effective metaphor for business competition and the model is exemplified,
complete with illustrations of military hardware, in Ries and Trout (1986).
More recently, this metaphor has encountered increasing criticism from the
likes of Smith and Saker (1990) who identify a number of inadequacies
including the focus on conflict at the expense of recognizing various forms of
inter-firm behaviour including cooperation. However, the danger remains that
in spite of evidence to the contrary, traditional notions of competition are
shaped by repetition of the military metaphor and by high-involvement,
experiential and 'competitive' learning events such as those provided by
marketing simulations.

THE REALITY OF INTER-FIRM BEHAVIOUR

Marketing simulations are partial representations of reality. Simplifying assumptions are introduced to make the devices operational but other assumptions will reflect, at least in part, the constructs of the designer. Thus, in the case of promotional literature for MARKOPS (Larreche, 1988), it is not too difficult to identify the pervasive influence of the military metaphor:

> Take command of one (company) and measure your performance against three ferocious competitors.

and then

> Position your products against competitors' offerings and capture market share from them – before they capture it from you!

The challenge for the adopter of a marketing simulation, irrespective of the software used, is to check the extent to which the military metaphor or some other model of the competitive world is appropriate. Both marketing simulation software and the simulation process can encourage a combative interpretation. It may well be necessary to supplement this view with a richer model of inter-firm behaviour.

Easton (1990) provides such a model. Easton starts his article with a question:

> What are the relationships between competitors? It is not taken for granted that the relationship will be primarily a competitive one in the traditional sense.

Easton is concerned with the reality of competition as it exists, although the empirical evidence to support the model exists in a relatively fragmentary form.

Easton uses a continuum to depict the various forms of relationship. This continuum runs from conflict, through competition to coexistence, cooperation and then collusion. This continuum allows us to orientate the various models and metaphors which are available to describe the relationships that exist between the players in a supplying network.

At one extreme is conflict and this is described by Easton as:

> overt, directed towards the destruction or wounding of a rival whose objectives are seen as mutually incompatible, operated through direct interference, works outside accepted rules of market conduct, is independent of resources and is personal in nature.

The central point, coexistence, is described as, '. . . working towards a goal independent of others'. At the other extreme of the continuum collusion is described by Easton as, '. . . cooperative behaviour designed to injure or thwart a third party.'

Various types of inter-firm behaviour are possible and, in practice, any one organization may display a number of behaviours with respect to the various actors in the supplying network, including the final consumer. To suggest that a marketing simulation allows direct experience of competition, or words to a similar effect, might suggest something approximating the classical conditions of imperfect competition but in fact many conditions may prevail in reality.

It would be unrealistic for a marketing simulation exercise to mirror precisely a specified reality. Amongst other reasons, the existence of an end-point can drive the policies of the teams. In some instances it may also be undesirable for a simulation to mirror reality. For example, there could be an educational or training need which requires a focus on some aspect of inter-firm relationships which is only rarely encountered in practice. Also, some behaviours which might be available and encouraged in the simulation environment could be illegitimate in the world of work – and vice versa.

For most purposes, adopters of marketing simulations must consider the extent to which the simulation experience encourages or discourages what Easton identifies as a

... broader, more holistic and questioning attitude .. which explicitly recognizes the interactions between marketing strategy and the processes of relationships management amongst competing organizations.

Unless there are good reasons for some particular focus, the marketing simulation should demonstrate the range of possible inter-firm relationships and should allow participants to experience the operational implications of at least some of the alternatives. Above all, the marketing simulation experience should encourage awareness, understanding and evaluation of those alternatives.

DISCUSSION

With undergraduates and also with postgraduates and managers, the earlier perceptions of the authors when running THE MARKETING GAME! were that the participants shift towards either the 'conflict' mode identified by Easton or, less frequently, to the 'coexistence' mode. Data collected on an *ad hoc* basis generally supported these perceptions.

Examples of 'conflict' include sending representatives to other teams with the overt purpose of negotiating an alliance but with the covert purpose of occupying their decision time and degrading the quality of their subsequent decisions. Collecting (stealing) opponents' results and the more refined submission of fake decision sheets have also been encountered.

As for 'coexistence', the independence associated with this mode typically occurs when a team is regarded as a non-competitor simply because it occupies a niche in the market place which has little prominence in the marketing strategy of the other firm. Other modes of behaviour identified by Easton, notably 'cooperation' and 'collusion' and to a lesser extent 'competition', were rarely identified even though such behaviour is not unusual in the world which managers inhabit, postgraduates are generally familiar with, and undergraduates are about to join.

The 'conflict' and the 'coexistence' modes are not endemic in THE MARKETING GAME!. The software does not encourage, but does allow for, various kinds of relationships to emerge between the four teams in any one industry. The approach of the authors when designing curricula for managers, postgraduates and undergraduates had not been to promote any one particular kind of relationship. In spite of this, it was believed that the patterns identified had become prevalent to the point where greater intervention was required if marketing simulation experiences were to encourage a realistic view of competition.

With undergraduate marketing courses at Lancaster, the general policy of the authors is to adapt marketing simulation software and to intervene in the learning process to ensure or at least to encourage what Kolb (1971) has termed 'reflective observation' and 'abstract conceptualization'. Without such a policy it is felt, and to some extent known, that learning from the use of marketing simulations can be very shallow and short-lived. Such a policy requires time and resources to build various inputs to the basic simulation exercise. Without such inputs, the world represented by the marketing simulation is likely to be accepted uncritically. This is particularly important given the role of simulations in establishing and confirming concepts of competition.

If the course objectives built into the curriculum specify learning about competition through hands-on experience, at least some guidance must be provided to ensure that a realistic view of the subject is obtained by the participants. Given the attitude and behaviour patterns identified in some 20 runs of THE MARKETING GAME!, the extent of intervention on the undergraduate programme was increased in 1991/2 to include more specific material on the nature of inter-firm relationships using sources such as Easton (1990). While there was no attempt to coerce or in other ways directly influence the emergence of relationships, participants were encouraged to consider the alternatives in a simulation environment which did not inhibit any one form.

AN EXPLORATORY STUDY

The data which follow go beyond the status of happiness sheets but fall short of presenting a full and accurate assessment of actual behaviours and learning outcomes. The focus is on inter-firm relationships.

Having alerted undergraduates to the range of possible inter-firm relationships and building on material covered in a parallel course on marketing behaviour, it was possible to collect rather more data on this aspect of the simulation than in previous years. However, no direct comparison is possible with previous years.

Thirty-two undergraduate marketing major students followed the course. There were two industries, each containing four teams. Twenty-six students provided feedback via a self-completion questionnaire. The data were collected during a formal plenary session in which there was no conferring between teams or between team members.

| Relationship | Years | | | | | | | |
| | 1 to 4 | | 5 to 8 | | 9 to 12 | | Total | |
	n	%	n	%	n	%	n	%
Conflict	11	15	17	24	9	12	37	17
Competition	21	28	17	24	25	34	63	29
Coexistence	43	57	29	40	35	47	107	48
Cooperation			2	3	5	7	7	3
Collusion			7	10			7	3
Total	75		72		74		221	

Table 25.1 *Individual perceptions of all inter-team behaviour*

Of primary interest in the resulting data was participants' perceptions of the range of inter-team behaviours encountered during the simulation. While output measures of the relationships between teams can include the likes of respective market shares by segment, as in reality such measures can conceal as well as reveal. The concern was with inter-team behaviour and also the perceptions held of that behaviour. It does not follow that some particular behaviour implies ignorance of the alternatives.

In order to reflect the dynamics of the simulation in terms of levels of play and participants' experiences, the simulation time was divided into three periods – Years 1 to 4, Years 5 to 8 and Years 9 to 12. Each of the 26 respondents could report on three relationships, one with each of the other companies in the industry over three time periods, giving a maximum of 234 responses (26 × 3 × 3). Table 25.1 shows the relationships between all companies as reported by participants.

One general observation that can be made about the data is the reported occurrence and recognition of relationships from all parts of Easton's continuum. The inclusion of Easton's model and of other material into the course could be interpreted as having had the desired effect of giving participants a wider view of the possible relationships that might exist.

When the three phases of the simulation are examined the pattern seems to be one of a high concentration of 'coexistence' followed by some experimentation with a wider range of relationships, followed in turn by a reversion towards the initial pattern.

The balance between the relationships reported does raise a number of issues. By far the commonest form of relationship is reported as 'coexistence', accounting for just under half of all the reported relationships. 'Competition' accounts for 29 per cent of perceived relationships and 'conflict' for 17 per cent. What is clear from the data is the very low reporting of 'cooperation' and 'collusion', together accounting for only 6 per cent of the relationships.

While the data suggest the achievement of some success in promoting a wider range of behaviours, notably a reduction in the amount of reported 'conflict', and an apparent increase in the amount of 'competition', is there evidence of too much comfort, manifested by the high levels of 'coexistence' throughout the simulation? The patterns in the data might also point to a more sophisticated realization by the teams that one consequence of effective segmentation and positioning can be a reduction in the intensity of competition. However, the low level of 'cooperation' may be of some concern since it suggests that the opportunities stemming from such arrangements were not recognized or realized.

To identify the extent to which these relationships emerged during the simulation rather than being a result of deliberate design on the part of the teams, respondents were asked two further questions concerning their own behaviour and that of the other teams in the industry. There is little to distinguish the two sets of responses. The question about the respondents' own teams averaged 3.12 (where 1 equals 'emerged' and 5 equals 'designed') and the industry figure was 3.44. Both sets of data confirm that the patterns which developed were deliberate, at least in part, and not accidental. There is also some hint of participants attributing more deliberation and design on their competitors' part than on their own!

An issue surrounding the data is the extent of intra-team consistency in the perception of the relationship. There is a very high degree of consistency within the teams. Altogether there were 63 sets of ratings. On 36 occasions, the members of the team were in complete agreement and only one relationship was mentioned. On 23 occasions a single member of the team reported differently from his or her colleagues. There were only four occasions when two members of a team dissented from the consensus.

While there is good agreement within the teams it is important to assess the validity of these ratings. Consequently, participants were asked to provide examples of incidents or activities that they felt were illustrative of the relationships formed. These data suggest that the ideas contained in the Easton continuum had been applied correctly. The following quote is interesting in that it provides some insight into how relationships are formed, the shape that emerges and the consequences:

> Impact were very destructive, starting a price war . . . results went missing in period 5, suspicion centred on Impact as they were our main competitors . . . we (Achtung) did a deal to swap market research with ATM and then agreed with them and Impact to use pioneering advertising in the second product.

In the same industry, Impact's general behaviour clearly caused some concern for this member of ATM: '. . . then Impact didn't do pioneering advertising in final year as agreed.'

Perhaps this illustrates the problems of trust and the absence of sanction in the simulation and the risks of attempting to widen the portfolio of relationships in an industry.

The speed with which relationships in the simulation can sour is evidenced by this comment from the second industry made by a member of PC-U-Like who, describing a conflict cited, 'the contractual dispute with Extra

Ordinaire . . .' Unlike the teams in the first industry, this agreement to share market research had been formed into a contract with penalty clauses. Clearly the parties were less naive but in the contract there was still sufficient ambiguity to cause a considerable degree of friction and bitterness. Giving their account of this incident one member of Extra Ordinaire described how,

We made a contract with PC-U-Like which they broke. This resulted in bad relations with them . . .. We shared market research with Puce Elec so that they would have more money to use to compete with PC-U-Like.

PC-U-Like generated a high degree of animosity that stemmed not only from the decisions they were making in terms of strategy, segmentation and positioning but also from the way they conducted themselves. The source of their conflict with Puce Elec seems to have been 'Personal comments made about Puce and its performance (usually derogatory and supercilious)'.

As well as looking at intra-team consistency in the perceptions, it is also interesting to consider the inter-team perceptions. In a recent paper reporting research undertaken in Italy, Havila and Sandstrom (1991) observed the extent to which parties to a relationship held quite different views over such basic issues as the number of contacts made between the parties, the nature of those contacts and their outcomes. Such asymmetry clearly poses problems when describing the minutiae of a relationship. Further analysis of the data to create difference scores for perceptions of inter-team behaviour showed some asymmetry, usually slight, between the perceptions held by two teams on the nature of their relationship. This is in line with the findings of Havila and Sandstrom.

While this analysis suggested less consensus than the intra-team ratings, there was reasonable consensus about the nature and dynamics of relationships between the teams in the simulation.

This section has reported the data from what is thought to be the first attempt to measure systematically the inter-team relationships in a 'competitive' simulation exercise. The data are not conclusive but they do demonstrate the importance of alerting participants through appropriate interventions to the range of inter-firm relationships that can exist in reality and which might not be fully represented in any one simulation exercise.

CONCLUSIONS

In this exploratory study, an attempt has been made to measure the inter-team relationships established during a typical run of a 'competitive' marketing simulation exercise. The results present a different picture from that usually given. The prevalence of 'coexistence' is counter to the literature which typically reports relationships which Easton has described as 'conflict' and 'competition'.

Drawing a distinction between the intended, apparent and actual outcomes of a simulation can identify the extent to which 'competition' and more especially 'conflict' are anticipated by, and are far more visible to, the simulation facilitator. That visibility colours perceptions of the nature of the exercise. Only by measuring the relationships does it become clear that such highly visible and often exciting behaviours are common but not necessarily typical. The more neutral relationship of 'coexistence' is less obtrusive and is unheeded. Given the earlier evidence of student feedback, there is a further suggestion that unless participants are alerted to the range of inter-firm relationships they will also develop a partial view and implement limited behaviours.

Available marketing simulation software designs tend to be based on particular models of the nature of inter-firm relationships. Furthermore, previous life experiences and the process of involvement in marketing simulation exercises can encourage certain patterns of behaviour. One outcome is that false representations can be created or inappropriate preconceptions reinforced. To varying degrees, the available marketing simulations are capable of supporting behaviours drawn from across Easton's continuum but what has to be addressed is the extent to which those behaviours are in practice confined to certain positions. From this, the true effectiveness of marketing simulations in providing useful experience about the full range of inter-firm relationships and skill development in coping with those relationships needs close attention.

If these difficulties associated with marketing simulations are accepted, then in curriculum design and subsequent theoretical inputs and debriefs there is a responsibility to not only make participants aware of the range of relationships but, if possible, to create a simulation experience which fosters experience of the range of relationships.

Finally, the excitement of simulations should not be allowed to conceal their limitations. Enthusiastic course evaluation data giving the impression that all is well should not hinder critical development of the method. The exploratory study reported here provides a limited example of a common problem. Any educator involved in learning through simulation must face the difficulty of how to approach and measure actual learning outcomes. It is easy to report the success of learning through simulation based on assertion and the more superficial measures of apparent learning.

REFERENCES

Burgoyne, J G and Stuart, R (1976) 'The nature, use and acquisition of managerial skills and other attributes', *Personnel Review*, 5,4 19–29.

Easton, G (1990) 'Relationships among competitors', in Day, G, Weitz, B and Wensley, R (eds) *The Interface of Marketing and Strategy*, Jai Press, London.

Easton, G and Araujo, L (1991) 'Language, metaphors and networks', working paper, *Department of Marketing, University of Lancaster.*

Evans, W A and Sculli, D (1984) 'An evaluation of business games with respect to the development of managerial talent', *Simulation/Games for Learning*, 14,1, 3–13.

Fripp, J (1993) *Learning Through Simulations*, London, McGraw-Hill.

Havila, V and Sandstrom, M (1991) 'Supplier customer relationships: a dyad or a triad', *Seventh IMP Conference - International Business Networks: Evolution, Structure and Management*, Uppsala.

Hirst, M (1991) 'Personal computer software for use in marketing education (Part 1)', *Journal of Marketing Management*, 7, 77–92.

Kolb, D (1971) *Experiential Learning: experience as the source of learning*, New Jersey, Prentice-Hall.

Kotler, P and Singh, R (1980) 'Marketing warfare in the 1980s', *Journal of Business Strategy*, Winter, 30–41.

Larreche, J C (1988) *Markops: the simulation for marketing training*, London, StratX.

Lewis, R (1991) 'Computers in higher education teaching and learning: some aspects of research and development', *The CTISS File*, 11 March, 3–7.

Long, G and Tonks, D G (1991) 'The hidden rhetoric of "The Marketing Game!"' *Marketing Education Conference Proceedings*, Cardiff Business School, 646–669.

McLaughlin, H and Thorpe, R (1993) 'Action learning – a paradigm in emergence: the problems facing a challenge to traditional management education and development', *British Journal of Management*, 4, 19–27.

Mason, R M (1991) 'The role of metaphors in strategic information systems planning', *Journal of Management Information Systems*, 8,2, 11–30.

Mason, C H and Perreault, W D (1987) *The Marketing Game!* Homewood, Ill., Irwin.

Middleton, B and Long, G (1990) 'Marketing skills: critical issues in marketing education and training', *Journal of Marketing Management*, 5,3, 325–342.

Moutinho, L (1988) 'Learning/teaching effectiveness of marketing simulation games', *Quarterly Review of Marketing*, 13,2, 10–14.

Moutinho, L and Paton, R (1990) 'Developing computer exercises and simulations in marketing, or how to boost student motivation', *Marketing Education Group Conference Proceedings*, Oxford Polytechnic, 1014–1034.

Perry, C and Euler, T (1989) 'Marketing simulations in tertiary education: a review and future directions', *European Journal of Marketing*, 23,4, 40–49.

Ries, A and Trout, J (1986) *Marketing Warfare*, New York, McGraw-Hill.

Smith, G and Saker, J (1990) 'Competition or cooperation?: The military metaphor in marketing – a bridge too far', *Marketing Education Group Conference Proceedings*, Oxford Polytechnic, 1299–1321.

Tonks, D G and Wan, A (1991) 'The hidden curricula of marketing', *Simulation/Games for Learning*, 23, 3 September, 220–236.

ABOUT THE AUTHORS

David Tonks and George Long are in the *Department of Marketing, School of Management, University of Lancaster, Lancaster LA1 4YX*.

Chapter 26

Computerized tutor support systems: the tutor's role, needs and tasks

Jeremy J S B Hall

ABSTRACT

This chapter identifies areas where software can support the tutor running computerized business simulations and so improve tutoring efficiency, effectiveness and consistency.

Traditionally, computerization has focused on the simulation model and, by eliminating manual calculations, this has improved tutoring efficiency. However, modern microcomputers allow the role of the computer to be extended to provide timely and pertinent information that not only supports the tutor administratively but also facilitates and helps the management of learning.

Taking a 'systems approach', this chapter starts from a discussion of the tutor's role, needs and tasks. This discussion serves to suggest areas where software can support the tutor and based on this an architecture for a Tutor Support System (TSS) is described and discussed.

ADMINISTRATOR, FACILITATOR OR MANAGER?

Rollier (1992) proposes that 'facilitator' is the most appropriate term to apply to the tutor's role since he feels 'administrator' is too limiting and 'instructor' implies controlling and directing the learning process (teaching). In this context he suggests that the 'facilitator' should stay 'in the background as much as possible'. Jones (1991) takes a more extreme view, suggesting that 'contamination occurs when a teacher treats the event as a guided exercise and encroaches on the role autonomy of the participants'.

Undoubtedly, the simulation tutor's role differs from that of the teacher in the lecture room. Although participants have to be free to make decisions and make mistakes, the tutor still must ensure that each participant learns. This is particularly important on executive short courses for otherwise the participants will view the session as a waste of their (valuable) time.

Hall (1977) describes the directing staff's (tutors') tasks under the heading 'exercise management'. In this context the student-centred nature of simulations can be discussed in terms of delegation where the tutor delegates the authority and responsibility for learning to the participants. However, in the context of managerial delegation, this does not mean that the manager (or here, the tutor) totally relinquishes managerial authority or responsibility (Dunham and Pierce, 1989). The tutor is, still, ultimately responsible for ensuring that learning takes place and tutoring is a management process that can be enhanced through an appropriate computerized Tutor Support System (TSS).

Although suggesting that the tutor should be viewed as a 'manager' of learning, it is reasonable to propose that this role involves:

- administration,
- facilitation, and
- management.

The administration task

The administration task covers decision entry, making calculations, producing results and record keeping (for the end review and debriefing session).

For computer-based simulations the calculation task has been largely eliminated with the tutor reduced to machine minding (typing decisions, initiating the simulation, requesting reports, feeding and nurturing the printer). Generally, decision entry is still done by the tutor but this need is lessening, due to the availability of direct access games (Elgood, 1993), computer networks and Decision Support Systems (DSSs). Direct access games involve teams using their own computer with a stand-alone simulation. Networks allow teams to enter their decisions from and receive results in syndicate rooms. DSSs allow, in the absence of a network, decisions to be extracted on disc for entry into the tutor's computer. Printers, with their inclination to jam, still present a problem. Record-keeping is still necessary to ensure that the tutor is provided with information for the review session – experience suggests that one cannot rely on teams keeping adequate, unbiased records for this purpose.

The facilitation task

Facilitation involves ensuring teams have the necessary materials and information to proceed with learning. It relies on teams requesting support and therefore is a passive, reactive activity that does not interfere with participants' autonomy. Information requests can be classified as follows:

- rule clarification,
- simulation support, and
- knowledge support.

- *Rule clarification*: Elgood (1993) discusses this as follows:

    The imaginary nature of a game or simulation always leaves scope for genuine misunderstandings about what the rules mean, where the game boundaries lie, and how the various figures are made up.

Consequentially, the tutor must be on the look-out for these misunderstandings and be able to correct them. If this is not done then participants will become demotivated and treat the simulation as a 'game'. Generally, the need for rule clarification occurs on decision entry.

■ *Simulation support*: although simulations are simplifications of the real world it is not reasonable or possible to provide totally comprehensive documentation, spoken briefing or computer printouts, especially since, for written documentation, experience suggest that these are not read. If the computer reports are too long then 'information overload' will occur. For the spoken brief, Greenblat and Duke (1981) suggest:

> Keep the introduction short! As questions arise later, you will be able to deal with them. Covering all points at the beginning is a poor idea, for players will forget those not seen as relevant because the questions have not yet arisen.

Thus, as the simulation proceeds there will be *ad hoc* needs to explain results and clarify the simulation. It is a major help if additional information is provided by the TSS to allow the tutor to answer routine questions quickly and completely.

■ *Knowledge support*: besides supplying additional information explaining results, there may be a need to provide business 'knowledge' to stimulate thought. Keys and Leftwich (1985) address this problem by providing, in the participant's manual, readings on business policy and strategy. However, there is the risk that participants will not read such material or that it is insufficiently comprehensive to cover all knowledge needs. So the tutor will be required to discuss relevant management issues in a team's syndicate room. The purpose of knowledge support is to fill gaps in participants' knowledge rather than reprise the complete course and experiences, thus it is a focused task that differs from team to team and course to course. It demands the tutor either having suitable knowledge or access to it.

The management task

As described at the start of this chapter, I suggest the role of the tutor is to manage learning. This involves a need to pro-actively determine barriers to learning, supplying guidance and support and thus ensuring learning objectives are met. This requires the tutor to:

■ manage the learning process, and
■ continuously assess learning,

in a way that does not usurp the participants' authority but, rather, encourages learning.

■ *Managing the learning process*: the management of the learning process (Figure 26.1) involves the tutor analysing the current situation, diagnosing

ANALYSIS

DIAGNOSIS

FEEDBACK

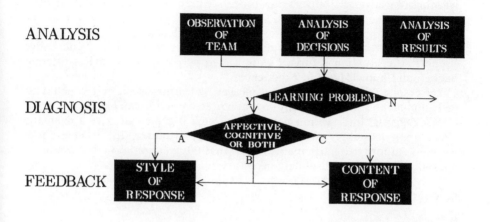

Figure 26.1 *The management process*

learning problems and, if necessary, providing additional feedback to participants (Hall and Cox, 1993).

Ideally, the tutor will gather information by observing the teams, precautionally scanning decisions and evaluating results. Based on this, an attempt will be made to decide whether there are learning problems. If these exist it is necessary to decide whether the problem is cognitive (a lack of knowledge or experience) or affective (a motivational, team-working problem) or both. Based on this the tutor must choose the style of the response and its content.

The problem facing the tutor is that of resources. It is not unusual for a single tutor to manage as many as six teams of six or more participants, each located in separate syndicate rooms which may be spread across a hotel or training centre. Further, the need for learning efficiency means that there is continuous pressure to minimize simulation duration. Burgess (1990) states:

> Quite often operators of simulation games are caught up with the sheer mechanics of operating the simulation; these games typically operate on hourly cycles. The operators do not have time to consider deeply the player performance and the quality of the decisions made.

Consequently, the tutor does not have time to do all the tasks necessary to ensure learning effectiveness nor adequately concentrate on tutoring the weaker teams. Thus it is necessary to transfer routine work to the TSS, leaving the tutor free to concentrate on 'managing learning'.

■ *Assessing learning*: undoubtedly, the choice and use of any andragogic or pedagogic device or method should be based on the need to fulfil defined learning objectives. However, the student-centred nature of simulations presents particular problems. Participants' freedom of action means that the pattern of progress and specific issues explored can, and often do, vary between runs of the same simulation. As discussed above in 'Knowledge support', the situation is further complicated by participants having different background knowledge and experience.

Yet despite this and the fact that measuring learning is, at best, a nebulous task, it must be done continually so that corrective action can be taken. Elgood (1993) suggests 'Intervention part-way through a game can have a dramatic effect upon learning (and upon motivation)'. However, the delegation of learning authority to participants means that intervention must be minimized and only occur when absolutely necessary.

Thus part of the tutor's task is assessing learning and deciding when it is necessary to take action. Two key indicators of learning are:

■ 'business success', and
■ reducing 'mistakes'.

'Business success': although it is beyond the scope of this chapter to discuss 'business success', its measurement by the tutor is important for two reasons.

First, it is reasonable to suggest that as a group learns it will run a more successful business (otherwise what would be the purpose of management education?). Consequentially, it is argued that learning correlates with business success and that by assessing business success one can judge learning.

Second, although 'learning' is the key (cognitive) objective, generally there is an affective need for competitive success. Lundy (1984) discusses competition and its undesirable affective effects. However, she does not differentiate between competition in terms of 'winning' the game, and competition in terms of a natural and necessary real-world strategic activity. For strategy-level simulations, the competition between teams is vital. (Smith and Walsh (1978) while discussing business strategy in general, state that 'competition is so crucially important in the determination of strategies that we have taken the liberty of listing it as a separate element and discussing it first'.)

However, this is not meant to discount the demotivating and counter-productive impact of 'losing'. It is argued that only by measuring business success can the tutor predict possible motivational problems and take appropriate actions.

In the real world it is the purpose of managers to be more successful than their competitors, so the results of successful companies will diverge from those of unsuccessful ones. However, for simulations, divergence will cause motivational problems and suggest learning differences and difficulties. This suggests that simulations should be convergent (Figure 26.2). Convergence suggests that teams are reaching similar levels of (cognitive) learning. Further,

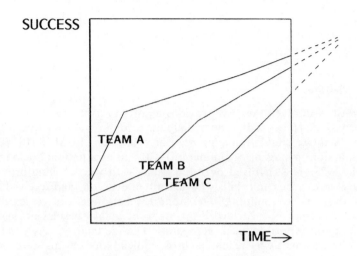

Figure 26.2 *Success convergence*

teams will perceive equality in terms of competitive success and therefore convergence ensures affection.

'*Dans ce meillure des mondes possibles*' (Voltaire): the design of the simulation should facilitate this convergence. However, in practice it is necessary for the tutor to take actions to ensure convergence, although it is not necessary for this convergence to occur during the simulation provided participants perceive that convergence will, eventually, occur. Therefore the TSS should not only measure success but provide facilities to support convergence.

Reducing 'mistakes': besides measuring success there is the possiblility of measuring failure – the propensity for teams to make 'mistakes'. These mistakes can be measured in terms of costs or lost profits. The simulation GLOBAL OPERATIONS measures lost profit so, for instance, if a team mismatches demand and production capacity this either leads to lost sales (and profit) or idle plant (and unrecovered overheads).

A tutor experienced with a particular simulation is often able to scan a team's decisions and predict problems. The experienced tutor will assess relative business strengths and weaknesses from team results. Inexperience and time pressures mean that the identification of 'mistakes' is often not possible. The TSS should provide a means of measuring and tracking 'mistakes'.

THE TUTOR SUPPORT SYSTEM

There is a need, therefore, for a software-based tutor support system that provides:

■ audit reports,

- commentaries,
- decision screening, and
- success measurement.

Audit reports

At the most basic level, the TSS provides reports to explain how team results were arrrived at. These 'audit reports' help the tutor answer team questions and therefore facilitate simulation support. For example, TEAMSKILL (a complex production management simulation) was run as a national management contest in 1978. This involved over 100 teams with wide-ranging production knowledge, experience and skills who submitted decisions and received results by post over several months. To support teams and ensure learning, a telephone help line was provided. For this to be viable, besides normal team results, an audit report detailed the operation of the factory, why production targets were not met, why machines broke down, why set-ups were late etc. Consequentially, it was usually possible to answer questions immediately without the tutor having to spend time re-analysing the problem, re-running the model or performing additional, *ad hoc*, calculations. This not only saved tutoring time but the rapid authoritative response increased the participants' trust in the learning experience.

Commentaries

Commentaries take the approach forward. Audit reports are, largely, passive. They are designed to support response to team-initiated questions. However, they can be used more proactively. Here, the tutor uses the audit report to identify team learning needs and problems. Based on this diagnosis the tutor, without being asked, discusses the matter with teams. For instance, in TEAMSKILL, if production targets were regularly missed because of stock shortages, the tutor might discuss inventory management and budgeting with the team. This proactive use suggests a second TSS processing need. Here, data from team results and the model are refined further.

For instance, INTEX (an FMCG SBU strategy-level simulation) produces, for the tutor, a series of reports that treat each market sector as a profit centre. One report shows whether a sector made a profit or loss and a second provides information on profit and contribution margins and promotion as a percentage of sales income. Not only does this allow individual sectors to be assessed but also, by comparing sectors, it is possible to assess whether strategy is consistent between sectors. These commentaries involve further processing of team data. Use, by the tutor, is to diagnose problems, to provide feedback and to provide a basis for the simulation review. Feedback is in two stages. First, the appropriate report is supplied to teams without comment to stimulate thought about markets and to encourage analysis. Later, if necessary, a general discussion of profit margins and promotional strategy is initiated to encourage teams to look at these issues.

Decision screening

Decision entry is a key point in the decision-making cycle with conflicting tutoring needs. Teams await the results of their decisions with anticipation and therefore rapid input and turn-around is vital. However, if there is a misunderstanding of the rules or poor management thinking, a 'bad' decision may be entered and processed (with catastrophic results). Even if this does not demand re-running it will be disrupting and demotivating.

Decision screening is necessary and, in terms of basic data processing theory (Hall, 1979), is well established. Yet as late as 1990, in a critique of software it was stated that 'There are many improvements that should be made to these input programs' (Teach, 1990).

Besides character checking (to protect against typing errors), range checks serve to define the range of permissible values. Yeo (1991) suggests a single, permissible, band. However, A MANAGEMENT EXPERIENCE draws on statistical quality control theory (Grant, 1952) with two levels of range checks. The wider range defines permissible entries and serves to protect the simulation model from extreme entries (such as negative prices) while not constraining decision-making freedom. The narrower, warning limits are advisory. They suggest to the tutor that a problem may exist that should be investigated, and where action may be necessary.

Beyond this basic data verification, there is the facility to check against the database (Hall, 1979). In A MANAGEMENT EXPERIENCE, the decision screening software includes a 'sophistry screen' that looks for conflicts between decisions, historical trends, team assumptions and their objectives. This software traps sophistic decisions where, for example, prices are raised, promotion cut while there is over-capacity and, long term, sales demand is falling.

Besides helping simulations where the tutor enters decisions, decision screening becomes essential where the simulation is network-based or direct access.

Success measurement

Success measurement attempts to measure and predict cognitive (learning) and affective (motivational) problems. Its purpose is to provide the tutor with information about trends in relative business success and the incidence of poor decision making (mistakes). Its use is *not* to 'choose a winner' and, arguably, teams should never know that it is occurring. Because of this it is, perhaps, immaterial which measure or measures of business success are used. Further, since it is usual for teams to start from the same position running businesses in the same market, with the same financial structure, there tends to be a correlation between different measures.

Besides providing a measure of total business success (such as ROI earnings or market share) there are opportunities to use output from the commentaries and decision screening to measure weaknesses. Thus A MANAGEMENT

EXPERIENCE not only measures profits lost due to lack of business efficiency but also the incidence of weaknesses and sophistic decisions.

Because of the need for team results to converge, the measurement of team success must not just involve measuring on a period-by-period basis but also the projection of trends and the identification of teams whose performance is either extremely bad or extremely good.

A PRACTICAL EXAMPLE

Although TSSs have been evolving over several years it is only comparatively recently that large, powerful microcomputers have become commonly available. This availability provided the impetus to add a comprehensive TSS to an existing, established, business simulation.

A MANAGEMENT EXPERIENCE was originally developed in 1976 to run on the GEISCO computer time-sharing service. In the early 1980s the initial FORTRAN version was rewritten in BASIC for Tandy III microcomputers and subsequently transferred to IBM-compatible microcomputers. In this form the complete program consisted of 853 statements and of these 209 statements were the core simulation model (with the rest for decision entry, report printing and file handling). In 1992 this version was updated to include a comprehensive TSS and has been run regularly since. This update did not change the core simulation model and basic I/O. Commentaries and success measurement were added and audit reporting and decision screening were very extensively expanded. The extent of the software expansion is illustrated by the size of the new version that consists of over 3,000 statements. This represents a nearly fourfold increase in size. However, since the TSS is driven by the simulation model it is more meaningful to compare the TSS code with the core simulation model. For every statement in the core model the TSS requires ten statements.

Runs of the new simulation on courses and discussions with experienced simulation users suggest that the TSS provides significant help. But, since this investigation has been on an informal basis and the simulation has not been used by inexperienced tutors, there is still a concern that the additional data provided to the tutor may be overwhelming.

CONCLUSION

By encapsulating the tutor's routine job in software, the TSS ensures that business simulations are used more effectively, efficiently and consistently. More time can be spent by the tutor on strategic learning issues. The TSS serves to reveal more of the simulation model and its dynamic response to the tutor. For the experienced tutor this provides opportunities to enrich the learning experience. For the less experienced tutor the TSS provides the facility to answer questions authoritatively. For new users of simulations or those new to a particular simulation, the additional information provided shortens the time required to become familiar with the simulation.

Philosophically, the TSS assumes that the tutor is and will remain a key catalyst for learning. Yet intelligent systems and distant learning may reduce or eventually eliminate this role.

Certainly, the TSS and the overhead that it adds to a simulation means that design is not a matter of concentration on the simulation model but of building a complete learning 'system'.

REFERENCES

Burgess, T (1990) 'Management simulation-games and artificial intelligence', *Simulation/Games for Learning*, 20, 3.

Dunham, R B and Pierce, J L (1989) *Management*, Scott, Foreseman and Company, Glenview, Ill.

Elgood, C (19930 *Handbook of Management Games*, Gower, Aldershot.

Grant, L (1952) *Statistical Quality Control*, McGraw-Hill, New York.

Greenblat, C S and Duke D (1981) *Principles and Practices of Gaming-Simulation*, Sage, Beverly Hills, CA.

Hall, J J S B (1977) *DECISION - Administration Guide*, Hall Marketing, London.

Hall, J J S B (1979) *How to Pass Examinations in Data Processing*, Cassell, London.

Hall, J J S B and Cox, B M (1993) 'Computerised management games: the feedback process and servomechanism analogy', in Percival, F, Lodge, S and Saunders, D (eds) *The Simulation and Gaming Yearbook 1993*, Kogan Page, London.

Jones, K (1991) 'Using computer-assisted simulations and avoiding computer-hindered simulations', *Simulation and Gaming*, 22, 2, 234-8.

Keys, B and Leftwich, H (1985) *The Executive Simulation*, Kendal/Hunt Publishing, Dubuque, Iowa.

Lundy, J (1984) 'The effects of competition in business games', *Gaming and Simulation*, 10.

Rollier, B (1992) 'Observations of a corporate facilitator', *Simulation and Gaming*, 23, 4, 442-56.

Smith III, S and Walsh, Jr, J E (1978) *Strategies in Business*, Wiley, Chichester.

Teach, R D (1990) 'Designing business simulations', in Gentry, W (ed.) *Guide to Business Gaming and Experiential Learning*, Nichols/GP Publishers, West Brunswick and Kogan Page, London.

Yeo, G K (1991) 'A framework for developing simulation game systems', *Simulation and Gaming*, 22, 3, 308-27.

Simulations cited

TEAMSKILL (1978) Hall Marketing, London.

A MANAGEMENT EXPERIENCE (1976, 1992) Hall Marketing, London.

GLOBAL OPERATIONS (1981) Hall Marketing, London.

INTEX (1984) Hall Marketing, London.

ABOUT THE AUTHOR

Jeremy Hall is owner of Hall Marketing, a firm specializing in the development of simulations for management development. With over 25 years' experience in designing simulation models, he has developed more than three dozen computerized business simulations covering most aspects of management education.

He is the author of two books on computing and numerous articles on management use of computers and computer-aided management education. He is on the editorial advisory board of *The Journal of Management Development*.

He has a degree in electrical engineering from Imperial College London and is currently doing research into computer aided management education, on a part time basis, at Imperial College. His research interests are Tutor Support Systems and Participant Support Systems and their application for andragogic education.

Address for correspondence: Hall Marketing, Studio 11, Colman's Wharf, 45 Morris Road, London E14 6PA.

Chapter 27

Simulating the human problems of acquisitions and mergers

David Cain

ABSTRACT

The author describes how a computer-based business simulation was adapted to provide part-time MBA students with a convincing experience of the human problems associated with mergers and acquisitions. In terms of the psychological discomfort experienced by individuals, the difficulties of managing inter- as well as intra-group relationships and, not least, the problems of establishing a revised business strategy to cope with a major environmental change, the outcomes of the simulation parallel much real-world experience. Through this form of experiential learning the simulation promotes the personal development of students. This is achieved through the integration of theory with experience, and by enabling students to assess their own capacity for diagnosing problems and applying the skills required to handle the psychologically complex situations which can arise even where the scale is small and the technology straightforward.

The need for senior managers to combine the rational analytical skills associated with economic performance with a high degree of social and cultural sensitivity is, today, widely recognized. Arguably, the need has always existed, even if it has not always been satisfied. What now gives it added relevance is the familiar phenomenon of increasing environmental change. If the strategic response required is to be carried through successfully, managers will also have to demonstrate their ability to cope with the human problems involved. In turn, this raises a question about how far managers can be prepared for such a role. The frequently reported problems of implementing change suggest that even experienced managers have the utmost difficulty in coping with the newly-encountered problems posed by major organizational change, such as rationalization, mergers or acquisitions. But how, precisely, should we aim to supplement their experience so that managers have a better chance of identifying the nature of the problems they will face, and developing possible solutions?

The question is particularly pertinent in the context of a Masters in Business Administration (MBA) programme, with its emphasis on strategic issues and aimed at meeting the needs of future senior managers. At Newcastle Business School, we were conscious of the need to extend existing opportunities for personal development to include experience of inter- as well as intra-group processes. At the same time, we wanted to make sure that the context was one in which strategic decisions were required to ensure competitive survival in a dynamic environment. In this way students would, it was hoped, come to recognize the links between the dynamics of the group and the nature of the decisions emerging from the processes employed. Moreover, by going beyond the conventional format of competition between single company teams, we could greatly increase the probability that strategy formulation and its subsequent development would be experienced as a social and political, not simply analytical, process – with significant psychological consequences for those involved.

In many respects the acquisition process is an ideal vehicle for this purpose. Typically, strategies need to be reviewed and, where possible, integrated; objectives, performance standards and resource allocations have to be sorted out; above all, there are the difficult decisions about the people affected by the change. If potential synergies are to be realized, the social and cultural consequences of the change will have to be recognized and the strong feelings likely to be aroused taken into account.

THE DESIGN

We chose to build on our experience of the widely-used EXECUTIVE 300 computer-based simulation, from April Training Executive Ltd, which makes extensive use of data from the car industry, to provide an environment which students find convincing.

The student group – managers and professional specialists drawn from a range of public and private sector backgrounds – were already familiar with the basic structure of the simulation through their experience, six months earlier, of competing within an industry made up, in the conventional way, of single company groups. In particular, they had developed some facility in the use of the 'what if' model available with the simulation which allows teams to explore possible strategies and identify key relationships before committing themselves to a final set of decisions in each round.

On this occasion we introduced the 'Financial Executive' version of the simulation which allows more choice in funding and investment decisions, including the purchase of up to 5 per cent of a competitor's equity in any one round. Since this mechanism alone would not allow participating companies to achieve control of competitors in an acceptable time period (even assuming they wanted to), the teams were informed that their companies were subsidiaries of conglomerates. Like their real-world counterparts, these conglomerates were capable of making divestment and acquisition decisions which reflected their own objectives rather than the performance of their subsidiaries. Thus a company might be sold in spite of, or even because of, the success it had achieved.

While the simulation itself took place over three days in a residential setting, pre-event preparation was seen as an important foundation for the learning we wanted to promote. The probability of take-over activity was clearly signalled. The students were invited to reflect on the nature of the problems likely to be experienced and to develop their personal ideas for coping with them. To assist this process, research papers discussing the issues associated with post-acquisition integration and strategic control were made available. A summary of the ideas developed at this stage formed part of the post-event assignment, in which students were invited, *inter alia*, to review their pre-event ideas in the light of the experience of the simulation.

Team selection was determined by the tutors, care being taken both to establish different memberships from those employed in the earlier simulation and to provide, as far as possible, a balance of skills and personal character-istics. No leaders were appointed or roles assigned.

OPERATION

Each team began as an independent company competing in the simulated car industry. Updated market research information was made available which enabled teams to extend their understanding of the industry structure. A period of two hours was allowed for the first set of decisions to enable the teams to assess their strategic alternatives using the 'what if' model to explore the implications of each (if well implemented, both differentiation and cost leadership strategies have been very successfully employed). The model incorporates the impact of competition in the industry but the additional impact of the other teams in the event can, of course, only be known when the decisions from each team have been 'saved' and all discs loaded to the umpire's master program. This provides each team with hard copy output including P/L statement, B/S, cash flow, R&D results, product performance, details of environmental changes affecting the industry or particular companies, and competitor performance data (if required). This plethora of information presents teams with the challenging problem of managing the analysis and review process.

The processes and dynamics displayed by each group were monitored by staff observers moving around the groups to allow them to identify their characteristic styles and cultures. After the first four decision periods, staff met as a group to determine which of the four companies would become the parent and which the subsidiary in the new industry structure composed of two competing groups. (This decision process was recorded on video and played back to the students as part of the post event review).

In making these choices, full account was taken of the normal economic performance criteria, such as growth of sales, profitability and share rating. Past experience of the simulation has shown that at this early stage, groups which display superior planning and decision-making skills have not always translated them into measurable results. In making our selection, we therefore had to anticipate the tensions which might result from allowing one group which is more successful in performance terms, to take responsibility for a better organized, but so far less successful group. Ground rules issued with the take-over announcement specifically ruled out the possibilities of resignation or dismissal as means of coping with the task of integration.

Predictably, the decision to form a group made up of a financially successful parent and an organizationally strong subsidiary, received a hostile reception from the subordinate group. The negative effects of take-over were experienced intensely by the individuals involved who reported feelings of shock and disbelief, anger, resentment, depression and tension.

These were attributed to the perceived unfairness and irrationality of the decision and a strong sense of having 'lost' to a group seen as less competent ('Can "they" expect to manage us?'). Not surprisingly, attempts by the parent group to establish a basis for cooperation were given a cool reception. Each group believed that the other was guilty of withholding information and remained sceptical about the possibility of achieving fruitful cooperation. Formal communications therefore proved difficult.

Informally, even humorous asides were likely to be attributed with an edge their authors may not have intended. Slowly, evidence of cooperation emerged but was not sufficient to overcome the loss of motivation in the subsidiary and the decline in performance which accompanied it. The parent group continued to make effective decisions governing the performance of its own business unit but were discouraged by the problems of inter-group relationships which greatly impeded progress towards a corporate strategy for the combined companies. As a result, no positive synergies emerged. It seemed clear that the strong feelings released by the take-over decision suspended, at least temporarily, the development of a systematic approach towards the problems it created.

The second take-over decision was less controversial. Here, a well-organized group with a strong track record was given responsibility for one which was both divided and less effective. Indeed, they appeared to have already resigned themselves to the prospect of subsidiary status and may even have welcomed the introduction of outside direction. The parent company felt that an arm's length relationship provided an effective basis for control, since this would allow maximum autonomy to the subsidiary and thereby maintain, it was assumed, a high level of motivation. Meetings of representatives from the two groups were held in order to agree major policies and review results. However, the parent group discovered that the decisions which followed were not always consistent with the policies they thought they had agreed, and the results achieved by the acquired group continued to prove disappointing. They eventually concluded that the arm's length relationship wasn't working, and that somewhat closer integration was required to achieve effective control. Unfortunately, time did not allow them to put their ideas into practice.

OUTCOMES

Initial feedback from the students took the form of oral presentations at the close of the event when participants were invited to review both business results and their experience of the process. While this went some way towards providing a sense of closure, it was clear that the feelings generated by the event were still strong.

What did emerge was that three out of the four groups had achieved a high level of cohesion accompanied by strong group cultures and a firm commitment to the strategies they had developed. Resistance to change was, predictably, high in the acquired companies but also present, in more muted form, in the acquiring companies. Here, the wish to protect their own identity affected the way in which they set about, or failed to set about, the process of integration which they had tried to achieve within the constraint of minimum disturbance to their established social pattern and strategic commitments. Until this was recognized progress towards the reorientation required by both groups could not, and in the event did not, begin. The most commonly cited reason for avoiding possible conflicts was that the risks involved for future relationships in the class were too high. 'We still have to work together for the next 18 months' was a typical sentiment. Any action which threatened established norms of respect and cooperation was, it was argued, unacceptable. Interestingly, this inhibiting assumption, though widely shared, was never made explicit at the time of the event and the possibility of dealing with it therefore lost.

What cannot be provided in a short residential programme is the essential period of reflection required to allow personal learning to be identified and a wider perspective brought to bear by linking experience with the relevant literature. Students were given ten weeks (including the summer vacation) to reflect on the learning they felt they had achieved about themselves as individuals, the processes at work within and between groups and their implications for strategic decision making.

Their reports demonstrated that in most cases the event had been a powerful, if still disturbing, learning experience, Strong links had been made with the literature on the characteristics of effective groups, patterns of group formation and development, and the phenomenon of 'group-think' which, in hindsight, was recognized as a powerful influence on group behaviour.

But it was in the reactions to organizational change that perhaps the most interesting observations were made. The degree of stress and anxiety and the strength of resistance to change released emotions which seemed to overwhelm any plans to handle the process of post-acquisition integration (though, as far as observers could tell, not a lot of planning had been attempted, in spite of the pre-event literature distribution). The difficulty of reconciling strategies derived from very different group cultures and the problem of establishing communication patterns between groups which built trust rather than destroyed it, also provided significant sources of insight. Perhaps most striking of all was the need for the acquired groups to have the time to 'mourn' the loss of their identity as an independent group before integration could be contemplated.

The widely-shared conclusion that potential synergies can only be achieved by first addressing the social and cultural problems of change, comes through forcibly. As the product of direct personal experience it is learning that has taken place at an emotional, not simply cerebral, level. The corollary is also emphasized: that the traditional dominance of product and task as the main focus of management attention needs to be balanced by a comparable concern with process. Whether this can be reconciled with the win/lose dynamics of a highly competitive situation remains to be explored. There is the additional difficulty that learning to manage process successfully may first require individuals to learn more about themselves, especially their behaviour under conditions of ambiguity and uncertainty: a slow and sometimes very uncomfortable process. The event can therefore be seen as the medium by which a range of problems are experienced, their significance appreciated, and some useful insights achieved. Future design changes will therefore focus on enhancing the quality of learning which the event makes possible. In particular, the need to facilitate the reflection process within the event so that individuals and groups have more opportunities to learn from each other as the action unfolds, will be given more attention. We shall also be looking for evidence that students are developing transferable skills which can be applied successfully in other situations, most notably the ones they work in day-to-day.

ABOUT THE AUTHOR

David Cain recently took early retirement from his post as senior lecturer in the strategic management division of Newcastle Business School.

Address for correspondence: 16 Edlingham Close, Newcastle on Tyne NE3 1RH.

Chapter 28

Multi-criteria business gaming in Poland: MANAGER-93

Witold T Bielecki and Oktawian Koczuba

ABSTRACT

The game MANAGER-93 can be classified as a computerized simulation business game. It was developed by professors of the University of Warsaw's faculty of management, and is reviewed in this chapter.

Participants create executive teams. Each team has the responsibility of managing an enterprise and makes over 20 decisions at each stage of the game. Decisions are made concerning the:

- type of approach to enterprise development (extensive and/or intensive);
- scale of investments;
- changes in the employment structure;
- production quality, eg, research and development's role in quality improvement;
- expenditures for protecting the natural environment;
- average salary levels of different groups of workers;
- breakeven-point analysis;
- inventory control;
- pricing of goods produced;
- target market (domestic and/or export);
- net-profit distribution.

This game is interactive. The effectiveness of a given team's decision depends on the decisions made by the executive teams heading up competing businesses. For instance, sales volume for a given period depends on the relationship of the enterprise's price levels to the average market price levels. Such situations force participants to use the systems analysis approach.

Before the executive teams make their first decision, they learn about the simulated firm in an introductory session. During this session they become acquainted with the structure of the firm and the current financial situation of the firm they will manage. They are also informed about the main relationships existing between different economic categories and parameters in this system. But they must recognize the intensity of the impact of these parameters and they do that (as they 'learn by doing') during the entire game. It is not easy because, as was said above, these impacts depend on decisions made on both operational and strategic levels by competing executives. Therefore, the participants learn that there is no pre-defined strategy for success.

An instructor is able to create different kinds of economic systems, from a pure central planning economic system to a full market-driven one. The instructor can also introduce temporary or permanent symptoms of economic recession into the game.

The steps below delineate the game process. Participants:

1. Become acquainted with the instruction and the input data which are the same for all enterprises and include the last two years' activity. They are informed about the validity of parameters that determine the kind of economic system being modelled.
2. Create executive teams. They thus have the opportunity to self-select team membership.
3. Work out a few strategic scenarios for developing the firm they will manage.
4. Make the types of decisions listed above; they record the decisions made on a special form.
5. Enter data on the form into a computer, which starts simulating the manufacturing processes and markets (domestic and foreign). Then the computer generates the balance sheet.
6. Instruct the computer to print a special report with all the information they need about the firm, their position in the market, and some information about competitors.
7. Analyse the results; based on these results they make additional decisions. Therafter, steps 4–7 are repeated as needed.
8. Engage in a summary session. Participants present their scenarios and compare them and discuss the decision processes in which they have been engaged. They develop an appreciation of the importance of analysing the financial condition of enterprises to determine current and future viability.

Many objectives are accomplished by this game. Executives:

- Engage in managing situations of uncertainty and in managing situations within competitive market environments, often without adequate information, thus learning to work under conditions of ambiguity.
- Gain experience in developing alternatives. They then consider scenarios for the strategic development of the enterprise and learn the importance of their analyses of these scenarios.
- Improve their skills in multi-criteria decision-making situations.
- Learn how to adapt to changes in the economic and financial system of enterprises.

- Learn how to analyse a balance sheet and draw conclusions for further decisions.

Another major objective of this game is to observe the reactions of participants (decision-makers) eg, to observe whether conflict arises between the goals of the enterprise and the interests of the workers, both for the short term and for the long term.

The game focuses on economic and financial relationships with little emphasis on manufacturing processes. Additional emphasis on production processes would not change the main objectives of the game but would make the game difficult to comprehend. Psychologists who have observed many game sessions attest to the game's complexity, and they conclude that the game is geared to the average participant's ability level; therefore they do not recommend increasing the complexity of the game for educational purposes.

The game is delivered within undergraduate, graduate, and postgraduate (MBA) courses offered at the University of Warsaw. It is also played by executives enrolled in short 'in-company' courses. A special version of this game is also used by enterprises' supervisory boards to test managers' abilities for potential positions in the upper management levels of their organizations.

ABOUT THE AUTHORS

The authors, Witold T Bielecki (a specialist in operation research and computer decision support systems) and Oktawian Koczuba (a specialist in the economic analysis of enterprises) are professors of the faculty of management of Warsaw University. They have many years of experience in developing and using both manual and computerized decision-making games for management training.

Address for correspondence: University of Warsaw, Nowy Swiath, 00-497 Warsaw, PO Box 6, Poland.

Chapter 29

EXEC-Management Game System: exploration of software functionality?

Jeremy J S B Hall

ABSTRACT

This chapter describes and discusses the functionality and facilities provided by computerized simulation-games. These functions are discussed using a specific management game as a case.

After describing the game, its software functions are listed and criticized based on experience running the game on executive short courses over a six-year period. This experience is further generalized, based on experience with other games that address other learning objectives.

BACKGROUND

EXEC-Management Game System is an interactive total enterprise game that can operate on a 'real time' basis with participants entering decisions from separate locations directly into the game. The game is 'data-centred', with software modules in addition to its basic simulation model. These modules provide additional functionality and the game has a decision support system.

The game focuses on tactical management issues and is aimed at middle management who wish to widen and exercise their management skills and knowledge; the learning issues addressed are:

- general management;
- decision making under pressure;
- team integration;
- decision making;
- forecasting – product and financial;
- modelling techniques;
- budgets and financial reports;
- tactical control;
- financial analysis.

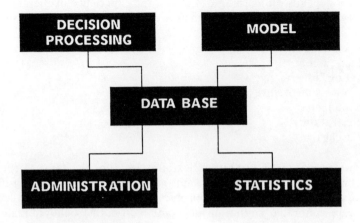

Figure 29.1 *Game structure* (*EXEC-Management Game System*)

Standard decisions cover marketing, finance, operations and business development:

- cost-improvement expenditure;
- production requirements;
- selling price;
- marketing expenditure;
- credit budget.

These decisions can be changed on a monthly or on a less frequent basis. However, although decisions need only to be changed as necessary, the basic reporting cycle is monthly. Through interaction with the database, participants have additional extensive flexibility in directing their company.

The game has been used extensively in the UK and occasionally in Europe on executive short courses and as a stand-alone management event by large, multinational companies.

SOFTWARE STRUCTURE

The software is structured about a central database (Figure 29.1) and consists of four program modules (decision processing, simulation model, administration, and statistics).

Model module

The model consists of seven model sub-models each with three levels of complexity. For each sub-model the administrator decides which level to use.

The choice depends on learning objectives, the experience of the participants and the time available. The sub-models are:

- sales demand;
- production control;
- marketing/advertising;
- cost improvement/investment;
- credit budget;
- administration;
- market elasticity.

The approach was chosen to retain flexibility to tailor the game to education needs while simplifying the process and, more importantly, ensuring that the resultant combination behaved appropriately. That is to say, all levels of models were 'calibrated' so that, in any combination, they behaved realistically and in a 'balanced' manner.

Sales demand – allows switching from full competition (no inter-company interaction) to an oligarchy (full interaction between teams) with and without a seasonal factor.

Production control – defines the number of products (on a Pareto pattern) and the timing of scheduling. Scheduling can be set to take place before or after the previous period's results are known. The option where teams have to schedule the next period's decisions before knowing their results replicates the real-world situation and forces the teams to consider the implications of this information 'time-delay' on forecasting and inventories.

Marketing/advertising – progressively increases the complexity of the price and advertising models. At the greatest level of complexity, a price 'stability' effect delays the impact of price reductions (reflecting the time taken to inform the market) and over reacts to price increases (reflecting customer dissonance).

Cost improvement/investment – ranges from a simple cash investment decision to one where, each period, several projects are presented and teams have to select which to implement, based on business needs, financial returns and available resources. Investment in cost improvement affects quality (rejection rates and market image), variable costs and product performance.

Credit budget – alters interest rates and borrowing conditions reflecting 'easier' or 'harder' economic situations.

Administration – allows a charge to be introduced for making decisions (to discourage changing decisions every period when running in 'real time'). At the highest level of complexity this charge is based on the time taken to make the decisions (so decisions made at the start of the period cost less than those made later). This forces a trade-off to take place between reflection time, rapid reaction and the number of decisions changed.

Market elasticity – provides a range of competitive situations that are balanced in terms of ability to grow sales and make profits. This flexible modularity is addressed in the participant documentation by having a basic manual and a series of 'memos' that are supplied to the participants depending on the modules chosen.

Modifying the database

Besides switching the complexity levels of the sub-models, the administrator can modify the parameters in the database. This can be done at two levels. Administrative options 8, 11, 12 and 13, in the Administrative Function list below, allow key data to be modified during the game (allowing qualitative and negotiated interaction). Further, any item of the database can be modified to completely recalibrate the game (for instance to change the industry or economic scenario).

Administration module

The administration is designed to simplify the housekeeping of the whole system. It consists of a number of options and allows the administrator to tailor it to particular learning objectives. The game environment (number of teams, models used, start and finish times of the access 'window', number of periods per hour and access codes for teams) can be set and reset during the course of a run (see Figure 29.2). Key data in the master database can be changed, allowing pressure on teams to be adjusted and qualitative and negotiated elements introduced. The administrative options are:

Code	Administrative Function
1	To conversationally set-up file BUSDAT to initiate the game
2	Modify restart time
3	Modify the number of teams competing
4	Modify model
5	Modify the number of simulated months per real hour
6	Modify start and finish periods
7	Change the pass numbers for a team
8	Modify unit costs for a team or teams
9	End administrative update
10	Set up file BUSDAT to initiate the game using data
11	Modify share prices
12	Modify assets
13	Modify fixed costs

Decision processing module

Networked decision entry

Decisions can either be entered centrally or entered by individual teams (using computer facilities in the individual syndicate rooms). The Administrator's Guide (AG) discusses this in terms of:

```
REAL TIME 8.17
PLEASE INPUT PASSWORD
PLEASE INPUT ADMINISTRATION CODE?
PLEASE INPUT START TIME — EG 6:30PM IS 18.5? 9.0
HOW MANY TEAMS (SEVEN OR LESS)? 4

YOU HAVE A CHOICE OF MODELS FOR EACH OF A SERIES OF
BUSINESS FUNCTIONS — EACH MODEL HAS THREE LEVELS OF COMPLEXITY
RANGING FROM 0 (SIMPLE OR NONE) TO 2 (COMPLEX)

FOR EACH FUNCTION INPUT 0, 1 OR 2 AS REQUESTED

SALES MODEL? 2
PRODUCTION MODEL? 2
MARKETING MODEL? 1
INVESTMENT MODEL? 1
BUDGET MODEL? 2
ADMINISTRATION MODEL? 1
ELASTICITY MODEL? 1

DO YOU WISH TO RUN A REAL TIME PROGRAM? YES
HOW MANY SIMULATED MONTHS PER REAL HOUR? 3

DO YOU WISH TO SET LIMITS ON ACCESS PERIODS EACH DAY? YES
WHAT IS THE START AND FINISH OF PERIOD
EG FROM 6PM TO 10PM WOULD BE  18,22? 8.75,10.1

PLEASE INPUT PASS NUMBER
FOR COMPANY 1 ?  1231
FOR COMPANY 2 ?  5991
FOR COMPANY 3 ?  34127
FOR COMPANY 4 ?  20041
```

Figure 29.2 *Game set-up*

Having arranged, as an option, for the computer to take over the routine tasks of administration of simulated time and the collection of team statistics, it seems logical to hand the administration of the task of submitting team decisions to the computer (AG, p. 56).

Decision support

Additionally, the computer facility has a 'library' of software that allows participants to undertake statistical and financial analysis, such as forecasting and modelling (AG, pp. 51–3). The library is based on both standard applications packages and specially written software.

Software controlled access

Since the administration module allows the access times to be set and modified, together with the number of periods per hour, individual team pass numbers ensure integrity. This means that 'real time' administration is automatic and teams can have computer facilities in their own syndicate rooms. Usually, these are in the same building. However, once, in South Wales, the network allowed the teams to spread over a half-mile wide area!

Statistics module

As the game progresses key statistics are gathered that can be assessed by the statistics module to provide inter-team comparisons on a period-by-period basis.

As with the administration module, the statistics module is password-protected, preventing teams obtaining access from their own syndicate rooms.

Graphic output

Besides tabular lists of results, the key statistics are graphed for use at the exercise review session.

REAL TIME

The game can be run on a pseudo-real time basis where each decision period represents one month's trading that takes, typically, ten minutes of real time. With this time pressure participants, typically, cannot make decisions every period but every two or three periods. Further, charging for decision making encourages less frequent decision making.

Time pressure

However, to ensure that teams have an opportunity to reflect and re-plan, a typical timetable, such as the one below, involves running the business for blocks of six or twelve months with re-planning/reflection time scheduled between these blocks.

Day 1:
   17:15 Briefing
   18:15 Analysis and planning commences

Day 2:
   09:00–10:00 Decisions made every 20 minutes
   10:00–11:15 Review and preparation of long-term plan
   11:15–12:00 Decisions made every 15 minutes
   12:00–14:00 Re-planning, reflection and refreshments
   14:00–15:00 Decisions made every 10 minutes
   15:00–15:30 Preparation for review
   15:30–17:30 Review

This matter is discussed in the Administrator's Guide as follows:

Another major factor that affects the realism of the game is the time pressure on the participating teams. The time pressure must relate to the complexity of the model and the types of decisions being made. It is important to differentiate between day-to-day decisions (i.e. short term management plans) and long term plans and goals. The very fact that, of necessity, the compression of time occurs in a management game also tends to cause emphasis to be placed on one or another form of time pressure. . . . to have realistic pressure on short term plans it is practically impossible to allow for any long term planning . . . Therefore, there is a need to be able to run the game with a series of time pressures. . . . a suitable plan would allow, after every six months of simulated time, a longer period to make further long term plans before returning to the greater time pressure of the short term operation (AG, p. 55).

ADMINISTRATIVE INTERACTION

When discussing the design rationale for the game, and specifically the database-centred system, the Administrator's Guide states: 'In order to facilitate the interaction between the game and the administrator the game must be structured so that the routine tasks are performed by the computer' (AG, p. 55). In practice this facility means that very complex learning events can take place with a tutoring team interacting and negotiating with the participants and playing several roles.

The Administrator's Guide discusses this in terms of roles for the (non-executive) chairman of the board, financial news editor, union negotiator, inter-team 'staff' transfers (executive hiring) and even take-overs and mergers. In practice this concept is extended to cover suppliers, customers and bankers.

The game was used regularly in this fashion with, for example, the union negotiator (an ex-union official!) not just negotiating wage increases but also longer holidays, retirement benefits, canteen facilities, and complex productivity schemes. These involved the administrator in an 'umpiring' mode, calculating the effect on variable and fixed costs, capital expenditure and cash flow that were used to modify the master database. Special orders negotiated with 'customers' (involving late delivery penalties, foreign currency transactions etc) were treated similarly.

FINANCIAL NEWSPAPER

A particulary useful facility is the 'financial newspaper' called *EconoDig*. (This stands for 'Economic Digest' but with Dig being a euphemism for its 'gutter tabloid' nature.) Often teams make off-the-cuff comments to the reporter about the unions that are then misquoted (adding a new dimension to the current negotiation!).

Despite the 'fun' aspect (it often has cartoons!) the newspaper is 'To provide the facility for non-mathematical information for the teams, a module provides a financial newspaper and an optional editorial' (AG, p. 55). Besides providing information about market shares and the Stock Exchange share price, the administrator can use the newspaper to provide information about the economy (the model has full inflation factors built in), rumours about the market (it is possible to introduce additional teams during the game – therefore, if appropriate, foreign competitors could enter the market or, as

Functionality	Key	Secondary	Occasional
DATA CENTRED	*		
MODULAR MODEL	*		
CHANGE ALL PARAMETERS			*
CHANGE KEY DATA	*		
ADMINISTRATIVE INTERACTION		*	
NETWORKED OPERATION			*
QUALITATIVE OUTPUT		*	
QUALITATIVE INPUT			*
PERFORMANCE STATISTICS		*	
GRAPHICAL PRESENTATION		*	
DECISION SUPPORT SYSTEM			*
REAL TIME OPERATION			*
SOFTWARE CONTROLLED ACCESS			*
ADJUSTABLE TIME PRESSURE	*		
INCREASING COMPLEXITY	*		
INFLATION			*

Key facility represents a 'core' design need necessary for all games.
Secondary facility represents a general need for all or most games but will only be required occasionally on courses or, if missing, may be addressed in a different way.
Occasional facility represents a need for only a few, specialized games and therefore would not be built into most games.

Figure 29.3 *Classification of key functions/facilities*

happened once, a team 'split' was accommodated), leaked information about in-company problems (capacity, inventory shortages), etc. The 'editorial' philosophy is to provide clues about problems and needs rather than prescriptive comments and obvious 'facts'.

FUNCTIONS AND FACILITIES

Based on using EXEC and other games, the key functions/facilities are classified into key, secondary or occasional requirements, as shown in Figure 29.3.

Data centred (key facility). Centring the game on a database is viewed as a key facility. Not only is it necessary to simplify changing data (key and all) and to enable administrative interaction, it has long been regarded as a core requirement of information systems (Couger and McFadden, 1975) and is featured in recent papers on the future trends in game design (Patz, 1990; Yeo, 1991). It allows the game designer to produce a family of adaptations of a game (the games CASINO CHALLENGE and QUAD were adapted from SERVICE CHALLENGE). Thus a database structure is seen as a key facility especially if one wishes to add extra functionality (such as a Tutor Support System described in Chapter 26 of this Yearbook).

Modular model (key facility). This facility was designed to provide tutors with the facility to tailor the game to meet learning objectives and timetable constraints. In practice it was rarely used. However, its key feature status is based on its 'object orientated' nature (Hicks, 1993) that allows a library of tested and calibrated models to be built up which may be reused in other games, shortening development time and reducing design risk.

Change all parameters (occasional facility). This is often perceived as a core wish by users, yet November (1993) refutes this; this, too, is the experience of the author. Besides pragmatic experiences, one must consider the dynamic nature of games and the need to ensure that the game is designed to respond reasonably to decisions (its 'natural response' – Hall and Cox, 1993).

Change key data (key facility). In contrast, the facility to change key data is deemed to be a key facility. It allows the tutor to manage the dynamic response of the game (Hall and Cox, 1993) and thus make the economic situation 'easier' or 'harder' and so adjust the pressure on participants. Further, it allows the tutor to introduce 'random' crises.

Administrative interaction (occasional facility). Although changing key data is deemed to be a key facility, full blown administrative interaction is deemed to be of secondary importance. It can be viewed as moving the game from a 'closed system' simulation to an 'open system' one (Patz, 1990) but requires a large tutoring group. This increases the cost of running the game and extends its duration. (Besides requiring a tutor for each role, it is necessary to have two further facilitators – one to manage the role-playing tutors and the other to manage the game data.) Therefore is only necessary to meet special learning objectives.

Networked operation (occasional facility). Bryan and Corless (1988) suggest that, in the future, 'The game could take place over a network, so the problems of physical proximity could be removed'. EXEC overcame this problem and, as described, was run with teams as far apart as half a mile (0.3 kilometres). However, this introduced a new problem. This spread meant that it was impossible for the tutor to visit team rooms to observe and assess learning and needs. Because of this and since networks are not universal, networked operation is classified as an occasional facility. However, improved game design and wider network availability suggests that this function will become a secondary, and perhaps a key, facility.

Qualitative output (secondary facility). Elgood (1993) states, 'Knowledge must be available, but there must be scope for effort and skill in recognising the knowledge, from which benefit must be won'. Thus, ultimately, participants must recognize the link between cause (their decisions) and effect (business results). This link must not be prescriptively obvious and here the 'fuzzy' nature of qualitative feedback elicits thought and reflection. However, this 'fuzziness' can be produced in other ways: from the quantitative business reports where teams will have to reprocess data to extract useful information, or from tutor interventions.

Qualitative input (occasional facility). This involves the tutor subjectively modifying the database. This means additional administrative effort and the modification may have to be justified to participants. However, it does provide the freedom to translate team 'wishes', unconstrained by the decision form. Coote *et al.* (1985) discuss this in terms of a computer 'assisted' simulation where the tutor acts as mediator between team policies and the simulation software. Qualitative input facilitates the tutors in role playing suppliers, customers, unions etc.

Performance statistics (secondary facility). The gathering of statistics during the run of the game for use during the review session seems to be 'a good thing'. However, there are logistical and behavioural problems. Logistically, there may be insufficient time from the end of the last decision-making period to the start of the review to extract the statistics and prepare suitable visual aids. Behaviourally, massive statistics may stifle discussion and turn the review into a critique of the teams' business performance rather than a session to share learning. Therefore, this is regarded as a secondary requirement. However, it may be that the availability of direct computer-generated output in the review room and suitable data retrieval software may overcome these problems.

Graphical presentation (secondary facility). This facility, if used to provide information for the review, exhibits the same problems as the performance statistics facility. However, as an addition to the teams' reporting and decision supporting system, it does offer opportunities. But, these opportunities are restricted by the inability to print graphics rapidly and the lack of a graphics standard.

Decision support system (occasional facility). The Decision Support System (DSS) was a failure. There were two reasons for this. First, time pressure meant that, even during the longer 'planning' periods, participants were unwilling to budget time for using the decision support tools. Second, since several of the DSS tools were full-blown planning tools, they required considerable time for familiarization. This situation has been replicated in other, more complex, games (INTEX and TECHNIQUE) where a spreadsheet model is provided. Here, although the spreadsheet is designed specifically for the game, an extra half day is necessary for teams to become familiar with the hardware and software and to prepare a meaningful plan. Further, a pre-defined DSS seems to reduce the amount of thinking done. Coote *et al.* (1985) discuss this in terms of psychological and social problems; narrower learning opportunities and restricted access. With CISCO (a complex contract management game) it was observed that making teams manually produce their first period's plan ensured that the DSS was better understood and led to better decisions.

Real time operation (occasional facility). Teach (1991) and Chiesl (1990) argue strongly for future games to provide for 'real-time' operation. However, experience with EXEC suggests that the real time facility has limited utility. In particular, the time pressure produced tended to force participants into operational 'fire-fighting' rather than thoughtful decision making. Although the simulation model can operate in accelerated real time, executives cannot think in accelerated time. The need for reflection (Kolb, 1975) is eased if the timetable allows for this. Therefore, the real time facility is more applicable for functional exercises involving operational decision making; examples are production management or project management games. Two project games, PLANNING EXPERIENCE and PROTEST, utilized computer paced real time operation to replicate the time pressures and inherent time management issues.

Software controlled access (occasional facility). This facility is a necessity for real time operation. It also has utility for decision support systems, direct access games and planning simulations, here with the software controlling access to the microcomputer.

Adjustable time pressure (key facility). Adjustable time pressure is a necessity to maintain cognitive pressure. Thus, during the game, the decision-making cycle progressively shortens. By allowing the interspersion of planning periods between periods of decision making, an opportunity to reflect on the learning experience is provided.

Increasing complexity (key facility). Perry and Euler (1988) suggest that 'simulations should allow for increasing complexity, to allow for a gradually deepening learning experience'. In this context, for EXEC, the dip in the seasonal peak of sales at the start of the game coupled with high liquidity, eased the entry into the game. Later, the seasonal peak in sales occurring after the market's simulation caused problems in scheduling and capacity planning. This 'natural' increase in complexity ensured that cognitive pressure was maintained and, in turn, ensured efficient use of delegate time. Hall and Cox (1993) discuss this in the context of the 'natural and managed response' of the game and describe other mechanisms and patterns of increasing complexity.

Inflation (occasional facility). One mechanism to increase complexity is inflation. Inflation causes financial data to be continuously adjusted and means that teams have to continually update their planning and measuring systems and perceptions. Inflation was a major issue while EXEC was in use and this was recognized by the decision involving cost improvement. Further, if union and supplier negotiations were involved, inflation was a necessity. However, introduction of inflation tended to reduce team focus and participants' identification of how their decisions affected results. Thus, it increased complexity and the time required for the game, but without an equal increase in learning opportunities. Therefore, although realistic, inflation represents an occasional need.

CONCLUSIONS

This chapter discusses software functionality in a single, venerable, game. The use of the word 'venerable' is deliberate since EXEC was developed in late 1969 for use on the GEIS (latterly Honeywell) Computer Time Sharing Service. It was first run in May 1970 and ran regularly up to July 1976 (when the author left Honeywell).

Because of its age, EXEC's tutor support functionality was limited and support for participants (participant support system) was limited to that of a decision support system. It is interesting that several key EXEC functions have recently been suggested as prerequisites of 'future' games (Chiesl, 1990; Teach, 1991 – real time operation; Patz, 1990 – open system operation) or 'state-of-the-art' games (Gray and Hope, 1988 – database, graphics, networked and real time). This reinforces the suggestion by Burgess (1990) that 'the design of most, if not all, of the existing computerised management simulations are little changed from the original implementation'.

The functionality described and discussed in this chapter provides a starting point for the assessment of today's games and, perhaps, a discussion of the current state-of-the-art.

REFERENCES

Bryant, N, Corless, H (1988) 'Changing technology and management games', *Gaming and Simulation*, 14.

Burgess, T (1990) 'Management simulation-games and artificial intelligence, *Simulation/Games for Learning*, 20, 3.

Chiesl, N E (1990) 'Interactive real time simulation', in Gentry, J W (ed.) *Guide to Business Gaming and Experiential Learning*, Nichols/GP Publishing, East Brunswick, and Kogan Page, London.

Coote, A, Crookall, D and Saunders D (1985) 'Some human and machine aspects of computerized simulations', *Gaming and Simulation*, 11:

Couger, J and McFadden, F R (1975) *Introduction to Computer Based Information Systems*, Wiley, New York.

Elgood, C (1993) *Handbook of Management Games*, Gower, Aldershot.

Gray, C and Hope, B (1988) 'The development of a "hot" business management game', *Gaming and Simulation*, 14.

Hall, J and Cox, B (1993) 'Computerized management games: the feedback process and servomechanism analogy', in Percival, F, Lodge, S and Saunders, D (eds) *The Simulation and Gaming Yearbook 1993*, Kogan Page, London.

Hicks, Jr J O (1993) *Management Information Systems: a user's perspective*, West Publishing, New York.

Kolb, D (1975) 'Towards an applied theory of experiential learning', in Cooper, C (ed.) *Theories of Group Processes*, Wiley, London.

November, P (1993) 'Adaptable simulations' in Percival, F, Lodge, S and Saunders, D (eds) *The Simulation and Gaming Yearbook 1993*, Kogan Page, London.

Patz, J (1990) 'Open system simulation', in Gentry, J W (ed.) *Guide to Business Gaming and Experiential Learning*, Nichols/GP Publishing, East Brunswick and Kogan Page, London.

Perry, C and Euler, T (1988) 'Simulations as action learning exercises: implications for conducting and evaluating business and economic simulations', *Simulation/Games for Learning*, 18, 3.

Teach, R D (1991) 'Using time as a decision variable in a business simulation', *Simulation/Games for Learning*, 21, 2.

Yeo, G K (1991) 'A framework for developing simulation game systems', *Simulation and Gaming*, 22, 3. 308–27.

Simulation/games cited

CASINO CHALLENGE (1992) Hall Marketing, London.
CISCO (1988) Hall Marketing, London.
INTEX (1984) Hall Marketing, London.
A PLANNING EXPERIENCE (1973) Honeywell Information Systems, London.
PROTEST (1993) Hall Marketing, London.
QUAD (1991) Hall Marketing, London.
SERVICE CHALLENGE (1989) Hall Marketing, London.
TECHNIQUE (1989) Hall Marketing, London.

ABOUT THE AUTHOR

Jeremy Hall is owner of Hall Marketing, a firm specializing in the development of simulations for management development. With over 25 years' experience in designing simulation models, he has developed more than three dozen computerized business simulations covering most aspects of management education.

He is the author of two books on computing and numerous articles on management use of computers and computer-aided management education. He is on the editorial advisory board of *The Journal of Management Development*.

He has a degree in electrical engineering from Imperial College London and is currently doing research into computer aided management education, on a part time basis, at Imperial College. His research interests are Tutor Support Systems and participant Support Systems and their application for andragogic education.

Address for correspondence: Hall Marketing, Studio 11, Colman's Wharf, 45 Morris Road, London E14 6PA.

SECTION 7: Sources of information

Chapter 30

References to recent articles on research and practice in simulation and gaming

ABSTRACT

The following references have been kindly made available by the ERIC Clearinghouse. They provide the listing of ERIC journal articles and documents dealing with games and simulations. All articles are in English unless otherwise stated. The help of ERIC/ CHESS is gratefully acknowledged as is DIALOG Information Services Inc.

Mike McDonagh
Napier University, Edinburgh

GENERAL APPLICATIONS

Monte Carlo Simulation. Comparison of two-stage testing and computerized adaptive testing
Kim, Haeok; Plake, Barbara S
Paper presented at the Annual Meeting of the National Council on Measurement in Education, Atlanta, GA, April 13–15, 1993

Role-play your way to learning
Swink, David F
Training and Development, 47, 5, 91–7, 1993

Productivity tools for simulation-centred training development
Munro, Allen; Towne, Douglas M
Educational Technology, Research and Development, 40, 4, 65–80, 1992

Jeu de role: comment s'en servir (Role playing: how to use it)
Elder, David
Francais dans le Monde, 254, 61–4, 1993

Monitoring the effect of color on performance in an instructional gaming environment through an analysis of eye movement behaviors
Livingston, Lori A *et al.*
Journal of Research on Computing in Education, 25, 2, 233–42, 1992

Experiential learning through computer-based simulations
Maines, Bill *et al.*
Alberta Journal of Educational Research, 38, 4, 269–84, 1992

Teacher as game-show host, bookkeeper, or judge? Challenges, contradictions, and consequences of accountability
Anders, Patricia; Richardson, Virginia
Teachers College Record, 94, 2, 382–96, 1992

Failure of the Mann-Whitney test: a note on the simulation study of Gibbons and Chakraborti (1991). Response to Zimmerman (1992)
Zimmerman, Donald W *et al.*
Journal of Experimental Education, 60, 4, 359–66, 1992

Training teachers of the gifted to use simulations
Marks, Diana F
Gifted Child Today, 15, 25–7, 1992

A crisis in space – a futuristic simulation using creative problem solving
Clode, Linda
Gifted Child Today, 15, 6, 52–3, 1992

Effects of computer simulations and problem-solving approaches on high school students
Geban, Omer *et al.*
Journal of Educational Research, 86, 1, 5–10, 1992

Simulations as a fundamental teaching tool: striking the appropriate balance
Hugenberg, Lawrence W
Bulletin of the Association for Business Communication, 55, 4, 65–9, 1992

SIGMA – a graphical approach to teaching simulation
Schruben, Lee W
Journal of Computing in Higher Education, 4, 1, 27–37, 1992

What's in a model? Issues in the use of simulation models to analyze student understanding: a reaction to Ohlsson, Ernst and Rees
Schoenfeld, Alan H
Journal for Research in Mathematics Education, 23, 5, 468–73, 1992

Simulations globales (Global simulations)
Care, Jean-Marc
Francais dans le Monde, 252, 48–56, 1992

Getting our students to think through simulations
Wolfe, Connie *et al.*
Contemporary Education, 63, 3, 219–20, 1992

Microcomputer applications. Curriculum guide and simulations and test bank
Mahaffey, Darlena; Patton, Jan
East Texas State University, Commerce. Educational Development and
Training Center, 1992

How to evaluate multimedia simulations: learning from the past
Yildiz, Rauf; Atkins, Madeleine J
Paper presented at the European Conference on Educational Research,
Enschede, The Netherlands, June 22–5, 1992

10 Secrets of Successful Simulations
Shirts, R Garry
Training, 29, 10, 79–83, 1992

A comparative analysis of general case simulation instruction and naturalistic
instruction
Domaracki, Joseph W; Lyon, Steven R
Research in Developmental Disabilities, 13, 4, 363–79, 1992

Learning to solve complex problems in simulation
Hughes, Ian
Higher Education Research and Development, 11, 1, 1–7, 1992

Developing automated feedback materials for a training simulator: an interaction between users and researchers
Slechter, Theodore M *et al.*
Paper presented at the Annual Conference of the American Educational
Research Association, San Francisco, CA, April 20–24, 1992

Integrating technology usage across the curriculum through educational
adventure games
Ritchie, Donn; Dodge, Bernard
Paper presented at the Annual Conference on Technology and Teacher
Education, Houston, TX, March 12–15 1992

Jeux et jouets dans l'education des jeunes enfants (Games and playthings in the
education of young children). Digest 25
Mauriras-Bosquet, Martine *et al.*
United Nations Children's Fund, Paris; United Nations Educational, Scientific, and Cultural Organization, Paris, 1988

The effectiveness of games for educational purposes: a review of recent
research
Randel, Josephine M *et al.*
Simulation and Gaming, 23, 3, 261–76, 1992

The relative influence of several factors on simulation performance
Gosenpud, Jerry; Miesing, Paul
Simulation and Gaming, 23, 3, 311–25, 1992

Living in a global age. A simulation activity for upper elementary and secondary level students
Stanford University, CA. Stanford Program on International and Cross Cultural Education, 1984

Heelotia: a cross cultural simulation game. Recommended for grade 5 to adult
Stanford University, CA. Stanford Program on International and Cross Cultural Education, 1991

Parallel instruction: a theory for educational computer simulation
Min, F B M
Interaction Learning International, 8, 3, 177–83, 1992

Creativity is alive in outdoor play: children solve problems as they invent games on the playground
Castle, Kathryn; Wilson, Elaine
Dimensions of Early Childhood, 20, 4, 11–14, 39, 1992

Effects of animated computer simulations on inductive learning with adults: a preliminary report
Rieber, Lloyd P; Parmley, M Wayne
Proceedings of Selected Research and Development Presentations at the Convention of the Association for Educational Communications and Technology, February 1992

Building microcomputer-based instructional simulations: psychological implications and practical guidelines
Thurman, Richard A; Matoon, Joseph S
Proceedings of Selected Research and Development Presentations at the Convention of the Association for Educational Communications and Technology, February 1992

Supporting hypothesis generation by learners exploring an interactive computer simulation
van Joolingen, Wouter R; de Jong, Ton
Instructional Science, 20, 6, 389–404, 1992

An adaptive testing simulation for a certifying examination
Resheatar, Rosemary A *et al.*
Paper presented at the Annual Meeting of the American Educational Resarch Association, San Francisco, CA, April 20–24, 1992

Simulations: selection and development
Wager, Walter W *et al.*
Performance Improvement Quarterly, 5, 2, 47–64, 1992

BEHAVIOURAL STUDIES

Employment counsellors' and youths' views of the transition to work: preparing to develop a work skills simulation

Cairns, Kathleen V *et al.*
Canadian Journal of Counselling, 26, 4, 222–39, 1992

Simulated legal education: a template
Robinson, Thomas A
Journal of Legal Education, 42, 2, 296–98, 1992

Computer-based simulation systems and role-playing: an effective combination for fostering conditional knowledge
Schlechter, Theodore M *et al.*
Journal of Computer-Based Instruction, 19, 4, 110–14, 1992

My school game: a grade 1 game
Basaraborvich, Yvonne *et al.*
Canadian Social Studies, 26, 4, 170–71, 1992

On your own: a game of survival
Hamilton, Taddie
Social Studies Texan, 8, 1, 38, 1992

The game board of family dynamics: structures, stages, rules, roles and functions. Fostering families. A specialized training program designed for foster care workers and foster care parents
Schatz, Mona Struhsaker *et al.*
Colorado State University, Ft Collins, Department of Social Work, 1991

Lowering beginning teacher anxiety about parent-teacher conferences through role-playing
Johns, Kenneth M
School Counselor, 40, 2, 146–52, 1992

The use of role-play in teaching research ethics: a validation study
Strohmetz, David B; Skleder, Anne A
Teaching of Psychology, 19, 2, 106–8, 1992

The long haul: a grade 5 game
MacArthur, Brent *et al.*
Canadian Social Studies, 26, 3, 123–5, 1992

Research on the comparability of the oral proficiency interview and the simulated oral proficiency interview
Stansfield, Charles W; Kenyon, Dorry Mann
System, 20, 3, 347–64, 1992

Role play: a versatile cooperative learning activity
Waters, Elaine *et al.*
Contemporary Education, 63, 3, 216–18, 1992

Jeopardy: a career information game for school counselors
Miller, Mark J; Knippers, Julie Anna
Career Development Quarterly, 41, 1, 55–61, 1992

Assertiveness training for disabled adults in wheelchairs: self-report, role-play, and activity pattern outcomes
Glueckauf, Robert L; Quittner, Alexandra L
Journal of Consulting and Clinical Psychology, 60, 3, 419–25, 1992

An unexpected wait before testifying increases nervousness in witnesses: a jury simulation
Bookstaber-Smith, Ruth Anne
Journal of Offender Rehabilitation, 17, 3/4, 197–211, 1992

BUSINESS STUDIES

Using a simulation to teach intercultural communication in business communication courses
Jameson, Daphne A
Bulletin of the Association for Business Communication, 56, 1, 3–11, 1993

The stock market game: classroom use and strategy
Wood, William C *et al.*
Journal of Economic Education, 23, 3, 236–46, 1992

Business computer applications I. Curriculum guide and simulations and test bank
Patton, Jan; Murray, Darlena
East Texas State University, Commerce. Educational Development and Training Center, 1991

Business office clerical/business office services. Simulations and test bank
Patton, Jan; Murray, Darlena
East Texas State University, Commerce. Educational Development and Training Center, 1991

Office support systems. Curriculum guide and simulations and test bank
Peace, Betty; Patton, Jan
East Texas State University, Commerce. Educational Development and Training Center, 1990

The relationship between financial performance and other measures of learning on a simulation exercise
Anderson, Philip H; Lawton, Leigh
Simulation and Gaming, 23, 3, 326–40, 1992

ASSESSMENT CENTER SIMULATION: A university training program for business graduates
Steuer, Eckhard
Simulation and Gaming, 23, 3, 354–69, 1992

Simulating the corporate strategic planning function in the business communication curriculum
Scheiber, H J; Hager, Peter J

Bulletin of the Association for Business Communication, 55, 3, 46-8, 1992

Multiple feedback mechanisms in a business simulation
Thalheimer, Will *et al.*
Proceedings of Selected Research and Development Presentations of the Association for Educational Communications and Technology, February 1992

Teaching economic concepts to fifth graders: the power of simulations
Gretes, John A *et al.*
Social Science Report, 28, 2, 71-83, 1991

ENVIRONMENTAL

Environmental concern and cooperative-competitive behavior in a simulated commons dilemma
Smith, Jeffrey M; Bell, Paul A
Journal of Social Psychology, 132, 4, 461-8, 1992

Seal revenge: ecology games invented by children
Surbeck, Elaine; Glover, Mary Kenner
Childhood Education, 68, 5, 275-81, 1992

Effectiveness of microcomputer simulations in stimulating environmental problem solving by community college students
Farynaiarz, Joseph V; Lockwood, Linda G
Journal of Research in Science Teaching, 29, 5, 453-70, 1992

Activities to grow on. Earth-friendly games, crafts, and activities
Murray, Sandy *et al.*
Instructor, 101, 8, 55, 1992

HEALTH STUDIES

Use of HyperCard to simulate a tissue culture laboratory
Nester, Bradley S; Turney, Tully H
Collegiate Microcomputer, 10, 4, 193-8, 1992

Psychometric study of the clinical treatment planning simulations (CTPS), for assessing clinical judgment
Falavey, Janet Elizabeth; Herbert, David J
Journal of Mental Health Counselling, 14, 4, 490-507, 1992

What we say and what we do: self-reported teaching behavior versus performances in written simulations among medical school faculty
Hartman, Sandee L; Nelson, Marc S
Academic Medicine, 67, 8, 522-7, 1992

The development and use of gaming in multidisciplinary geriatric education
Kues, John R *et al.*

Educational Gerontology, 18, 1, 27–40, 1992

HUMANITIES

Should the minimum drinking age be changed? A simulation on the legislative process
Tamura, Eileen H
Social Studies, 83, 5, 201–6, 1992

Swap-shop: teaching the imperative: a proficiency-based game
Conlon, Kristine M
Interrichtspraxis/Teaching German, 25, 1, 66–7, 1992

Catch the spirit of learning's cooperation games. The geography decathlon, Part 2
Raker, Elizabeth *et al.*
Learning, 20, 8, 66–70, 1992

Teaching history through role-playing: a report on a 'mock' constitutional convention for students
Henderson, Rodger C
Journal of the Middle States Council for the Social Studies, 11, 36–45, 1989

MANAGEMENT

Construct validity of a simulation of interactive decision making
Shannon, David M *et al.*
Journal of Educational Research, 86, 3, 180–83, 1993

The effects of community training using a videodisc-based simulation
Wissick, Cheryl A *et al.*
Journal of Special Education Technology, 11, 4, 207–22, 1992

Developing a simulation model for the development of higher education administrators
Cabrales, Eusebio J; Eddy, John P
Journal of Research on Computing in Education, 25, 1, 105–12, 1992

Computer simulation and library management
Main, Linda
Journal of Library Administration, 16, 4, 109–30, 1992

Teaching the dilemmas of commons property management using the commons game
Kirts, Carla A; Tumeo, Mark A
Journal of Library Administration, 16, 4, 109–30, 1992

Modelling total quality elements into a strategy-oriented simulation
Mergen, A Erhan; Pray, Thomas F

Simulation and Gaming, 23, 3, 277–97, 1992

Managerial skills acquisition: a case for using business policy simulations
Hemmasi, Masoud; Graf, Lee A
Simulation and Gaming, 23, 3, 298–310, 1992

A participants' DSS for a management game with a DSS generator
Yeo, Gee Kin; Nah, Fui Hoon
Simulation and Gaming, 23, 3, 341–53, 1992

Game methods of collective decision making in management consulting
Prigozhin, Arkadii Il'ich
Soviet Education, 33, 12, 25–45, 1991

Using computer simulations in management education
Curry, Bruce; Moutinho, Luiz
Management Education and Development, 23, 2, 155–67, 1992

MOTOR SKILLS

Computer support of operator training: constructing and testing a prototype
of a CAL (computer aided learning) supported simulation environment
Zillesen, P G van Schaick *et al.*
Paper presented at the International Conference for Corporate Training for
Effective Performance, Enschede, The Netherlands, December 1, 1991

CACTUS: command and control training using knowledge-based simulations
Hartley, J R *et al.*
Interactive Learning International, 8, 2, 127–36, 1992

Developing a train driving simulator
Nowak, Stefan
Interactive Learning International, 8, 2, 145–8, 1992

SCIENCE AND ENGINEERING

The effect of computer simulations on introductory thermodynamics understanding
Lewis, Eileen L *et al.*
Educational Technology, 33, 1, 45–58, 1993

Use of microcomputer simulation and conceptual change text to overcome
student preconceptions about electric circuits
Carlsen, David D; Andre, Thomas
Journal of Computer-Based Instruction, 19, 4, 105–9, 1992

A real life simulator for construction site management
Ndekugri, Issaka; Lansley, Peter
Computers and Education, 19, 4, 321–28, 1992

Simulated holograms: a simple introduction to holography
Dittman, H; Schneider, W B
Physics Teacher, 30, 4, 244-8, 1992

Integrating computer simulations into high school physics teaching
Ronen, Miky *et al.*
Journal of Computers in Mathematics and Science Teaching, 11, 3/4, 319-29, 1992

Computer game of shell trajectory: a subset of a 'pre-engineerng college on disk'
Song, Xueshu
Journal of Computers in Mathematics and Science Teaching, 11, 3/4, 331-6, 1992

Simulating the understanding of arithmetic: a response to Schoenfeld
Ohlsson, Stellan
Journal for Research in Mathematics Education, 23, 5, 474-82, 1992

Role-playing reactions: identifying with the elements
Spain, Ragan S
Science Teacher, 59, 9, 38-40, 1992

Simulating communication in mathematics
Greenes, Carole *et al.*
Arithmetic Teacher, 40, 2, 78-82, 1992

Trading Alfs for a Bart: a simulation
Richbart, Lynn; Richbart, Carolyn
Arithmetic Teacher, 40, 2, 112-14, 1992

Creating a computer simulator package for a hypothetical computer architecture
Pyzdrowski, Anthony S; DeNardo, Anette M
Paper presented at the fifteenth Annual Conference of the Eastern Educational Research Association, Hilton Head, SC, March 5 1992

The effects of teaching a hypothetical computer architecture with computer simulators
DeNardo, Annette M; Pyzdrowski, Anthony S
Paper presented at the fifteenth Annual Conference of the Eastern Educational Research Association, Hilton Head, SC, March 5 1992

Chapter 31

Publishers of games and simulations in the UK, the USA, Europe and Australasia

Ray Land, Napier University, Edinburgh

UK SIMULATIONS PUBLISHERS

Aberdeen University Press
Farmers Hall, Aberdeen AB9 2XT
Tel: (0224) 641663/641672
Fax: (0224) 643286

Edward Arnold Ltd
Mill Road, Dunton Green,
Sevenoaks, Kent TN13 2YA
Tel: (0732) 450111
Fax: (0732) 461321

Avebury
Ashgate Publishing Group,
Gower House, Croft Road,
Aldershot, Hants GU11 3HR
Tel: (0252) 331551
Fax: (0252) 344405

**AVP, Publishers of Educational
  Resources**
School Hill Centre,
Chepstow, Gwent NP6 5PH
Tel: (0291) 625439
Fax: (0291) 629671

B T Batsford Ltd
4 Fitzhardinge Street
London W1H 0AH
Tel: 071–486 8484
Fax: 071–487 4296

BHASVIC Resources
Dyke Road
Hove, East Sussex BN3 6EG

BKT Information Services
7 Darley Avenue
Toton, Nottingham NG9 6JP
Tel: (0602) 732871
Fax: (0602) 211148

Blackwell Publishers
108 Cowley Road
Oxford OX4 1JF
Tel: (0865) 791100
Fax: (0865) 791347

**Building Environmental Performance
  Analysis Club (BEPAC)**
Building Research Establishment,
Garston, Watford WD2 7JR
Tel: (0923) 664132/664780
Fax: (0923) 664095

Cambridge University Press
The Edinburgh Building,
Shaftesbury Road,
Cambridge CB2 2RU
Tel: (0223) 312393
Fax: (0223) 315052

**Careers and Occupational Information
  Centre**
Dept of Employment, Room E415,
Moorfoot, Sheffield S1 4PQ
Tel: (0742) 594563

Fax: (0742) 752035

Cassell plc
Villiers House, 41–47 Strand,
London WC2N 5JE
Tel: 071–839 4900
Fax: 071–839 1804

Centre for Innovation in Mathematics Teaching
School of Education, University of Exeter
St Luke's, Exeter EX1 2LU
Tel: (0392) 217113

Chartwell-Bratt (Publishing & Training) Ltd
Old Orchard
Bickley Road, Bromley BR1 2NE
Tel: 081–467 1956
Fax: 081–467 1754

Computational Mechanics Publications Ltd
Ashurst Lodge
Ashurst, Southampton SO4 2AA
Tel: (0703) 293223
Fax: (0703) 292853

Computers in Teaching Initiative, Centre for History with Archaeology & Art History
University of Glasgow,
1 University Gardens, Glasgow G12 8QQ

Construction Industry Research & Information Association
6 Storey's Gate,
London SW1P 3AU
Tel:071–222 8891

Development Education in Dorset
East Dorset Professional Education Centre,
Lowther Road, Bournemouth BH8 8NR
Tel: (0202) 296071

Economics Association, The
1A Keymer Road,
Hassocks, West Sussex BN6 8AD
Tel: (0273) 846033

Edward Elgar Publishing Ltd
Suite 2,

Fairview Court, Fairview Road
Cheltenham, Glos GL52 2EX
Tel: (0242) 226934
Fax: (0242) 262111

Elm Publications
Seaton House, Kings Ripton,
Huntingdon, Cambs PE17 2NJ
Tel: (048 73) 238/254
Fax: (048 73) 359

Emjoc Press
Garden House, Welbury,
Northallerton, North Yorkshire DL6 2SE

Energy Consultancy
24 Elm Close,
Bedford MK41 8BZ
Tel: (0234) 262677

Framework Press Educational Publishers Ltd
St Leonard's House, St Leonardgate,
Lancaster LA1 1NN
Tel: (0524) 39602

Gordon & Breach Science Publishers Ltd
PO Box 90,
Reading RG1 8JL
Tel: (0734) 560080
Fax: (0734) 568211

Gower Publishing Co. Ltd
Gower House, Croft Road,
Aldershot, Hants GU11 3HR
Tel: (0252) 331551
Fax: (0252) 344405

Groundwork Group Development
3 Meathop Fell, Meathop,
Grange-over-Sands, Cumbria LA11 6QZ
Tel: (05395) 33600

Harvard University Press
14 Bloomsbury Square,
London WC1A 2LP
Tel: 071–404 0712
Fax: 071–404 0601

Hobsons Publishing plc
Bateman Street,
Cambridge CB2 1LZ
Tel: (0223) 354551

Fax: (0223) 323154

Hodder & Stoughton Ltd
Mill Road, Dunton Green,
Sevenoaks,Kent TN13 2YA
Tel: (0732) 450111
Fax: (0732) 460134

Holt, Rinehart & Winston
24-28 Oval Road, London NW1 7DX
Tel: 071-267 4466
Fax: 071-482 2293

Ellis Horwood Ltd, Publisher
Campus 400, Marylands Avenue,
Hemel Hempstead, Herts HP2 7EZ
Tel: (0442) 881900
Fax: (0442) 882099

Interscience Publishers
Division of John Wiley Ltd,
Baffins Lane,
Chichester, W.Sussex PO19 1UD
Tel: (0243) 779777

**Keele Mathematical Education
Publications**
c/o Dept of Education,
University of Keele,
Keele, Newcastle, Staffs ST5 5BG
Tel: (0782) 621111

Kogan Page Ltd
120 Pentonville Road,
London N1 9JN
Tel: 071-278 0433
Fax: 071-837 6348

Longman Group UK Ltd
Longman House, Burnt Mill,
Harlow, Essex CM20 2JE
Tel: (0279) 426721
Fax: (0279) 431059

McGraw-Hill Book Co Europe
Shoppenhangers Road, Maidenhead,
Berks SL6 2QL
Tel: (0628) 23432
Fax: (0628) 35895 & 770224

**Maxwell Macmillan International
(Europe) Ltd**
Nuffield Building, Hollow Way, Cowley,
Oxford OX4 2PH
Tel: (0865) 748754

Fax: (0865) 748808

**Mechanical Engineering Publications
Ltd**
Northgate Avenue,
Bury St.Edmunds, Suffolk IP32 6BW
Tel: (0284) 763277
Fax: (0284) 704006

Mercat Press
c/o James Thin, 53-59 South Bridge,
Edinburgh EH1 1YS
Tel: 031-556 6743
Fax: 031-557 8149

MIT Press Ltd
14 Bloomsbury Square,
London WC1A 2LP
Tel: 071-404 0712
Fax: 071-404 0601

Multilingual Matters Ltd
Frankfurt Lodge,
Clevedon Hall,
Victoria Road,
Clevedon, Avon BS21 7SJ

Network Exhibitions & Conferences Ltd
Ceased trading 1992; titles acquired by:
Bee Vee Promotions Ltd.
Fleece Yard, Market Hill,
Buckingham MK18 1JX
Tel: (0280) 815226
Fax: (0280) 815919

Open University Press
Celtic Court
22 Ballmoor, Buckingham MK18 1XW
Tel: (0280) 823388
Fax: (0280) 823233

Oxford University Press
Walton Street, Oxford OX2 6DP
Tel: (0865) 56767
Fax: (0865) 56646

Peter Peregrinus Ltd
Michael Faraday House,
Six Hills Way,
Stevenage, Herts SG1 2AY
Tel: (0438) 313311
Fax: (0438) 313465

Pergamon Press
Headington Hill Hall,

Oxford OX3 0BW
Tel: (0865) 794141
Fax: (0865) 60285

Pineridge Press Ltd
54 Newton Road,
Mumbles, Swansea SA3 4BQ

Pitman Publishing
128 Long Acre,
London WC2E 9AN
Tel: 071-379 7383
Fax: 071-240 5771

Plenum Publishing Co. Ltd
88/90 Middlesex Street,
London E1 7E2
Tel: 071-377 0686
Fax: 071-247 0555

Prentice-Hall
Campus 400,
Marylands Avenue
Hemel Hempstead, Herts HP2 7EZ
Tel: (0442) 881900
Fax: (0442) 882099

Research Studies Press Ltd
24 Belvedere Road,
Taunton, Somerset TA1 1HD
Tel: (0823) 336197
Fax: (0823) 253252

Royal Aeronautical Society
4 Hamilton Place,
London W1V 0BQ
Tel: 071-499 3515
Fax: 071-499 6230

Sage Publications Ltd
6 Bonhill Street,
London EC2A 4PU
Tel: 071-374 0645
Fax: 071-374 8741

SAUS Publications
School for Advanced Urban Studies,
University of Bristol,
Rodney Lodge,
Grange Road, Bristol BS8 4EA
Tel: (0272) 741117
Fax: (0272) 737308

Scholastic Publications Ltd
Villiers House, Clarendon Avenue,

Leamington Spa, Warwickshire CV32
5PR
Tel: (0926) 887799
Fax: (0926) 883331

Southgate Publishers
Glebe House, Church Street, Crediton,
Devon EX17 2AF
Tel: (0363) 777575
Fax: (0363) 776007

E & F N Spon
(an imprint of Chapman & Hall Ltd)
2-6 Boundary Row,
London SE1 8HN
Tel: 071-865 0066
Fax: 071-522 9623

Sydney University Press
Distributed by:
Oxford University Press
Walton Street, Oxford OX2 6DP
Tel: (0865) 56767
Fax: (0865) 56646

Taylor and Francis Ltd
4 John Street,
London WC1N 2ET
Tel: 071-405 2237
Fax: (orders & trade dept) (0256) 479438

UCL Press Ltd
University College, London,
Gower St
London WC1E 6BT
Tel: 071-380 7707
Fax: 071-413 8392

University of Manchester
Department of Agricultural Economics,
Manchester M13 9PL
Tel: 061-275 4793
Fax: 061-275 4929

John Wiley & Sons Ltd
Baffins Lane,
Chichester,
West Sussex PO19 1UD
Tel: (0243) 779777
Fax: (0243) 775878

Winslow Press
Telford Road,
Bicester,

Oxon OX6 0TS
Tel: (0869) 244644
Fax: (0869) 320040

WRC (Water Research Centre) plc
PO Box 16, Henley Road,
Medmenham,
Marlow, Bucks SL7 2HD
Tel: (0491) 571531
Fax: (0491) 411059

Wye College
School of Rural Economics & Related
  Studies,
Department of Agricultural Economics,
Ashford, Kent TN25 5AH
Tel: (0233) 812401
Fax: (0233) 813320

UK GAMES PUBLISHERS

Argus Books
Angus House,
Boundary Way,
Hemel Hempstead, Herts HP2 7ST
Tel: (0442) 66551
Fax: (0442) 66998

Academic Press Inc. (London) Ltd
24–28 Oval Road,
London NW1 7DX
Tel: 071–267 4466
Fax: 071–482 2293/071–485 4752

Butterworth & Co. (Publishers) Ltd
Borough Green,
Sevenoaks,
Kent TN15 8PH
Tel: (0732) 884567
Fax: (0732) 884079

Chapman & Hall Ltd
2–6 Boundary Row,
London SE1 8HN
Tel: 071–865 0066
Fax: 071–522 9623

David & Charles plc
Brunel House,
Newton Abbot,
Devon TQ12 4PU
Tel: (0626) 61121
Fax: (0626) 64463

Elsevier Science Publishers Ltd
Crown House, Linton Road,
Barking,
Essex IG11 8JU
Tel: 081–594 7272
Fax: 081–594 5942

Fourmat Publishing
133 Upper Street,
London N1 1QP
Tel: 071–226 7497
Fax: 071–359 3031

Hobsons Publishing plc
Bateman Street,
Cambridge CB2 1LZ
Tel: 0223 354551

Key Note Publications Ltd
Field House, 72 Oldfield Road,
Hampton, Middx TW12 2HQ
Tel: 081–738 0755
Fax: 081–783 1940

Kaye & Ward Ltd
38 Hans Crescent,
London SW1X 0LZ
Tel: 071–581 9393
Fax: 071–823 9406

Kogan Page Ltd
120 Pentonville Road,
London N1 9JN
Tel: 071–278 0433
Fax: 071–837 6348

Partizan Press
26 Cliffsea Grove,
Leigh-on-Sea
Essex SS9 1NQ
Tel: (0702) 73986
Fax: (0702) 739

Shaw & Sons Ltd
Shaway House,
21 Bourne Park, Bourne Road,
Crayford, Dartford DA1 4BZ
Tel: (0322) 550676
Fax: (0322) 550553

Shelter Publications
88 Old Street,
London EC1V 9HU
Tel: 071–253 0202

Stanley Thornes (Publishers) Ltd
Old Station Drive,
Leckhampton,
Cheltenham,
Glos GL53 0DN

Patrick Stephens Ltd
Sparkford,
Yeovil,
Somerset BA22 7JJ
Tel: (0963) 40635
Fax: (0963) 40023

Time Patterns
97 Devonshire Road,
Birmingham B20 2PG
Tel: 021-523 4446

US SIMULATIONS
PUBLISHERS

Addison-Wesley
Rte 128,
Reading, MA 01867
Tel: 617-944-3700/800-447-2226
Fax: 617-944-9338

American Mathematical Society
Box 6248,
Providence, RI 02940
Tel: 401-455-4000/800-321-4267
Fax: 401-331-3842

Ann Arbor Science Publishers Inc.
230 Collingwood St,
Ann Arbor, MI 48106
Tel: 313-761-5010
(UK distributor: Butterworth & Co. Ltd)

Brookings Institution
1775 Massachusetts Ave NW,
Washington DC 20036-2188
Tel: 202-797-6000/800-275-1447
Fax: 202-797-6004

Brooks-Cole Publishing Co.
Division of Wadsworth Inc.,
511 Forest Lodge Road,
Pacific Grove CA 93950-5098
Tel: 408-373-0728/800-354-9706
Fax: 408-375-6414

(UK distributor: International
   Publishing Services)

Butterworth-Heinemann
80 Montvale Ave,
Stoneham MA 02180
Tel: 617-438-8464
Fax: 617-279-4851

CRC Press Inc
2000 Corporate Blvd NW
Boca Raton FL 33431
Tel: 407-994-0555
Fax: 407-994-3625
(UK distributor: Mosby-Year Book
   Europe Ltd)

Delmar Publishers Inc.
Box 15-015,
Two Computer Dr. W,
Albany NY 12212
Tel: 518-459-1150/800-347-7707
Fax: 518-459-3552
(UK distributor: International Thomson)

Elsevier Science Publishing Co.
655 Avenue of the Americas,
New York, NY 10010
Tel: 212-633-3806
Fax: 212-633-3880

Free Press
Division of Macmillan Inc.,
866 Third Avenue,
New York, NY 10022
Tel: 212-702-2000
Fax: 212-605-9364

Harvard University Press
79 Garden Street,
Cambridge MA 02138
Tel: 617-495-8562/800-448-2242
Fax: 800-962-4983

Houghton Mifflin Co.
One Beacon Street,
Boston MA 02108
Tel: 617-725-5000/800-257-9107
Fax: 617-227-5409

IEEE Press
Division of Institute of Electrical &
   Electronics Engineers Inc,
445 Hoes Lane,

Piscataway NJ 08855-1331
Tel: 212-705-7548
Fax: 908-981-1855
(UK distributor: Electronica Books Ltd)

IEEE Computer Society Press
10662 Los Vaqueros Circle,
Los Alamitos, CA 90720
Tel: 714-821-8380/800-272-6657
Fax: 714-821-4010
(UK distributor: Electronica Books Ltd)

Richard D Irwin Inc
Subsidiary of The Times Mirror Co.,
1818 Ridge Road
Homewood IL 60430
Tel: 708-798-6000/800-634-3961
Fax: 708-798-6296
(UK distributor: Addison-Wesley)

Kluwer Academic Publishers
Subsidiary of Wolters-Kluwer,
101 Philip Dr.,
Norwell, MA 02061
Tel: 617-871-6600/6300
Fax: 617-871-6528
(European distributor: Kluwer Academic
    Publishers, The Netherlands)

Johns Hopkins University Press
701 W 40 St, Suite 275,
Baltimore, MD 21211-2190
Tel: 301-338-6900/800-537-5487
Fax: 301-338-6998

McGraw-Hill Inc
Blue Ridge Summit, PA 17294-0850
Tel: 800-722-4726
Fax: 800-932-0183

Charles E Merrill Publishing Co.
1300 Alum Creek Dr.,
Columbus OH 43216
Tel: 614-258-8441

MIT Press
55 Hayward Street,
Cambridge MA 02142
Tel: 617-253-5646/800-356-0343
Fax: 617-258-6779

National Academy Press
2101 Constitution Avenue NW,
Washington DC 20418

Tel: 202-334-3313/800-624-6242
Fax: 202-334-2451

Praeger Publishers Inc.
One Madison Avenue,
New York, NY 10010
Tel: 212-685-5300
Fax: 212-685-0285
(UK distributor: Distropa Ltd)

Prentice-Hall
Route 9 W,
Englewood Cliffs, NJ 07632
Tel: 201-592-2000/800-223-1360

PWS-Kent Publ. Co.
Division of Wadsworth Inc.,
20 Park Plaza
Boston MA 02116
Tel: 617-542-3377/800-343-2204
Fax: 617-338-6134
(UK distributor: International Thomson
    Publishing Services Ltd)

Reston Publishing Co. Inc
Box 547, 11480 Sunset Hills Road,
Reston VA 22090
Tel: 703-437-8900
(now merged with Prentice-Hall)

Sage Publications Inc.
2455 Teller Road,
Newbury Park, CA 91320
Tel: 805-499-0721
Fax: 805-499-0871

South-Western Publ. Co
Subsidiary of The Thomson
    Corporation,
5101 Madison Road,
Cincinnati, OH 45227
Tel: 513-271-8811/800-543-0487

Springer-Verlag New York Inc.
175 Fifth Avenue,
New York NY 10010
Tel: 212 460 1627
Fax: 212 473 6272

St Mary's Press
Christian Brothers Publications,
702 Terrace Heights,
Winona, MN 55987-1320
Tel: 507-452-9090/800-533-8095
Fax: 507-457-7990

TAB Books Inc.
Division of McGraw-Hill,
11311 Monterey Ave,
Blue Ridge Summit, PA 17214
Tel: 717-794-2191/800-233-1128
Fax: 717-794-5344/2080
(UK distributor: McGraw-Hill Book Co.
Europe)

University of Chicago Press
5801 South Ellis Avenue,
Chicago, IL 60637
Tel: 800-621-2736
Fax: 312-660-2235
also
5720 S Woodlawn Ave,
Chicago, IL 60637
Tel: 312 702 7600
Fax: 312 702 0172

University Press of America
4720 Boston Way,
Lanham MD 20706
Tel: 301-459-3366/800-462-6420
Fax: 301-459-2118

Van Nostrand Reinhold
Division of The Thomson Corporation,
115 Fifth Avenue,
New York, NY 10003
Tel: 212-254-3232/800-555-1212
Fax: 212-254-9499/212-475-2548

West Publishing Co.
Box 64526
50 W Kellog Blvd
St Paul, MN 55164
Tel: 612-228-2500/800-328-9352

Westview Press
Subsidiary of SCS Communications Inc.
5500 Central Ave
Boulder, CO 80301
Tel: 303-444-3541
Fax: 303-449-3356

John Wiley & Sons Inc.
605 Third Ave
New York, NY 10158-0012
Tel: 212-850-8832/6000
Fax: 212-850 8888/6088

Year Book Medical Publishers Inc
now Mosby-Year Book Inc
11830 Westline Industrial Drive
St Louis, MO 63146
Tel: 314-872-8370
Fax: 314-432-1380
(UK distributor: Mosby-Yearbook
Europe)

EUROPEAN SIMULATIONS PUBLISHERS

Akademie Verlag Gmbh,
Leipziger Strasse 3-4,
Postfach 1233,
0-1086, Berlin, Germany
Tel: +37 (02) 22360
Fax: +37 (02) 2236357

Akademiai Kiado Es Nyomda
PB 245,
1519 Budapest, Hungary
Tel: +36 (01) 1812131
Fax: +36 (01) 1666466

Birkhauser Verlag AG
Klosterberg 23,
4010 Basle, Switzerland
Tel: +41 (061) 271 7400
Fax: +41 (061) 271 7666

Dekker (Marcel) AG
Hutgasse 4,
Postfach 812,
CH-4001 Basel, Switzerland
Tel: 010 41 61 2618482
Fax: 010 41 61 2618896

Elsevier Science Publishers
PO Box 211,
1000 AE Amsterdam, The Netherlands
Tel: (20) 58 03 911
Fax: (20) 58 03 203

**Gordon & Breach Science Publishers,
SA**
Switzerland
(UK distributor: Scientific & Technical
Book Service Ltd, Reading)

Adam Hilger
(now IOP Publishing Ltd)
Techno House,
Redcliffe Way,
Bristol BS1 6NX
Tel: 0272 297481
Fax: 0272 294318

Industriens Utredningsinstitut
(Institute for Economic & Social
  Research)
POB 5501,
114 85 Stockholm, Sweden
Tel: (08) 783–80–00
Fax: (08) 661–79–69

Kluwer Academic Publishers Group
PO Box 322,
3300 AH Dordrecht, The Netherlands
Tel: 010 31 78 524400

Martinus Nijhoff Publishers
Spuiboulevard 50,
3311 GR Dordrecht, The Netherlands
Tel: (78) 33 49 22
Fax: (78) 33 42 54

Rotterdam University Press
(Universitaire Pers Rotterdam NV)
Heemraadssingel 112,
POB 1474,
Rotterdam, The Netherlands

Sijthoff Pers BV
Koopmanstraat 9,
Rijswijk PO Box 16050,
2500 AA The Hague, The Netherlands
Tel: (70) 319 09 11
Fax: (70) 390 64 47

Springer-Verlag Gmbh & Co. KG
Heidelberger Platz 3
Postfach W–1000 Berlin 33, Germany
Tel: +49 (030) 820710
Fax: +49 (030) 8214091

VCH Verlagsgesellschaft GmbH,
PO Box 10 11 61,
6940 Weinheim, Germany
Tel: (6201) 602–0
Fax: (6201) 602–328

Verlag der Fachvereine an der ETH-Zurich
Universitatsstr 19,
CH–8006 Zurich, Switzerland

Vieweg Publishing
PO Box 5829,
D6200 Wiesbaden 1, Germany
Tel: (611) 16 02 16
Fax: (611) 16 02 29

AUSTRALASIAN SIMULATIONS PUBLISHERS

Butterworth & Co. (Asia) Pte Ltd,
Singapore
(UK distributor: Butterworth & Co. Ltd)

Sydney University Press
c/o University of Sydney,
Press Building
Sydney NSW 2006, Australia
Tel: 6604997

World Scientific Publishing Co.
Singapore
(UK distributor: World Scientific
  Publishing Co. Pte Ltd [UK],
73 Lynton Mead,
Totteridge, London N20 8DH
Tel: 081–446 2461
Fax: 081–446 3356)

Chapter 32

Useful contact organizations for networking

Ray Land, Napier University, Edinburgh

AETT – Association for Educational Training and Technology
c/o Roy Winterburn, AETT Administrator,
Higher Millbrook, Beavor Lane,
Axminster, Devon EX13 5EQ

British Gas Education Service
PO Box 70, Wetherby,
West Yorkshire LS23 7EA

Centre for British Teachers
EFL Publications,
Headgate House, Head Street
Colchester, Essex CO1 1NS

Centre for World Development Education
Regent's College, Inner Circle,
Regent's Park,
London NW1 4NS

Christian Aid
PO Box 100,
London SE1 7RT

COIC
Room W 1108,
Moorfoot, Sheffield S1 4PQ

CVS Advisory Service
237 Pentonville Road,
London N1 9NJ

Daedal Training Ltd
Peak House,
66/68 Croydon Road,
Beckenham, Kent BR3 4AA

GBS Management Games
Guardian Business Services,
21 John Street, London WC1

Housing Support Team
64–66 Newington Causeway,
London SE1 6DF

ISAGA – International Simulation and Gaming Association
c/o Jan Klabbers,
Secretary, ISAGA,
Oostervelden 59
6681 WR Bemmel, The Netherlands
and
David Crookall
116 Morgan Hall, Box 870244,
Alabama University,
Tuscaloosa, AL 35487
USA

Maxim Training Systems Ltd
57 Ship Street, Brighton,
East Sussex BN1 1AF

Neighbourhood Initiatives Foundation
Suite 23/25, Horsehay House,
Horshey, Telford,
Shropshire TF4 3PY

New Games UK
PO Box 542,
London NW2 3PQ

New Grapevine Ltd
416 St Johns Street,
London EC1V 4NJ

Oxfam Education
274 Banbury Road,
Oxford OX2 7DZ

Practical Games Ltd
40A Bluecoat Chambers,
School Lane,
Liverpool L1 3BX

**SAGSET - The Society for Active
Learning**
c/o Jill Brookes, SAGSET
Administrator, Gala House
3 Raglan Road
Edgbaston
Birmingham B5 7RA

**SEDA - Staff and Educational
Development Association**
c/o Jill Brookes, SEDA Administrator,
Gala House, 3 Raglan Road,
Edgbaston,
Birmingham B5 7RA

Skillsline
Lemna House, 15 Lemna Road,
Leytonstone,
London E11 1HX

**The New International Management
Game**
ICL-Cranfield Business Games Ltd,
Cranfield, Bedford MK43 0AL

Training Business Products
141 Great Charles Street,
Birmingham B3 3JR

Training Tomorrow's Managers
Management Games Ltd,
Methwold House, Northwold Road,
Methwold,
Thetford, Norfolk IP26 4PF

Youth Clubs UK
Keswick House, 30 Peacock Lane,
Leicester, LE1 5NY

33: Notes for the contributors to the 1995 *Yearbook*

Please submit your article on paper *and* disc, stating the word-processing package used (this should always be IBM-compatible or Macintosh).

The title of the paper or article should be in bold capitals. Your name(s) should then follow, in italics and centred if at all possible. Try to use size 12 type for the rest of the text. Your manuscript should be double spaced: it helps us to make changes without having to bother you for 'clean copy'.

New paragraphs should be separated by an extra line spacing. You can also:

- use bullet points
- with the main items listed
- in a simple and appealing form

In the above example, there's an extra line space above and below the list. Now on to headings: please feel free to use them but keep them short. Keep a double line space between the end of the last paragraph and the next heading.

This is a heading

Put the heading in bold type, using lower case except for the capital first letter. Keep a line space between the heading and the start of the next piece of text. Sometimes our authors give references which could contain surnames and a date (Jones and Davies, 1984), although if three or more authors are involved it should be Jones *et al* (1984). The full reference goes at the end of the article. Also, you might want to include a quote (Bevan *et al*, 1992):

> all quotes longer than four lines should be indented so that they clearly stand apart from the main body of your narrative.

Any tables, figures or diagrams should be on separate sheets with an indication in the text of whereabouts you would like them placed. For example insert the instruction:

[table 1 about here]

Finally, on a separate sheet of paper, please say a few things about yourself and include an address for correspondence with interested readers. We do not want long autobiographies – just a couple of sentences!

REFERENCES

Bevan B, Thomas L, Reed H and Evans C (1992) *This is the title of a book*, Kogan Page, London.

Jones I and Davies D (1984) This is the title of an article, *Journal of Something or Other*, 16(2), 234–6.

Authors should send their papers and articles to: Danny Saunders, Simulation and Gaming Yearbook Editor, University of Glamorgan, Pontypridd, Mid-Glamorgan CF37 1DL, UK.